Designing Beds & Borders

The TIME LIFE
Complete ☀ Gardener

Designing Beds & Borders

By the Editors of Time-Life Books
ALEXANDRIA, VIRGINIA

The Consultants

Wendy Murphy is a freelance writer whose many interests include gardening and the botanical sciences. Author of several gardening books, she has written extensively on beds and borders, as well as on Japanese gardening traditions and indoor gardening under lights. Murphy divides her time between "Head Acres," her home in Kent, Connecticut, and a family island off the coast of down East Maine; she manages to coax a few flowers out of intractably rocky soils at both locations.

Barbara W. Ellis is a horticulturist, passionate gardener, and editor and author of many books on gardening. A graduate of Kenyon College and Ohio State University's School of Horticulture, Ellis has been managing editor of garden books for Rodale Press as well as director of publications for the American Horticultural Society and editor of *American Horticulturist* magazine and newsletter. She is a member of the Perennial Plant Association, the Hardy Plant Society, and the Garden Writers Association of America. Ellis has a large garden in sun and shade in eastern Pennsylvania. Some of her most recently published works include *Rodale's All-New Encyclopedia of Organic Gardening* (1992), *Outdoor Living Spaces* (1992), *Burpee Complete Gardener* (1995), and *Attracting Birds and Butterflies* (1996).

Cover: Kaleidoscopic color brightens this street-side Bel Air, California, border composed of the hybrid tea roses 'Mr. Lincoln', 'Honor', and 'Touch of Class', as well as bellflowers, delphiniums, sage, and other perennials. Endsheets: Edging a Lakeside, California, lawn with hot colors, this curving border contains a dazzling blend of plants, including bugloss, daisies, daylilies, roses, and basket of gold. Half title page: Brilliant rhododendron blooms dominate this Lancaster, Pennsylvania, bed. Title page: Romantic pale pink 'New Dawn' roses provide a soft backdrop for a stand of arborvitae in this Cooksville, Maryland, garden; an exuberant mix of lilies, larkspur, foxglove, and yarrow fills the border. At left: Annuals and perennials grace a pocket-sized Nashville, Tennessee, bed.

Contents

Beds and Borders in Your Garden

A well-designed bed or border can transform the most ordinary patch of ground into a gracious garden that intrigues and delights visitors and gratifies you, the gardener. Create a successful bed or border plan by experimenting with combinations of line, form, texture, and color. With a bit of practice and patience, you will be able to understand and manipulate these elements of design with sensitivity and imagination.

A Glorious Way Home
Rich hemlock hedges frame a colorful double border of perennials edged with blocks of showy annuals that flank an emerald green path leading to a shady side entrance of this Pennsylvania farmhouse. Pale pink Oenothera speciosa shimmer in summer sun beyond the foreground of dark pink Astilbe x rosea 'Queen Alexandra', spikes of Veronica spicata 'Blue Spires', and Stachys byzantina.

Understanding Beds and Borders

Whether your goal is to define a "room" or area of the garden, mask an unwanted view, or soften the edges of hard features such as patios and driveways, beds and borders serve many practical purposes. But each also has a visual and emotional impact beyond utility, and that influences its location and design.

What Is a Bed? What Is a Border?

While these two kinds of plantings are often spoken of in tandem, they differ in several significant ways. Generally, a bed is a garden area consisting of a free-standing island of cultivation. It is visible from all or several sides, in the manner of a statue on a pedestal.

A border, on the other hand, is more like a bas-relief. It is a planting area laid out against some vertical element, such as a hedge, a wall, a fence, or a building, that rises behind it and serves as a backdrop or a frame. To a limited extent, a bor-

der can be seen from the side, but its main vista extends outward from the vertical backdrop toward the front. These differences aside, however, beds and borders have many features in common.

Shared Traits

Both beds and borders offer you an almost unlimited opportunity to express your taste in plants and individuality in design. Within the context of your property, no plant type, size, or growth habit is inappropriate.

Beds and borders rely on the same design elements—plays of color, rhythm, texture, size, form, and mass—and either one can be designed to follow a formal or informal style. They are alike in being defined by distinct boundaries, whether of edging material or of a well-trimmed demarcation line between grass and bare earth.

Since both beds and borders are quite flexible, they can be designed to fit any landscape, large or

A Bed Tailor-Made for its Setting
This sinuous Rhode Island mixed bed, neatly edged with dwarf boxwood shrubs and sunken bricks, carefully follows the curves of the brick walk beyond it. Behind the edging, white and pink Phlox paniculata stand out against the blues of low-growing lavender and tall echinops.

small. Both can be planned for almost any combination of cultural conditions—whether sun or shade, moist soil or dry, rich soil or poor. You can install either one in a number of different locations and for a variety of purposes. You can, for example, dress up a plain entryway with a bed or a border; the site generally determines which is more appropriate.

Finally, beds and borders are both subject to a common-sense rule of cultivation: The plants you choose should have the same cultural requirements for sunlight, water, nutrients, soil conditions, and drainage. Although some plants may need pruning or staking at different times of year, all of the plants should thrive under the same general regime. You may be willing to water a prized specimen daily in order to enjoy its flowers, but it is easiest to care for the garden as a unit, raking the leaves in a single day in spring, and mulching and watering it all at the same time.

A Look at Bed Design

Because a bed is an island, it can be any size, with two important provisos: It should be large enough to be visible from a reasonable distance and to permit a varied display of interesting materials through the growing season, and it must not be so large that the gardener cannot reach into the center to tend all of the plants—unless it includes one or more maintenance paths.

The garden bed is amenable to all kinds of two-dimensional arrangements or "floor plans," although throughout history, there has been a tendency to favor some styles over others in keeping with the broader architectural and aesthetic customs popular at any given time. Two prime examples of changing garden fashions are the distinctly different treatments of beds of the Renaissance and those of 18th-century England.

The Renaissance flower bed was an outgrowth of the simple cultivated plot for culinary and medicinal herbs commonly found within the walls of medieval monasteries. Responding to increasing prosperity and civil order, wealthy landowners embraced garden design as a new means of displaying their status and wealth; their once-humble herb beds evolved into elaborate flowering affairs. Like the formal house it ornamented, the Renaissance garden was an exercise in geometry and symmetry, a maze of rectangular beds and intersecting lines or paths that boasted, in effect, of man's capacity to impose order on the external world.

The principles of the Renaissance garden can be adapted easily on a much smaller scale to the contemporary setting. Formal beds encompassing neatly trimmed shrubs and perennials as well as knot gardens combining herbs and closely clipped boxwoods both embody the control and precision characteristic of those earlier gardens.

Eighteenth-century English flower beds, by contrast, reflected the more naturalistic tastes and ideas that were popular in that era. Although these beds were intensively cultivated and planted, they were likely to meander along the banks of sinuous streams or nestle in the embrace of

I love old-fashioned elaborate knot gardens, but they seem to take years to become established and mature. What plants could I use to get a great-looking knot garden in a single season?

Use fast-growing herbs to create an instant knot garden. Opal basil, santolina, even leaf lettuce can be used to form the knot, and low-growing annuals like petunias and coleus can add color to the center.

A Shady Retreat
Thriving in dappled afternoon shade, borders filled with an eclectic mix of annuals, perennials, and shrubs flow freely around an inviting oasis of lawn and a bench in Bend, Oregon.

Color Reverberations
This island bed of purple iris, white Shasta daisies, and the ornamental grass Calamagrostis acutiflora 'Stricta' is set against rolling hills near Redding, Vermont, and echoes their colors. The grass will add interest in winter, after the colors of summer are gone.

Tip

Sign up for local garden tours or visit your region's historical or period gardens to get ideas for design and for plants that will thrive in your zone. These gardens often sell seeds of the plants that they grow.

rocky hillocks, and the groupings of plants within the beds were arranged to look as though nature had sown them. Gardeners of the time favored a pleasing, even whimsical, irregularity on the theory that nature abhors a straight line.

Contemporary cottage gardens embrace the same spirit found in 18th-century beds. Their free-flowing, casual form and less-structured plant combinations reflect a more relaxed and spirited approach to gardening.

Today both formal and informal beds are popular, but neither style need be rigidly followed, nor must your entire property be limited to just one style. Only a few elements remain as "rules" for designing a bed.

Bed Basics

Whatever its style, a bed must be designed to be seen from many angles. This means that the tallest plants in a bed should be planted toward the center, with adjacent plants progressively stepping down in height toward the edges, so that none of the mature

plants will block your view of those behind them. It also means that the bed should be designed to look attractive from different viewpoints. For example, in a large yard you will want a bed that looks as good from, say, your kitchen or bay window or from the patio, as it does from over the neighbor's fence.

And because a bed is designed to attract admiring attention, it makes sense to locate it in line with something else that is pleasing to look at, such as a pond, a distant vista, or a specimen tree. By the same logic, it should not be placed in line with some unsightly artifact or landscape feature, because the bed will only draw the eye in this undesirable direction. You can, however, position a bed to serve as a diversion, to draw a visitor's attention away from something unpleasant. For example, a riotously colorful flower bed in the center of the yard could distract viewers from an

A Beautiful Solution for a Problem Landscape
Rough stones hold the edge of a steeply sloping border of zinnias, marigolds, blue bachelor's-buttons, and red, yellow, and white lilies that lead past slate steps up to this house in Oldwick, New Jersey.

cent lawn when that edge is straight, but terrain, soil, and existing structures of your yard, as well as aesthetics, may dictate a more complex contour. Paving edgers, low-growing plants, lawn, and sometimes all three can form the front or sides of a border.

Plants chosen for the sides of a border will either enclose it and make a visual stopping point, as would tall shrubs, or open it to other views, as with a low edging of fragrant lavender.

Border Backdrops

The vertical backdrop to a border visually and physically orients the planting, and provides a relatively unchanging foil to contrast with the dynamic world of plants growing in front of it. A backdrop can be grand and dominant, like a tall stone wall or an *allée* of flowering trees, or it can be simple and serviceable, such as a single section of trellis or a split-rail fence.

The backdrop is permanent, lending unity throughout the seasons and special interest to the winter garden. A large backdrop will make a bold statement in its own right and also will influence the choice of plants for the border by altering sunlight, wind, or rainfall.

A simple fence or a trellis makes an excellent backdrop against which to display many different kinds of plants. Although either can be a charming accent, it need not become a dominant feature of your landscape. An old-fashioned picket fence, or a low one of split rails, along the back of the border, for example, serves the same purpose as a grand wall, but fencing feels less imposing and lets in more sunshine.

Living Backdrops

Living backdrops for borders can range from a clipped, somewhat formal hedge to a stand of waving ornamental grass to a sturdy screen of mixed, unsheared shrubs, looking as loose and natural as they might in nature. All will help to

Borrowing a Backdrop
This border in mid-summer cleverly masks and embellishes the property line between a Cape May, New Jersey, house and its neighbor, and uses the house as a backdrop. An edge of impatiens adds colorful highlights, as dark pink-and-blue Hydrangea macrophylla 'All Summer Beauty' comes into full bloom.

unsightly security fence, a dog run at the rear of the property, or children's play equipment.

Beds also can be used to mask unsightly features such as freestanding wellheads and utility boxes. When planning such a screening bed, use durable plants, since these areas may need to be serviced and endure heavy foot traffic.

A Look at Border Design

Because a border has a vertical element as a backdrop, you generally cannot walk around it to view it from all angles; instead, you must take it in from the front or sides. The border's front edge can be a straight line, it can step forward and back in rectilinear or diagonal jogs, or it can follow a curving course. You may have an easier task keeping the edge neatly dressed and mowing the adja-

shield plants from strong winds and set them off against a flattering backdrop of green.

If you prefer a living backdrop for your border, take a good look at the mature shrubs and small trees on your property. Consider their placement, form, and size, and their distance from your house. You may find that a complete backdrop, or part of one, is already in place on the property.

Alternatively, you could buy mature background plants to establish the border, but these will be fairly expensive, and you may need professional help installing them. If you have patience, you could buy smaller, immature shrubs to back up your border, giving them time to grow by filling in with annuals, perennials, and bulbs for more immediate impact.

Getting the Most from Your Border

If you use a building or other solid wall as the back of a border, you create an opportunity to grow an espalier tree or shrub or a fragrant vine, or to show off a specimen tree with a favorite bench tucked into its shadow. Placing a border, particularly one with fragrant flowers or foliage,

near a window will enable you to enjoy the plants up close from inside the house. You also may want to consider using a wall of your house or potting shed as part of a garden room, enclosed by borders on every side.

You can use a border for an occasional plant-rescue operation, as an opportunity to take advantage of a bargain plant, or to try out a particular type of plant. Nurseries near you may imperfect shrubs at discounted prices. If you live in a region that has cold winters, visit local nurseries at the end of the gardening season, when they are eager to dispose of any remaining shrubs at bargain prices.

Choose dense bushy plants for the front of your border to disguise any temporary unsightly features of your bargain shrubs as you nurse them back to health. If an evergreen hedge backs your border, some deciduous flowering shrubs added to the planting scheme will repay you twice over: Their spectacular fall color will add interest to your end-of-season border, and their flowers will brighten your garden when spring returns.

Tip

Properties taken by eminent domain or scheduled as sites for new highways can be great sources for mature plants. The plants are free, but you have to move them. Check with your planning commission for maps and a list of these properties.

Elevating a Humble Garden Shed
A classic double border featuring roses edged with blue Nepeta mussinii leads to a decorative garden shed, making it a focal point in this Washington, Connecticut, garden.

Cultivating Your Bed or Border

If bed and border plants are to prosper, they must enjoy optimum conditions of site, soil, air circulation, and climate. To ensure that all of these factors are given their due, it makes good sense to start with a thoughtful plan and a checklist, and work through it step by step like a general drawing up a battle plan.

Assessing Your Site

Begin with a close examination of the site, that unique patch of ground that constitutes your garden area. Of course, your property exists within a broad geographic region of known climate, and it falls within one of the hardiness zones mapped out by the United States Department of Agriculture (*page 102*).

Often, the spot where you want to install your bed or border will have a microclimate all its own. Acted on by sun exposure, wind patterns, and variations in topography, it might, for example, have a patch of standing water in one shady place and sun-baked arid soil 20 feet farther on.

Such microclimate variations can present both challenges and opportunities. They might, for example, rule out some plant choices that would otherwise seem ideal for your region, but they also allow you to experiment with plants that you normally would not consider using.

When evaluating your site, make note of seasonal changes during the entire growing season. An area that gets many hours of sunshine in early spring may have only midday sun when nearby trees leaf out. When it comes time to choose specific plants, you will need to know whether your site gets full sun (a minimum of six hours daily, at least four of them in the afternoon), partial shade (three to four hours of morning sun, followed by shade), dappled shade, or full shade (no direct sunlight but enough indirect light to support some plant growth).

Then consider how your family uses the yard. Note where they congregate and particularly where they settle when they have the time and inclination to appreciate the garden—whether viewing it from a living room window, for example, or outdoors on a path, patio, or deck. Decide

Filling In a Fence
Echinops ritro 'Taplow Blue' combines beautifully with pink garden phlox along a split-rail fence to turn this New Jersey border into a living wall of color.

where you would like family members and visitors to stroll, and what locations are at risk of being trampled or just ignored altogether.

Finally, incorporate in your site evaluation some thoughts about the views that exist beyond your property and whether you want to frame or disguise them. There might be some physical shortcoming, such as a neighbor's ugly storage shed, that you would prefer to hide or at least minimize. If so, you may want to put a hedge or screen there and locate your eye-catching flower displays somewhere else. Once you have made these decisions, it is time to deal with the soil.

Understanding Soil Types

Soil has three distinct layers, beginning with the typically dark-colored topsoil directly underfoot and continuing down through varied layers of subsoils to the layer derived from the parent rock. For purposes of growing most flowers and many shrubs, only the topsoil is important. This amazing substance—usually no more than 12 inches deep—teems with living organisms and is highly variable in what it offers plants.

Topsoil is composed of a mix of inorganic mineral particles—ranging in size from microscopic clay to larger silt to still larger sand—as well as air, water, and organic matter. The latter is a stew of decaying plant and animal matter that is being broken down into important plant nutrients by living microorganisms, insects, and earthworms. Topsoil is classified according to its texture, which may be sandy, clay, or loam.

Sandy soil is relatively high in coarse mineral particles; it is light, resists compacting, and tends to warm up and be workable earlier in spring than denser soils. Roots can penetrate it with relative ease, but it does not hold them firmly; nor does it retain water and water-borne nutrients.

Clay soil is heavier, with much finer particles that can coalesce into a sticky or gummy mass when wet and become as hard as concrete when dry. Because it is too compact to allow much air circulation and it retains water stubbornly, clay soil can be a liability for plants, suffocating them and promoting root rot.

Loam is made up of roughly 40 percent sand, 40 percent silt, and 20 percent clay. When ac-companied with substantial organic matter, it will have a slightly moist feel and will form small, irregularly shaped clumps that leave ample room for the slow passage of air, water, and nutrients. Such soil is the preferred medium for the majority of plants grown in beds and borders. If your soil falls short of this ideal, you can improve it by digging amendments into it.

Amending the Soil

The best of amendments—virtually a panacea for any soil—is compost. This dark, rich, humusy amalgam of decayed plant materials will not only add fertility to any soil, but will give body and density to sandy soil, while lightening and loosening clay soil.

Another important amendment involves soil pH, which is the shorthand term for the soil's level of acidity or alkalinity. Since the pH factor of your flower bed or border can affect plants' abilities to assimilate nutrients, you should test your soil periodically. You can do this with an inexpensive kit available at garden centers or by sending soil samples to your state agricultural extension office.

Most flowering ornamentals do best when the soil pH lies in a range from neutral (around 6.5 to 7) to slightly acid (5.5 to 6). But numerous plants, including most evergreens, woodland plants, and such flowering shrubs as azalea, rhododendron, and mountain laurel, favor more acid soil. In deciding which plants to put in your

Matching Plants to Their Backdrop
Mass plantings of Iris sibirica 'Pansy Purple' and 'Llewelyn' in front of a line of arborvitae reinforce the shrubs' upright form and make an easy-to-care-for border of late-spring color. The clean lines of this Pennsylvania garden are repeated in both the walkway and the bench.

I love azaleas but my soil is strongly alkaline. How can I grow these plants in my garden?

Plant azaleas in handsome containers filled with an acid soil mix and place them in your garden. Alternatively, set the shrubs in raised beds of acid soil.

Planting for Long-Lasting Color
Backed by a picket fence, white 'Maureen' Darwin tulips, 'Salome' daffodils, and purple Muscari armeniacum give this Greenwich, Connecticut, border (below) its first spring colors. Azaleas, unobtrusively tucked behind the tulips, will come forward after the bulbs are finished, augmented by colorful annuals.

Brightening a Weathered Backdrop
White cleomes, Nicotiana sylvestris 'Daylight', and sunflowers tower in the shelter of a pleasantly weathered, unpainted fence in this Kittery, Maine, garden. Lower-growing snapdragons and zinnias edge the border at their feet.

bed or border, you will have the choice of confining yourself to species that are compatible with the soil's present pH level, or altering the pH so you can put in other plants that you prefer more.

Where soil tests excessively acid, apply ground limestone before you plant in the fall, at a rate of 3 to 4 pounds per 100 square feet, water deeply, and retest in a few days. If the soil is too alkaline, correct with ammonium sulfate or iron sulfate, following directions on the package, or apply an acid-type fertilizer, and test again in a few days.

Improving Soil Fertility

Soil naturally contains amounts of the three major plant nutrients—nitrogen, phosphorus, and potassium—as well as essential trace minerals. You can put back into the soil whatever nutrients are lacking or have been consumed by plants at a rate faster than nature can replenish them. Do this before planting and at the same time that you make other soil amendments; if more fertilizer is needed later, add it periodically as a top dressing.

sium, always in that order; 10-10-10 is another common formulation. A soil analysis will help you determine which fertilizer, if any, you should add to your soil.

Knowing Your Climate

Plants do well in fresh air, so avoid siting a bed or border in a tightly confined place where air does not circulate freely. On the other hand, the majority of ornamental plants, especially the tall ones, are sensitive to constant wind. If your site is exposed, consider planting a living windbreak of large trees or shrubs, or putting up an attractive, practical fence.

Climate is a prime factor in determining which perennials will overwinter successfully. This has more to do with soil temperature than with air temperature. In severe climates, even hardy perennials may die if there is no blanket of insulating snow or if they are exposed to chronic freezing and thawing, causing them to be heaved out of the ground. To prevent heaving, apply a winter mulch, such as shredded leaves, bark, or wood chips, keeping it away from the crowns of the plants.

Observe your neighbors' plantings and experiment in your own garden. From what you learn, you may be able to try plants that are one zone less hardy than your location if you have a south-facing site or one that is close to the house or otherwise protected.

You can use a combination of organic matter, such as compost or other humus and bone meal, or inorganic dry fertilizer to amend your soil. (If you want to use only natural fertilizer, look for the words "organic" or "all natural" on the bag.) Often termed a complete fertilizer, the inorganic product is a formulation of the three key nutrients in various ratios expressed by a sequence of three numbers. Thus, a 5-10-5 on the label means that the product contains 5 percent nitrogen, 10 percent phosphorus, and 5 percent potas-

Liquid Grace
Shades of red create a sense of harmony amid competing textures and shapes in this Minnesota bed, where red fountain grass spills over dark red zinnias and bright pink Nicotiana.

Keys to Good Design

The best-planned beds and borders often appear to have grown up naturally. In fact, however, their design follows the principles that underlie every art form: balance, rhythm, accent, and harmony. In the garden, these principles are expressed through the thoughtful use of plants. As you plan your own bed or border, you will decide on species, colors, textures, groupings, and the relationship of each grouping to its neighbors and to adjacent landscaping and ornamentation. These will be artistic as well as practical decisions.

Establishing Balance and Rhythm

Balance in garden design is the appearance of equilibrium or stability. You can achieve balance by placing plants of equal size and color at equal distance from a central axis, as with a symmetrical pair of matched trees or matching hedgerows on either side of a front door. But you also can create balance with asymmetrical arrangements. Consider how children of unequal weight use a seesaw; the seesaw is off center, with the lighter child on the longer end of the board and the heavier child on the shorter end, close to the fulcrum. So, too, balance in a garden is a matter of coordinating mass, distance, and space to create a sense of equilibrium.

Rhythm is the suggestion of spatial movement in a design. When you establish rhythm in the arrangement of plants, you generate a sense of excitement and expressiveness in your bed or border; without it, the visual impact of the planting could be disappointingly flat. Rhythm requires variation in shape, color, texture, size, form, mass, or a combination of all.

A rhythmic border might include a clump of low-growing purple verbena positioned next to billowy mounds of contrastingly colored 'Sunbeam' coreopsis. The entire border might be backed by intermittent waves of deep blue or white delphiniums. With the pattern of coreopsis and verbena repeated along the front and ocasionally interrupted by tall, silvery spikes of lamb's ears, a rhythm is created across the expanse of the border. The heights of plants rise and fall from verbena to delphinium, while leaf and plant forms fluctuate from the ferny foliage of coreopsis to the tidy leaves of verbena and the softer but broader leaves of lamb's ears. By creating a rhythm with several elements—form, color, and height—the border develops a soothing flow as opposed to the staccato pattern that might occur if only one element varied throughout.

Accent and Harmony

Accent is a matter of providing a point of interest or emphasis in your design. An ornament such as a sundial, or a burst of brilliant color achieved with flaming orange poppies amid a bed of more subtle lemon yellow bearded iris, are both good examples of accent. Use accents to draw the viewer's eye to particular points in the garden, focusing attention on more interesting features and distracting the eye from less pleasing ones.

Finally, harmony refers to the unity and completeness of the design, first as it relates to the bed or border, second as it relates to the scale, proportion, and overall character of the yard or landscape around it. In a harmonious composition, all of the parts are compatible. Thus a colorful and carefree cottage garden composed of plants of similar height looks perfectly at home spilling over a picket fence next to a bungalow-style house. The same garden situated next to a more formal, plantation-style house with finished brick walls and walkways would be out of keeping with its setting.

Working with a Smorgasbord of Plants

In the past, garden experts held that only a narrow range of plants was appropriate for beds and borders. The earliest beds were planted strictly with "bedding plants," or annuals, often in a Persian carpet effect. Eventually, herbaceous perennials found their way into bed designs. Where the grounds were sufficiently large to permit the luxury of multiple borders, it was common for gardeners to plant single-species borders, such as one of roses, another of irises, and so on.

Today, gardeners feel free to plant virtually any type of plant in their beds and borders—not only

Adding Ornaments to Your Bed or Border

Ornaments offer you an opportunity to impart your personality and your sense of aesthetics to the look of your garden. Whether you want to reinforce an impression of stateliness in a formal bed (below) or natural simplicity in a border beside a country cottage (below right), you can find objects that will fit in with your intentions.

When selecting an ornament, keep its specific role in mind. Some objects serve to add beauty and create a focal point, such as at the end of a long border or at the center of a bed. A small statue or a large boulder, for example, can add perspective to the plot, put plants in proportion to one another and to their setting, and help ground the garden. Other items, such as the straddling stone tucked into the garden at right, can play a functional role. Footed urns and hanging baskets allow you to add vertical interest to the scene.

Ornaments also can be permanent structures, such as wooden or stone steps leading up to or past a hillside border.

Highly visible, steps can accent the border and be just as stylish as statuary. For those with a water source on their land, a footbridge adds a charming and practical accent to a stream or small pond. Some permanent ornaments look fine unadorned, while others, such as elegant or unusual arbors and trellises made of wood or wrought iron, are enhanced when they are overgrown with vines, flowers, or foliage.

For the gardener with artistic notions, a trompe l'oeil mural painted on the wall of a house or the back of a gardening shed can add year-round interest and beauty. An illusionistic painting depicting an extension of the garden or a far-off vista can add depth to a border that is short on real space.

One critical rule of garden ornaments and accents is that they should be consistent with the theme or feel of the garden that they grace. Wooden figures, wind chimes, whimsical signposts, bottle trees, and even pink flamingos are best suited to the casual country garden. Formal gardens, by contrast, demand a much more subtle treatment—even if the desired effect is whimsy. In this setting, stone cherubs, topiaries, pillars, fountains, and even mirrored gazing balls are more appropriate.

Using Objects to Change a Bed

A garden bed can be dramatically transformed by the addition of a single hardscape element, even though the bed's shape, size, and plants remain exactly the same. The choice of that element defines the transformation. In the example below, three different hardscape features create strikingly different moods in a bed. Experiment with objects in your own garden; there is no right or wrong choice as long as it pleases you.

◀ **First, a large rock holds center stage.** It is part of nature, contributes something substantial and earth-toned to contrast with the greenery, and produces a back-to-basics impression. Using a rock suggests that you value the natural world and its ornaments.

◀ **Now, replace that rock with a fancy birdhouse or a sundial.** Such an artifact acts as a focal point, just as the rock did, but with more sophistication, implying, perhaps, that you value creativity and worldliness over rusticity.

◀ **Third, put in a bench.** Such a homey-looking item invites visitors directly into the bed. The mood of the garden now changes and becomes more intimate, while the bench encourages guests to linger.

perennials and annuals, but also small deciduous trees and broad-leaved and needled evergreens, shrubs, vines, all kinds of bulbs, ferns, and grasses. With so wide a range of choices, each mixed bed or border can be unique.

Indeed, making selections from the vast array of plants available for contemporary American gardens can be a daunting experience. There's no simple method for choosing, but a good starting point is to select some of your personal favorites and then fill in around them according to an evolving plan. You will need to know each plant's growing needs, habits, and other characteristics in order to draft a workable plan.

Selecting Plants for Maximum Effect

Almost any plant can be used for a variety of effects, but some plant categories are especially well suited to particular purposes.

Evergreen trees and shrubs are important additions to beds and borders. Arborvitae, holly, yew, creeping juniper, euonymus, and rhododendron are among the evergreens frequently used to create a consistent green or blue-green background for the colors of a mixed bed or border.

Small deciduous trees in the center of a bed or against a solid wall at the back of a border make strong focal points all year round, showing decorative bare branches in winter. Some small trees, such as *Corylus avellana* 'Contorta' and *Salix matsudana* 'Tortuosa', drop their leaves in autumn to reveal delightfully twisted branches.

Vines, particularly when in bloom, become focal points, and the structure that supports them contributes to the garden's architecture. Some climbing roses, honeysuckle, and jasmine also contribute fragrance, a sensual aspect of gardening that should not be overlooked.

Ornamental grasses, a group that includes bamboos, rushes, sedges, and true grasses, offer year-round silhouettes. These grasses add movement as they wave with every breeze, and their seedheads decorate the winter landscape.

Ground covers such as periwinkle, pachysandra, or thyme need little or no care and retain their color and form throughout the seasons.

Flowering perennials are backbone plantings, providing reliable color year after year. Appreciated primarily for the relatively short periods when their flowers are fully formed and fresh, these plants remain important even after they recede from view because they offer a backdrop for annuals during the growing season and often display interesting seedpods during the fall months.

In a large garden, the brief bloom time of perennials is acceptable because other neighboring perennials that flower later can take over for blooms that have faded. But if your bed or border is a small one, you may want to give preference to perennials that contribute to the design over a longer period. 'Ballawley' bergenia, for example, produces bright crimson flowers in spring. When the flowers fade, the plant's large, flat, deep green, oval leaves offer visual interest throughout the summer. As cold weather approaches, the leaves turn deep red, adding yet another element of interest.

Annuals bring their own very specific set of virtues to the creation of beds and borders. Planted anew each year, they give the gardener the opportunity to alter completely the color scheme of a bed or border. Further, their adaptable nature makes them ideal for bringing a dash of color to a fading perennial or bulb bed. The most pleasing annual plantings are generally designed as informal clumps rather than neat and tidy lines of plants. Alternating the form and number of plants in each clump will contribute to a more relaxed and natural pattern of planting.

Making Inspiration a Reality

The gardener's challenge in designing a bed or border is to create a living structure or space that is in harmony with the surrounding environment—using plants as the medium and content. The best way to approach this task is to study the examples of other gardens. Take garden tours, read gardening books, and visit friends' gardens. If possible, make your surveys over an extended period, returning to some of your favorite places to see how plants look at different times of the growing season, perhaps even in winter.

To get a realistic sense of how great a variety of plants your space will accommodate, measure your planting areas and compare them with those of successful gardens you have seen. From there, you can begin to develop working plans.

Keep in mind, too, how much time and effort you can commit to your bed or border. Start small and expand only when you know you will have time to care for it. It's less costly to add to a garden over time than to feel guilty and avoid it because the design and plantings are overly ambitious and time-consuming.

Passing Through a Border

Openings in a border create focal points that direct visitors along the pathways that run through your garden. They guide your guests by influencing them to look down these paths.

Each opening should be wide enough to be easily noticeable. It also should be proportionate to the width of the path leading to it, but preferably provide room for two people to pass through comfortably—between 3 and 4 feet. Line the path with beds or borders to draw the eye forward to the path's destination. Pillars, shrubs with a vertical habit, small trees that flank the opening, or an arbor that crowns it give it even more visual emphasis. Perhaps best of all is a gate.

A securely latched gate on sturdy posts promotes an air of privacy concerning the space it encloses—especially a solid wooden gate that blocks the view. But even openwork iron gates such as those in the Los Angeles garden above, while offering a look at what lies beyond, establish clear boundaries. These gates block the side passages that intersect the front walk; though they are left ajar, a caller would have no trouble understanding that the lovely gardens on the other side are private.

Choose a gate of a shape and material that fit in with the surrounding architecture. It should have roughly the same height and profile as the wall, fence, or hedge on either side, and its construction should reflect the garden's style: typically, white wooden pickets for an informal garden or wrought iron for a formal knot garden. Such rules are not inviolable however. A gate that contrasts sharply with its surroundings can be a dramatic presence along the line of a border.

The Bed Perfected

*Use garden beds to showcase
particular plants, to serve as focal points
in the landscape, as a clever way
to screen out unwanted views, or as
visual enticements to draw
visitors deeper into the garden.
Whether you choose an informal design,
with plants that spill over onto the lawn,
or a formal style, with plantings
neatly hemmed in by hedges, you can
feel free to lay out your beds
in any shapes that suit your fancy.*

Composing a Pleasant View
*Silvery tones of Russian sage at the rear, and artemisia in
the front of this bed reflect the smoky morning mist
rising from distant New Jersey hills. The lines of the bed
and the forms of plants wihin it—red and pink bee
balm, golden helianthus, pink garden phlox, and mixed
zinnias—lead to an open pasture gate and the meadow
beyond. A large mound of purple-leaved Perilla
frutescens anchors the far end.*

Making Design Decisions

Curves That Echo Curves

By reprising the shape of the gazebo behind it, a circular bed centered on a young tree in an urn links the parts of this Portland, Oregon, garden. The tidy perennial and herb bed is bordered by a circle of germander and contains purple-leaved sage and bright pink spikes of Primula vialii 'Miracle'.

Beds play multiple roles in the garden. They can showcase a prized collection of plants, hide an unsightly view, or redirect traffic. Their flexibility is nearly limitless. But before you purchase a single plant for a new or cleared bed, imagine how the plants you've selected will look together. Consider what their size and habit will be at maturity. Decide what the bed's function will be within the larger context of your garden and what will be required to keep it looking its best.

Finding the Right Site

To choose the best location for a bed and determine its proper size, take into account your entire property, including its present plantings, and set those facts against your goals and preferences as a gardener. When you do so, you may find that apparent limiting factors inspire you and reveal hidden opportunities.

For example, if you have a patch of lawn that's hard to reach with your mower, you could put in a pretty bed. Or plant a steep, eroding slope with a collection of deep-rooted perennials or ground covers and it will become an attractive feature of your yard, requiring little maintenance. Consider tucking a small fragrance garden into a narrow space under a bedroom window or just outside a newly expanded breakfast nook so you can enjoy the scent of your garden in your house.

Beds can become focal points in your landscape, their location altering perspective in ways that change your sense of space. Put a showy bed in the middle distance of your backyard, and you will find that the back fence seems to recede into the distance. Well-placed beds can also help to pull seemingly disparate features such as fences, shrubs, trees, flowers, and buildings together into a balanced whole. For example, if you have a small house overshadowed by a huge shade tree, you can reduce the disparity between the two by installing a large flower bed between them for balance. A series of strategically placed flower beds can provide a sense of privacy and give flow to a large garden, creating

more intimate spaces between one functional living section and another.

On a more ambitious scale, a bed can even serve as a means for altering the terrain of your property. Add several yards of topsoil, mounded to form an island bed, and you can transform a flat, monotonous-looking expanse into something striking. You can also use an island bed to get around major drainage problems, providing a built-up planting area above shallow hardpan, for example, or creating a wetland garden atop a low, boggy site.

Choosing a Formal or Informal Bed Style

Some beds take their shape from the space they fill, such as a wedge of ground that might have been left when you built a patio or put an addition on your house. Most often, however, you will start from scratch with an ordinary expanse of lawn or landscape. You then can create either a formal or an informal design.

Formal beds take their design inspiration from geometric shapes: the square, the circle, the rectangle, or some variant. Their regular and familiar contours make them relatively easy to lay out with good proportion and scale in relation to the rest of the garden.

Informal beds take a little more thought and effort in planning, because the guidelines are more flexible. These beds are meant to mimic

A Balance of Color and Form
The columnar juniper in this informal mounded bed picks up the shapes of the sculpted evergreens in the background and keeps the handsome birdhouse in scale with the bed in this Connecticut garden. Budding hydrangea tops the mound, while a dwarf blue spruce, white iris, purple catmint, and Hosta 'Francee' drift to the edges.

the random forms found in nature, but their informality can be overdone if you use too many curves crowded into too short a span. You'll get better results with gentle, natural curves and ovals, which will give your informal garden an inviting, casual effect.

The decision to go with a formal or informal style will depend on your personal preferences, as well as the surrounding landscape and architecture. If a drive or walkway is lined with neat and tidy rows of shrubs or trees, an equally tidy formal bed might be more appropriate than a more casual informal bed.

Creating Boundaries with Edging

Whether a bed is formal or informal, its edge separates it visually and physically from the surrounding terrain. Maintaining a well-defined edge can be challenging, as vigorous plants spill out of bounds and turf grass sends out encroaching runners. To preserve the shape of your bed, place edging material around the perimeter when you originally prepare the soil, before adding plants. Commercially available edging materials such as plastic, metal, or wooden benderboard can be placed in the soil with their top edges just above the surface, so that with one mower wheel in the bed, the lawn can be mowed and trimmed at the same time.

Edging can contribute to your overall design. Consider, for example, installing paving bricks sunk vertically or diagonally. Formal beds can be edged with neatly clipped plants such as dwarf boxwood, lavender, feathery-foliaged santolina, or barberry to establish a distinct frame around the taller plants within. As handsome as such living edges are, however, they cannot physically maintain the bed's perimeter, and you will still need a concealed barrier between the soil of the bed and the adjacent lawn or path.

Understanding Proportion

Since antiquity, philosophers and scientists have observed that what humans recognize as mathematical proportion occurs in nature without any help from us. Such mathematical relationships have contributed to theories of ideal proportion in architecture, sculpture, painting, music—and garden design. One is the so-called Golden Section, or ideal rectangle, in which the shorter side has the same relationship to the longer side as the longer side has to the sum of both sides, producing a ratio of approximately 5 to 8.

Tailoring a Bed to Suit a Sculpture

A piece of sculpture is a good way to provide a focal point for a garden bed, particularly if the bed is designed to show both the sculpture and plantings to best advantage. Here are three bed designs that demonstrate how the identical bed shape, plant choices, and ornament—in this case a tall, classical statue of weathered stone—can be handled in strikingly different ways for different effects.

1. A Bed Teeming with Plants

This design focuses more on plants than on the sculpture. The plants are massed to provide interesting year-round color and texture combinations that are visible from several angles. The sculpture, however, is lost in the sea of plants, making it an incidental element rather than a featured focal point. Also, its off-center placement in this asymmetrical bed is at odds with its classical, formal style.

2. Highlighting the Sculpture

This design attempts to put the emphasis on the statue. The plants are arranged formally and symmetrically in increasing height from one end of the bed to the other. The ascent draws the eye to the sculptural focal point at the tall end of the bed, but because the plants nearest the statue are too tall, they obscure it so that it cannot be fully appreciated.

For example, a bed 10 feet wide by 16 feet long would fall within the definition of the Golden Section, as would one measuring 6 by 10. A quick way of checking proportions is to divide the small number by the larger; the quotient should be about 0.61. When the dimensions you lay out match the Golden Section, you'll like the look of your rectangular bed.

Another proportional relationship is the Fibonacci sequence, named for Leonardo Fibonacci, a 13th-century Italian mathematician. He saw that there was harmonious order in a sequence in which each number is the sum of the two preceding it, as in 1, 1, 2, 3, 5, 8, 13.... Look for these relationships in nature; you will find examples in the arrangement of petals in a primrose or the pattern of leaves on a stem. In gardens, these relationships produce visual effects that unconsciously strike us as gratifying.

One way to apply Fibonacci's sequence is to group plants so that two of one cultivar sit beside three of another, or to select plants whose mature heights will relate in the same manner to create harmonious proportions in your bed. Choose one tall specimen, such as bee balm, for every two medium and three short plants—two hosta, say, and three dianthus—and you maintain both 1:2 and 2:3 relationships.

While these principles can help you lay out a well-designed bed, you still should consult your own tastes and style to create a bed that's consistent with your vision for your garden.

I'd like an alternative to traditional flower beds. Any suggestions?

Plant a "green" bed, using green and silver foliage plants with interesting leaf shapes, such as lamb's ears and *Miscanthus sinensis* 'Gracillimus'.

3. Plants and Ornament in Balance

This garden design achieves equilibrium by giving the right emphasis to both plants and sculpture. The pleasingly oblong shape of the bed provides a sense of visual stability and restfulness that is typical of classical designs. Plantings are symmetrical, repeating texture and color in a way that is interesting but not overwhelming. The statue is centrally located at the back of the bed, but not so far away that detail is lost, and is complementary in style to the rest of the garden. The height of the statue provides the bed with an effective focal point. The shape of the plot, choice and location of plantings, and style and placement of the statue make for a well-balanced bed. A visitor to this garden can see that the sculpture is an integral part of the garden and not just an afterthought.

Developing Your Garden Plan

Planning ahead on paper helps you avoid costly mistakes and makes renovations easier. Begin with a schematic, or base plan, of your entire property. Draw the plan to scale, or trace the original blueprint of your house and landscape. Plot plans, which are available from your local assessor or register of deeds, may be helpful, but if you use more than one source, be sure that you correlate their various scales.

Planning on Paper

Your base plan should include all existing features of your landscape: buildings, patios, driveways, fences, property lines, ditches, utility poles, water lines, slopes, trees and shrubs, beds, low spots, and problem areas. Note any legal restrictions that will affect your decisions, mark paths and other established traffic patterns, and decide which views to enhance or block. On your map, indicate north and determine the summer sun's daily path so you can mark sun or shade areas. Use one color to draw existing features and a second color to highlight areas that need work.

Phases of garden work can be based on time, money, or plans for home expansion. Use a separate piece of tracing paper, marked with its own color, for each phase, and overlay them to show the complete design. Then, if you change your mind, you won't have to redraw the base map.

With your site plan in hand, spend some time in the garden. As you walk around, picture new spots for beds, perhaps as links between structures and garden features or as focal points at the apex of converging rows of tall trees. Perhaps you will see an opportunity to upgrade a well-worn rut through the yard into a path edged by a neat bed. Identify where people will sit, stand, and view the bed, and site it accordingly.

Designing the Bed's Size and Shape

The first step in planning a bed is to stand in the spot from which it will be viewed most frequently, perhaps your doorway or patio. For visual impact, beds located away from your house must be larger than those close by, such as near a front door. To find a good dimension for the long axis

Crowning a Bed with a Flowery Rampart
Majestic blue spires of 'Pacific Giant' delphiniums in this Portland, Oregon, bed help to screen the view from and to the street. Masses of pink peonies, snowy Shasta daisies, peachy lupines, red-orange geum, and a lustrous purple Japanese maple complete this crowning composition.

An Informal Planting in Formal Confines
Pale sea-green fronds of native sensitive fern stand out among the colorful, loosely formed and variably textured perennials contained within the orderly bounds of this circular bed in Connecticut.

of a rectangular bed, measure the distance to the new bed's center. Divide the distance in half, and make the long sides of the bed slightly shorter than that length. For example, an island bed 40 feet from your patio might be 18 feet long, or slightly less than half the distance from patio to bed—20 feet. If you were to apply the Golden Section ratio of 8 to 5 to the bed's other dimension, that would measure about 11 feet.

A circular bed is easier to lay out. Tie a string the length of the new bed's radius to a central stake, then walk a circle around it, using lime to mark the bed's edge. For an oval or irregular shape, arrange a garden hose where you want the bed to be. The hose will fall into gentle, wide curves that are quite natural looking.

In this kind of bed, avoid too many deep bends and arcs. They are difficult to mow around and tend to make the bed look "busy." If you are uncertain about curves, run your lawn mower along the line; if you have to raise the mower's wheels to maneuver, make the curves more gradual. It's easy to fix things in the planning stages but time-consuming after the bed is planted.

When you are satisfied with your proposed layout, mark the site and make adjustments until you are certain about size and shape. Be realistic about what you can manage. If the projected size

Downsizing a Grand Bed

To copy a large elaborate bed that you admire, first visualize it as a geometric composition of colors. Then check nurseries for modest-sized plants and objects you can use to re-create its look in your garden.

For example, you could transpose a bed in a public park, as in the picture below, by using fewer plants, or smaller plants of similar habit and texture, and repeating the layout and materials of the larger version. There, a large round pool is flanked by a semicircular bed of colorful plants with upright, uniform habits. Mid-size spruce trees form a backdrop, and two conical arborvitae shrubs at either end anchor the composition. The "home" version at right uses a large tree as a backdrop. The pool, now a birdbath, is encircled by a bed of lavender and a brick walkway. A semicircle of bedding plants rings the walkway, and dwarf arborvitae flank it. The new garden is proportional to its reduced size, but with the same formal feel as the original.

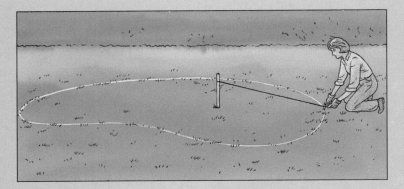

Tip

Once you have drawn up a base plan of your property, make several photocopies of it so you can sketch in changes directly. Then try out different plant placements, plant combinations, and shapes of beds, borders, and hardscape elements. After that, you can record on one final copy the actual changes you make in your garden.

is getting beyond what seems practical, draw the bed in closer to the house and make it somewhat smaller than originally envisioned. A rule of thumb for depth is that a bed should be at least twice as deep as the height of its tallest perennials. Thus, in a rectangular bed of 10 feet by 6 feet, your plantings should be less than 3 feet tall. For easier maintenance, add a few steppingstones among the plants so you can reach the bed's center.

Focal Point and Scale

A bed may be the central feature of your garden, but each bed needs its own focal point, such as an especially showy plant, a large boulder, a bench, or a garden sculpture. A focal point should draw the eye to it without dominating the view or dwarfing neighboring plants.

Scale is important. Take into account the mature height of proposed plantings and balance height and width against one another. By using perspective, or the tendency of the eye to focus on the most distant point, you can make your garden seem shorter or longer. Low plants or a bench placed across the axis, or central line, of a bed, for example, will make a long bed seem shorter.

When your plans are complete, place tablecloths, tarpaulins, or newspapers weighted down with stones or bricks to mark the bed area you have drawn. Then look at the site from different angles. If it looks too small, enlarge it until it comes into scale with its surroundings. A bed on a small lot may need to be scaled down if it takes up too much of the lawn relative to the house. Or you may want to enlarge a too-small bed.

Make your changes in the planning stage. Be sure to take your time and trust your judgment. After all, you are the one who must be happy with the results.

Building a Mounded Bed

Mounds can be used to raise a flat site for improved perspective or drainage, to solve a landscape problem, or to provide privacy. Plan for a mound tall enough (at least 18 inches high) to elevate the sight line, but slope it gently enough to prevent erosion— 6 inches in every 3 feet usually works well.

Traditional instructions to till and amend soil do not apply to mounds. Instead, put down layers of a soil that is dense enough to stay in place yet well-drained and capable of sustaining plants. Mounds can be made entirely of soil from your property, but if that soil erodes easily, you will need edging to keep it in place.

Because of their increased height, mounded beds are more exposed than the rest of the landscape and tend to dry out more quickly. You may want to install a drip or soaker-hose irrigation system to prevent erosion, and a timer to use when you're away.

◀ 1. Lay out the perimeter with garden hose and then mark it off with powdered lime. Insert a stake at the center of the bed and run a string from the stake to the perimeter to use as a guide for raising the elevation of the bed.

◀ 2. Use shovels and rakes to build the mound base. Add soil in 4-inch layers; on a dry site, water each layer well and let it dry before adding the next one. Cap with 6 inches of amended soil to the final height.

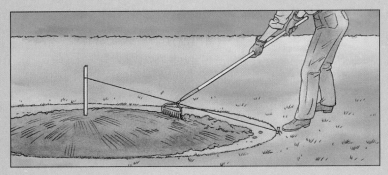

▲ 3. Install soaker hoses or another simple irrigation system. To stabilize the soil, add plants and a layer of mulch as soon as you finish building the mound.

Composing the Bed

Now that you've worked out the location, shape, and size of the bed, you're ready to start composing with plants. Arrange plants with similar cultural requirements in the same bed—for example, sun lovers in one bed, shade plants in another. Assuming that all your plants will grow well together, the ultimate measure of a bed's success is how much it delights the viewer. Much of this, of course, is intuitive and personal.

To broaden your understanding of how design works, talk with gardeners whose layouts you admire, take a garden design course, or visit private gardens open for tour. Look at garden styles as they relate to the surrounding property: Note the plants that work well in a formal garden and those that look better planted in a cottage garden.

Learning Composition from Artists

Art is another place to find design ideas. Just as artists look to nature for inspiration, so can gardeners gain inspiration from paintings. French modernist Paul Cézanne, for example, found it useful in painting his landscapes to see the trees, rocks, buildings, and other forms first as spheres, cones, and cylinders defined by color. In the same way, it may help you to view plants and flowers as basic shapes: round, spiky, mounded, lacy, arching, and sculptural with unique silhouettes.

Study Vincent van Gogh's exciting use of color, as in the painting "The Starry Night," where purples and blues contrast sharply with yellows. And linger over Claude Monet's exquisite use of luminous color and vibrating light effects, particularly in his paintings of his gardens at Giverny. They can teach much about the use of color in modern gardens.

Thinking in Terms of Line and Form

In the garden setting, line is expressed in the edges of paths and walls, in the boundaries between surfaces such as water, earth, lawn, and sky,

Planting to Emphasize an Unusual Shape
The heart layout of this Oregon front-yard bed is reinforced by an edging of evergreen dwarf arborvitae filled in with one variety of brightly colored tulips.

and in the silhouettes of such forms as tree trunks, sheared hedges, buildings, and trellises. A line directs the eye along a definite course. According to psychologists, line also has an emotional component. A horizontal line can have a positive, calming effect, while a vertical line adds drama and action. Two lines crossing at right angles create stability, a gentle curve soothes, circles invite rest, and a diagonal may seem jarring.

Form is three-dimensional, and tells you the shape, volume, and space an object occupies. You'll find it easier to select and place plants and structures when you think of them as forms. If you can visualize your plants' mature sizes and shapes, you will save money and time; first, because you won't purchase too many plants, and, later, because you won't have to rework an overplanted jungle.

When grouping flowering plants, consider the style of the garden. If you want a Victorian-style bed, for example, you will have to follow the strict Victorian traditions of design in which

I like drifts, but I don't want to create artificial-looking bands of color. How can I avoid this?

Arrange various-sized clumps of plants in the planting area. Interplant different kinds of flowers at the drift edges to blur the line where one ends and the next begins.

flowering plants were placed symmetrically in orderly rows, creating ribbons of color, or used as if they were individual daubs of paint.

Many contemporary gardeners, however, prefer the softer, flowing look of a "drift" design. First popularized in the late 19th and early 20th centuries by Gertrude Jekyll, an influential English garden designer, the drift involves interweaving plants in casually shaped serpentine groups, as nature might assemble them. The idea is that plants look striking at their flowering peak, but before and after that their colors are less vibrant. Their appearance also changes as the viewer moves about and changes perspective in the garden. From one angle some plants seem to be at the focal point of the border, but from another they appear farther away, overlapped by another part of the drift.

To imagine how the personality of a specific plant can change depending upon how you group it, consider the impact of 25 daffodil bulbs planted at 1-foot intervals over the length of a bed; the result will be a thin, ineffective file of flowers. But plant the same number of daffodils more closely together in a wide, diagonal drift, and your eye enjoys a lush, yellow expanse.

The number of plants needed to create a drift, and its optimum size, depend upon your plants' growth habits and the size of the bed. A drift should be large enough to be seen from where it will be most frequently viewed. A drift averaging about 1 square yard usually is sufficient. Since perennials take two or three seasons to reach a good size, put in drifts of these flowers somewhat sparsely at first and allow the plants to grow and fill in until they achieve an attractive density.

Getting a Feel for Texture

Texture in garden design refers primarily to the visual effect of leaves, stems, and bark. Fine, silky, rough, thorny, feathery, glossy, and velvety are some of the terms we use to describe our visual experience of plants. Picture the papery, peeling bark of a white birch tree offset by the smooth, waxy, dark green leaves of a rhododendron—two

A Succesful Mix of Foliage, Texture, and Color
Artemisia schmidtiana 'Silver Mound', with English lavender and lavender cotton clustered close behind, finds a niche in the emerald green boxwood edge of this Middleburg, Virginia, bed designed to display foliage and texture.

very different textures that combine well. Ferns bring a lacy texture to the garden, while the pointed leaves of iris are sharply dramatic. Some plants have what is called architectural foliage, so visible is their leaf veining or so peculiar their hairy, downy surface. The beautifully veined leaves of the hosta, for example, give them great appeal for the gardener.

You can use texture in a tactile sense, too. How a plant feels may be the deciding factor in choice and placement. If you dislike handling rose bushes, you may forgo them despite their beauty and fragrance. Or you might deliberately choose a prickly plant like a barberry bush to discourage people from cutting across your lawn.

Plants of varying textures react to light differently. The woolly foliage of lamb's ears, for example, absorbs light, which enhances its soft look, while the glossy leaves of holly reflect light, emphasizing their sheen. Consider also the size of the individual leaves. A large-leaved plant is typically described as coarse textured, while a plant with small leaves is fine textured. A successful flower bed displays a blend of textures, including both tactile and visual qualities.

Understanding Color

Line, form, and texture are important design considerations, but for most gardeners, color tops them all. When designing with color, what works and what doesn't are more than simply matters of individual taste. To get good results, it helps to understand the nature of color and its effects from a scientific vantage point.

Your sense of color is based on your eyes' experience of wavelengths, or light messages, reflecting off surfaces, including flowers and leaves. The messages are complex, because color has many dimensions and qualities.

The way colors interrelate optically—harmonizing, complementing, or clashing—is determined largely by their position in the color spectrum. This spectrum is visible in nature in the rainbow, whose lineup of colors runs from red to orange, yellow, green, blue, and violet. The standard color wheel, used to organize colors spatially for easy understanding of their relationships, contains these same six colors, and their intermediate gradations, in counterclockwise order. Three of the six—red, yellow, and blue—are primary colors; orange, green, and violet are secondary colors, each one a 50-50 mix of the primary colors on either side. There are also infinite other gradations along the way.

Colors related by shared pigments are harmonious; those with no common color parentage are contrasting

Tip

Experiment with color combinations before you plant—visit your local florist or a friend's garden and select sprays of different flowering plants. Arrange the cut flowers in different groupings until you find color schemes that you like.

A Tool for Working with Color

The color wheel puts colors side by side or opposite each other so you can see how they relate optically. Adjacent colors are considered harmonious, containing mixtures of their neighbors. Colors facing each other are defined as contrasting or complementary. The pastels in the inner circles are tints, containing quantities of white; the deeper colors of the outer circle are shades, modified by black.

Thinking of flower color in terms of its position on the color wheel can help you create a garden with a specific emotional effect. Gardens filled with harmonious colors or even shades or tints of the same color tend to be viewed as calm and serene, and are ideal when positioned by seating areas. Alternatively, gardens with complementary color, filled with vivid contrasts, frequently are used along walkways, where a sense of action is pleasing.

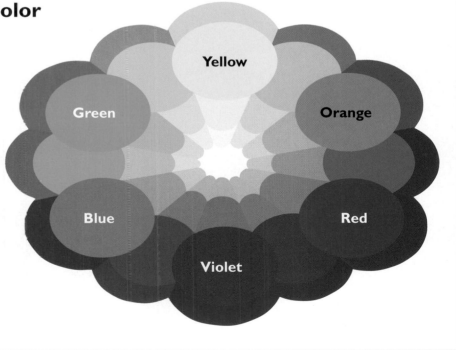

Composing with Color

	Popular Bedding and Border Plants	Complementary Partners	Harmonious Partners
RED FLOWERS	*Antirrhinum majus* 'Black Prince'	*Nicotiana alata* 'Lime Green'	*Boltonia asteroides* 'Pink Beauty'
	Cleome hasslerana 'Cherry Queen'	*Nicotiana langsdorfii*	*Petunia* x *hybrida* 'Fantasy Pink Morn'
	Dicentra eximia 'Adrian Bloom'	*Helleborus foetidus*	*Paeonia lactiflora* 'Sea Shell'
	Papaver orientale 'Allegro Viva'	*Moluccella laevis*	*Aquilegia canadensis*
	Gaillardia x *grandiflora* 'Goblin'	*Buxus sempervirens*	*Helenium autumnale* 'Moerheim Beauty'
	Hemerocallis 'Nanuet'	*Amaranthus* 'Viridis'	*Alcea rosea*
	Kalmia latifolia 'Ostbo Red'	*Hosta tardiflora*	*Anemone hupehensis*
ORANGE FLOWERS	*Belamcanda chinensis*	*Eustoma grandiflorum*	*Zinnia elegans*
	Fritillaria imperialis	*Hyacinthus orientalis*	*Narcissus poeticus*
	Impatiens x 'New Guinea Tango'	*Geranium* x *magnificum*	*Hemerocallis fulva*
	Ricinus communis 'Carmencita'	*Pulmonaria longifolia*	*Cosmos sulphureus*
	Tagetes erecta	*Ceratostigma plumbaginoides*	*Zinnia angustifolia*
	Zinnia angustifolia	*Delphinium* 'Blue Fountains'	*Coreopsis auriculata* 'Nana'
YELLOW FLOWERS	*Coreopsis verticillata* 'Golden Showers'	*Aster novae-angliae* 'Purple Dome'	*Chrysopsis mariana*
	Cytisus scoparius	*Campanula glomerata*	*Allium moly*
	Hemerocallis 'Golden Splendor'	*Salvia bulleyana*	*Canna* x *generalis* 'Pretoria'
	Iris pseudacorus	*Iris* 'Navy Strut'	*Potentilla fruticosa* 'Tangerine'
	Kerria japonica	*Heliotropium arborescens*	*Hypericum patulum*
	Rudbeckia hirta	*Buddleia davidii* 'Black Knight'	*Eremurus stenophyllus*
	Santolina chamaecyparissus	*Lavandula angustifolia*	*Coreopsis grandiflora*
GREEN FLOWERS	*Amaranthus* 'Viridis'	*Lilium* 'Enchantment'	*Adiantum pedatum*
	Helleborus foetidus	*Sedum spectabile* 'Carmen'	*Ilex opaca*
	Nicotiana alata 'Lime Green'	*Salvia splendens*	*Ageratum houstonianum*
	Moluccella laevis	*Anemone* x *hybrida* 'Rubra'	*Coleus* 'The Line'
BLUE FLOWERS	*Aster novi-belgii* 'Marie Ballard'	*Belamcanda chinensis*	*Nigella damascena*
	Hydrangea macrophylla	*Asclepias tuberosa*	*Delphinium* 'Blue Fountains'
	Consolida 'Blue Spire Improved'	*Hemerocallis fulva*	*Platycodon grandiflorus* 'Mariesii'
	Lobelia erinus 'Crystal Palace'	*Verbascum* 'Cotswold Queen'	*Caryopteris* 'Blue Mist'
	Lupinus polyphyllus	*Lilium* 'Gran Cru'	*Salvia farinacea*
VIOLET FLOWERS	*Cynara scolymus*	*Digitalis grandiflora*	*Pulmonaria longifolia*
	Geranium 'Johnson's Blue'	*Hemerocallis citrina*	*Syringa vulgaris* 'President Lincoln'
	Gomphrena globosa 'Buddy'	*Potentilla fruticosa* 'Tangerine'	*Perovskia atriplicifolia*
	Liatris scariosa 'September Glory'	*Rudbeckia nitida* 'Herbstsonne'	*Aster* x *frikartii* 'Mönch'
	Veronica longifolia	*Lantana camara*	*Heliotropium* 'Dwarf Marine'

or complementary. On the color wheel, harmonious colors are those positioned beside or near each other, while contrasting colors lie across from each other.

Colors also are described in terms of tone, value, and intensity. A tone is a color that is modified by the addition of white or black. When you add white, the tone is called a tint; pink, for example, is a tint of red. Add black, and the tone is called a shade; burgundy is a shade of red.

Value is the color's degree of lightness or darkness. Yellow, for example, is lighter in color than blue and thus is said to have a higher value. Saturation, or the intensity of a color, may range from vivid to muted to gray. And colors often are described in terms of temperature. Reds, oranges, and yellows are considered warm, while greens, blues, and violets are thought of as cool. Location, too, can influence color. Plants growing in coastal areas with moisture-laden air appear to have softer colors, while desert plants look brighter and sharper in the clear, dry air.

Texture and shape also can influence perception of color. We tend to sense the lemon yellow of *Lysimachia punctata,* or loosestrife, as being different from that of the hybrid lemon daylily, because the former is made up of tiny, delicate flowers on a spiky column, while the latter is a single, large, trumpet form rising well above its foliage.

Color Scheming

There are four basic kinds of color schemes for gardens. The most controlled is the monochromatic scheme, involving plants of a single color in various tints and shades. Such a garden might feature only yellows, blues, or whites. Or the scheme might be monochromatic in phases, which is a bit more ambitious, with an early spring-summer sequence of one color, followed later in the summer by a second flowering of another. This variation takes careful planning and a little luck, because you will have to choose flowers for the first group that will fade and die back in a timely fashion so as not to blur the color effect of the second planting.

Complementary color schemes combine opposite colors on the color wheel, for example, red with green, violet with yellow, or orange with blue. Such color combinations are powerful, and

they are not for every taste. If you like the idea, but want to develop it within certain limits, you can temper the color effects by positioning silvery foliage plants, for example *Artemisia absinthium,* between bold complementary plants.

A harmonious scheme uses a limited number of neighboring colors from the wheel. Violets, reds, and oranges are harmonious, as are blues, blue-violets, and pinks. Gardens designed to use colors in harmony offer an easy visual transition from color to color.

The color scheme that seems most natural is the polychromatic, which presents by design a many-colored, vivid display of hues and tints. Cottage gardens are typically polychromatic.

Blending Shapes and Colors for a Wild Effect
Brilliant, spiky spider lupines (Lupinus benthamii), native to the Los Angeles area, mingle with deep pink owl's clover (Orthocarpus purpurascens var. ornatus), orange California poppies, and paddle-shaped prickly pear cactus in these steep hillside beds in suburban Pasadena.

Designing the Border

*Borders establish the structure of
your garden, whether they are framed by
solid walls, hedges, fences, or trellised screens.
Designing one of these architectural
elements begins with an evaluation of
all the possible sites on your property
to find the best location, orientation,
and vertical backdrop for your planting.
The design should harmonize with its
location and reflect your tastes and
preferences in style and theme.*

Harmonious Backdrops and Borders
*A white picket fence serves as a sturdy backdrop on both
sides for low-growing borders of purple Iris sibirica,
pink-and-white Marguerite daisies, and roses, and
gracefully encloses a garden at the side of this home in
Missouri. The house's stone walls are softened by curtains
of yellow and red climbing roses.*

Adapting the Border to its Site

A border, by definition, is an edge or margin. The medieval cloister garden was a bordered sanctuary, set away from the noise and confusion of ordinary life by hedgerows or high walls covered with climbing plants. The modern-day border has the same potential to frame and enclose your property with beauty. Depending upon the shape of your garden and its relation to your house and other outbuildings, you may want to create borders in one, two, or several locations. You might create a border against an existing backdrop to fit in with the surrounding architecture or landscape. Or you may want to start from scratch and build a backdrop, one strategically located to solve a landscaping problem while it showcases your border planting. You might even plan your border as a source of cutting flowers if you entertain often and enjoy bouquets of flowers placed about the house.

Making a Border Work for You

Borders work in many ways. First, they can define your property's boundaries and create a sense of privacy and enclosure. A knee-high border, say, would mark property lines or delineate a footpath, while a border that is tall enough to block the view would create a discrete garden room that offers privacy. A border can screen you and your garden from prevailing winds. The plants in a border can muffle traffic noise. The strong line of a border backdrop can introduce a visual connection, tying together structures and the garden. A border provides the setting in which to present your choicest plants.

As you think about designing and siting your borders, keep in mind the ways you and your family will want to use the space they frame. Decide whether it's important for you to have large, uninterrupted views across your property, or whether you prefer to create a series of garden rooms with borders functioning as the walls. Borders placed at the perimeter of your property leave open areas of lawn for use in entertaining or recreation. If you prefer privacy and would like to have a series of sites that can be used individually, borders that divide the yard into discrete parcels create spaces for discovery and retreat.

When you have an idea of how the enclosed spaces will be used, make sure that your usual traffic patterns will not be unduly disturbed by

A Border Cutting Garden
Supplying floral adornment both indoors and out, this late-spring border thrives in a hot, sunny corner in Brentwood, California, sheltered by a tall, informal hedge backdrop. Prominent in the front are rich purple clusters of tender perennial Limonium perezii and brightly colored tulips.

any new border, and build ample openings into border backdrops where necessary.

Achieving the Right Scale

Use the size of your yard as the starting point in determining the dimensions of your border, particularly its depth. A useful rule of thumb is that the combined depth of facing borders should not exceed 25 percent of the width of the yard that they define. For example, if your yard is 75 feet wide, you will get the best effect if you limit the depth of matched borders along either side to no more than 9 feet each. (Check whether local zoning regulations require a setback along your property lines, and adjust the border size accordingly.) The depth of the border will translate directly into the number of rows, and hence different plants, that it can accommodate. A 3-foot-deep border, for example, can comfortably support two rows of plants.

The size of your house is also a consideration in deciding how large to make your border. A very deep border tends to look grandiose next to a small house; a narrow border skirting the walls of a three-story house will look inadequate.

Where you are left with difficult choices, it may be better to have one large border that makes a proportionately satisfying statement and displays color over several months than two or more smaller ones that escape notice and play out their color in short order.

Composing with Plants

To decide what plants will look best in your new border, begin by standing at the spots from which you will be viewing it most often. The border will have a different visual impact from each vantage point, changing according to plant shapes and sizes and the basic rules of perspective as you move about. For example, a foundation border on either side of the front door consisting of a perfectly balanced line of small shrubs may look fine when seen from a level position 15 feet back, but it may be lost to passersby who see the border from a lower, more distant vantage point, such as the street. And it may look different again when seen from your driveway or front doorstep.

To experiment with various plant sizes and shapes, and to get a preview of how a proposed border as a whole will look in three dimensions,

Graceful Lines of a Double Border
Curved border edgings create a sense of space and motion in this small Lancaster, Pennsylvania, garden, and lead the eye to a gate at the back. Boxwoods, azaleas, and rhododendrons add color in the shade.

temporarily put some large objects into the sites under consideration; use lawn chairs, for example, to simulate vertical shrubs and perhaps some small cardboard cartons to represent dense clumps of flowers. Then, take a look at them from your back door, from the bench behind the house, from the gate in the side yard, and from your windows. When you are satisfied with each view, you can begin creating your design.

Cultural Considerations of a Border

A border design is affected by the same basic factors that influence bed design, including sunlight, soil, terrain, wind, and existing vegetation, but with modifications to account for the fact that the border will be sheltered on one side.

For part of the day, most borders are in shade as the result of having a vertical element that blocks the sun. As a rule, perennials need fewer hours of sunlight than annuals, which explains why perennials are traditional border favorites. Most perennials need six hours of direct summer

A Large-Scale Screen
A tall, all-green border at the back of this rural New York property gives definition to a distant vista and blocks unwanted views. The snowy foliage of 'White Christmas' caladium makes for a refreshing contrast among the dark shades of this evergreen planting.

Brilliant Colors from Any Perspective
This border backs on a large window of a northern California house, to be enjoyed equally from within or outside. Bright red 'San Remo' Darwin tulips, coral bells, purple bearded iris, and sea lavender carry their late-spring colors the length of the border.

sun, but some, such as astilbe, Siberian bugloss, many iris varieties, hosta, golden groundsel, and Virginia bluebell, favor shade or filtered sun. In the South, even sun-loving perennials such as yarrow, golden Marguerite, and phlox need protection from the midday sun.

On the other hand, some parts of the border are relatively hotter and drier, such as those along a south- or west-facing brick, stone, or stucco wall that reflects light and absorbs heat, slowly releasing it to its immediate surroundings. The extra heat and light of the microclimate can accelerate the bloom time of spring bulbs by weeks, but you will have to water that part of the border more frequently later in the season.

The microclimate of a site also is affected by its topography. A site in a natural dip or hollow can be quite warm if it's protected from wind, but if the hollow is shaded, it can be rather cool. And a low, cool site might suffer frost sooner than a higher, sunnier slope. Rainfall might be relatively less in the lee of a site's high ground than it would on the windward side of the same location.

You can manipulate a site to alter the microclimate, adapting certain features to produce specific conditions. For example, the soil in raised beds that face the sun will warm quickly in the spring; the south-facing side of fences or walls can be used to grow tender climbers, wall shrubs, and trained fruit trees, since the plants are in sun for much of the day.

A wall or hedge backdrop also may affect your soil, and you may need to incorporate soil amendments for your border plants. If, for example, you have a concrete block foundation wall behind the border, take a soil test to check pH and nutrient levels. Limestone and magnesium can leach from the foundation into the soil, making it extremely alkaline and, therefore, unsuitable for azaleas, rhododendrons, and many other evergreens unless improved.

If your selected border site has been compacted, whether by construction equipment or by years of foot traffic, do some deep tilling or spadework to loosen the subsoil before planting. If fast-draining sand and gravel have been backfilled around your foundation just below the surface soil, allow additional space between the border and foundation wall, and add topsoil amended with moisture-retaining humus to your planting area.

Hedge backdrops present their own kind of problem for border plants, since their surface roots compete with the other plants for soil nutrients and water. To compensate, you may have to give the smaller plants in your border some extra fertilizer and water. Otherwise, move your plants a little farther away from the competition. Or plant drought-tolerant varieties such as yarrow, gaillardia, or coreopsis.

If you have steep slopes, wet soil, sandy areas, huge boulders, or rough winds, you can alter the terrain or choose plants to suit those conditions. Change the grade of a steep slope by building terraced beds held up by sturdy retaining walls *(see page 47)*; these walls will make perfect sites for a border of alpines and other plants that require quick-draining soil. Herbs, including rosemary, periwinkle, lavender, and chamomile, are great performers in well-drained areas. In a wet location where, for example, your border is at the edge of a pond or in a low-lying part of a garden, plant a border of goatsbeard, marsh marigold, yellow flag, or globe flower.

Tip

Consider planting a bog border on a naturally damp patch of ground and adding an asymmetrical edging of stones and flat rocks to create a stepping-stone path around the garden. Add moisture-loving grasses such as sedges and rushes to contrast with other perennials.

Establishing a Border Style and Theme

The style of your border should reflect the design and character of your house, the physical attributes of the site, and your tastes. You will set the tone of the border by choosing formal or informal elements. These two general designations encompass a wide range of styles, from the straight bands of a carefully clipped formal border, to the carefree exuberance of a cottage border—and all the variations in-between. Whatever style you choose, the colors, textures, and forms of the plants within your border should be arranged to unify it, using rhythm and balance.

(see page 51)

An Informal Border Retreat

White trelliswork and fencing add texture and interest to a corner of this Santa Ana, California, garden room, and provide backdrops against which to showcase a collection of roses. Silvery mounds of Artemisia 'Powis Castle' reflect the gray wall and act as grounding elements for both the trellis and bench.

Setting a Formal Tone

The tone of a border in the formal style is classic and ageless, reflecting a human love of order. Its lines are straight or traced in simple curves. There is mirroring symmetry, and the border itself is oriented in a line that leads directly to a focal point, such as the front door of the house, or a formal ornament. A classic border in a formal garden design might be a straight-sided geometric shape, generally a rectangle. Or it could be two identical borders on either side of an architectural feature, such as a doorway or driveway. Evergreen plantings or brick walls provide a strong year-round framework for the formal border. Hedges are rigorously clipped to keep them seamlessly uniform along their length *(see page 51)*, and the line along the front of the border is strengthened by a low hedge, such as dwarf boxwood, or by a brick or stone edge.

Traditionally, the formal border has been filled with annual plants or with single-species plantings, such as a collection of roses, irises, or heathers. Such plantings emphasize the unifying structure of the border's framework. But a formal border containing a variety of plants functions just as well, because the border's structure keeps the design coherent. Whatever the choice, a formal border typically uses a limited palette.

The modern adaptation of the English formal border has a greater variety of compact perennials and foliage plants within its symmetrical green framework. The plants should be arranged so that they step down neatly from tall at the back to medium in the middle range to low-growth habit at the front, all in well-defined, regimental ranks.

Setting an Informal Tone

The lines within an informal border meander in a way that suggests a group of plants naturally clustered in a landscape, growing in easy abundance in the shelter of a rock, fence, or wall. The border's casual asymmetry is enhanced by the wide variety of plants used—shrubs, perennials, bulbs, annuals, and vines—all combined in what has come to be known as the mixed border. The front-edge plantings could be drifts of small flowering plants rather than the boxwood rank of the formal border. The flowering plants in the informal border are an eye-catching mix of colors, shapes, and flowering times, rather than the formal border's reserved collection. Ornamentation should be equally casual in style. Rocks, a large wooden sculpture, or driftwood will all complement the natural look of an informal border.

Establishing a Theme

Within the range of formal and informal border styles, the choice of a theme is a good way to focus your design ideas. You might plant a bride's border, in which every plant blooms in different shades of white; a witch's border, filled with magical mandrake, wormwood, and foxglove; or a border devoted to plants mentioned in the works of Shakespeare. Plants can be restricted to one genus or species, such as azalea, camellia, iris, lilac, or rose. A culinary garden could have various herbs, ornamental lettuces, cabbages, and edible flowers. A wildlife garden could have flowers and other plants that attract hummingbirds or butterflies. A fragrance garden would be redolent with scent.

Color makes a useful theme for a border. Perhaps the most dramatic is the moon garden—planted with white flowers that open at night to be enjoyed by moonlight. Or choose specific foliage and flower colors, such as a blue garden, with wisteria, cornflower, lobelia, and blue salvia; a pink garden, with cleome, geranium, cosmos, and chrysanthemum; or a silver-and-gold garden, with 'Silver Mound' artemisia, silver sage, golden yarrow, and golden anthemis.

Site conditions also can prompt border themes. A shade border can have a woodland or green-garden theme. A rocky location can become home to a border of alpine plants. Other environmental theme possibilities include desert, deep shade, and seaside borders.

Establishing Rhythm in a Border

Though a backdrop ties a border's plantings together from behind, rhythm is the visual device that unifies the border along its length. Rhythm within a border occurs when one element repeats at regular intervals to set up visual punctuations that catch your eye as it is drawn along the border. As in music, this rhythmic repetition links

A formal hedge spans the back edge of our yard. How can I keep it as a screen but change its rigid appearance?

Stop shearing the hedge and begin selective hand pruning for a more relaxed look. Then add shorter shrubs in front of it in a casual, random pattern.

Manipulating Rhythm and Perspective: Buttressing

The notion of buttressing is borrowed from architectural engineering, and describes a prop abutting and supporting a major structure such as a wall. In the context of border design, buttressing is a device that breaks up an overly long horizontal line by positioning the occasional shrub or plant on the perpendicular. These "props," which advance toward the front of the border, have the effect of creating small, partial enclosures. In this way, they establish pleasing internal rhythms while providing a framework to bring diverse border plants into scale. Buttressing also creates the illusion of greater depth in the border.

If you have a formal border, buttress with shrubs of the same type as the background hedging. Position the buttresses at regular intervals and clip them to be somewhat smaller and lower than the hedge, as shown at right. For less formal designs, let large shrubs at the back of the border occasionally protrude into the bed, and let the intervals be irregular in keeping with the freer, more naturalistic form of the border.

Using Color for Balance and Rhythm

The repetition of bright yellow in this formal double border in Cooksville, Maryland, helps balance the borders and reinforces their mirrored symmetry. The rhythmic use of color strengthens the lines right up to the focal point.

Tip

Use decorative climbing vines in a border to add vertical interest—and not only against a backdrop. A 6-foot pole can support clematis or scarlet runner beans. Three or four long poles lashed at the top make a good frame for honeysuckle or a climbing rose. Let vines scramble for a season over nearby shrubs.

each part of the composition to the next. Create rhythm by repeating color, leaf texture, plant form, or a particularly striking plant.

There are several ways to create color rhythms. First, you can establish a few discrete planting areas within a border, and group plants that combine well within those areas as units. Intersperse contrasting plants between the units; plants with pale gray foliage or creamy white masses of flowers work well.

Or, devise a plan based on a single dominant color scattered at three or more locations along the border. With careful planning, you can time plantings so that one color predominates in spring, another in early to mid-summer, and a third in late summer.

As an alternative to color, use contrasting foliage textures or plant forms to create rhythm. The coarse leaves of acanthus, false spirea, hosta, or groundsel bush, grouped amid the medium foliage of alchemilla, euphorbia, or peonies, make a fascinating textural tapestry.

Creating a Balance with Color and Texture

Use color and texture to achieve balance in large borders, where your eye must travel over a long distance to get a complete picture. Color balancing is the careful placement of colors designed to create a variety of color associations, rather than just one or two focal points in the border. You can achieve color balance, for example, by

planting several equally warm-colored plants, such as bright red 'Cambridge Scarlet' monarda and brilliant scarlet geraniums, at some distance from each other so as not to concentrate all of the heat in one place. Or achieve balance by surrounding one or two flowering plants in a strong primary hue with a mass of paler-tinted flowers in the same color family, such as a small cluster of yellow ranunculus among a drift of yellow-centered white daisies.

You also can use color balancing to create the illusion that the border is longer or deeper. To give more depth to a narrow border, position warm, "advancing" colors such as red, orange, and yellow in the foreground, and cool, "retreating" colors such as blue, green, and violet at the rear of the border.

The same principle of balance applies to the texture of the plants in a border. If two plants of coarse texture or with large leaves are used in the same border, they should be separated for better display to avoid creating a "heavy spot." To achieve the best sense of balance, interplant finely textured plants between them.

Finally, use the height and mass, or the growth habit, of a plant to create balance within the border. A plant may have a vertical, rounded, or bushy form, or an open and loose form. In planning a border, aim for contrasting forms of height and mass throughout. If a huge berry-laden shrub already dominates one end of the border site, incorporate a noteworthy feature, such as another large shrub, a group of smaller shrubs with interesting and colorful bark, or a sculpture, at the other end to balance it.

Unifying a Border with Color
White is used to tie together the parts of this rural New Jersey border and to link it to the house in the background. Annual caladiums, cleome, impatiens, and salvia range in front of a low stone wall, with added rhythm supplied by the color and form of a row of potted white wax begonias.

Using Foliage in Border Design

	Type	Color	Texture	Shape
Pennisetum setaceum 'Rubrum'	grass	maroon	fine	mounded clump
Deschampsia flexuosa	grass	green	fine	upright clump
Miscanthus sinensis 'Morning Light'	grass	silver	fine	clump
Mahonia aquifolium	shrub	green	coarse	upright
Fothergilla major	shrub	dark green	medium	pyramidal
Berberis thunbergii 'Crimson Pygmy'	shrub	maroon	fine	compact mound
Clematis macropetala	vine	green	fine	climbing
Actinidia arguta	vine	green	coarse	climbing
Humulus lupulus 'Aureus'	vine	yellow	coarse	climbing
Athyrium nipponicum	fern	pale green	fine	arching
Adiantum pedatum	fern	gray-green	fine	arching
Osmunda cinnamomea	fern	pale green	fine	arching
Artemisia spp.	perennial	gray	fine	spreading
Ceratostigma plumbaginoides	perennial	green	fine	bushy
Hosta spp.	perennial	varies	varies	mounding
Lavandula spp.	perennial	gray-green	fine	mounding
Ajuga reptans	ground cover	bronze	fine	spreading
Cerastium tomentosum	ground cover	silver	fine	spreading
Saxifraga stolonifera 'Tricolor'	ground cover	green and red	coarse	spreading

Note: The abbreviation "spp." stands for the plural of "species"; where used in lists it means that many, but not all, of the species in the genus meet the criteria of the list.

The Border's Vertical Backdrop

The backdrop of a border serves as a place against which to showcase the distinctive shapes, textures, and colors of an assortment of plants. The sides of houses, stone walls, wooden fences, latticework, and hedges are all potential backdrops for borders. You already might have just the backdrop you need for your border—a sunny south-facing wall of your house, for example, onto which you can attach a trellis for climbing roses and, at the base, lay a carpet of lavender and catmint. You may want to build your own fence or wall, situated perfectly to block an unsightly view or to enclose a space, as well as to provide shelter and a setting for your favorite plants. Or, you may want to use a pre-built picket fence or a more rustic split-rail fence, depending on the border design you have chosen.

Establishing the Dimensions of Your Backdrop

There are some guidelines for choosing a pleasing and functional height for your border backdrop. A wall or fence less than 3 feet tall could be used to frame a dwarf hedge and direct foot traffic. For example, if you are considering building a backdrop in your front yard to be seen from the street, a 3-foot-tall element will mark property lines without cutting off your view of the street and the view into your yard. Build a higher wall or fence to ensure privacy. It should be tall enough to screen out the background and focus attention on your border plantings. For a wall or fence to be an effective backdrop, it should be taller than most of the plants in the border.

Walls and fences serving as backdrops must conform to local building codes concerning location, height, and materials. If you are building along a property line, consult with your neighbor as a courtesy; consider the possibility of splitting costs and maintenance responsibilities.

Building Materials for Walls and Fences

Choose materials that suit the style of your garden, the architecture of your house, and existing surfaces such as paths and patios. For example, a solid brick wall would be a good choice for a traditional style or formal house and garden in need of a windbreak, and a decorative white picket fence would be ideal for a Victorian house with an informal garden.

The Right Border for Each Backdrop
The plants in this composite illustration have been selected to show how border plants handsomely play off the characteristics of the vertical elements they front. Plant forms can be used to complement or echo the tone established by a backdrop. Positioned in front of heavy or solid backdrops, or on top as illustrated by the potted plant shown here, border plants also can soften the massive effect created by a solid wall.

Picket Fence
Dark shrubs create a striking color contrast against white picket fencing. The conical form of the shrubs mimics the pickets, tying the border and backdrop together.

Walls made of brick, adobe, or stone are the longest-lasting and most stable backdrops. They are strong enough to stand alone, or to retain earth on a slope. Stone walls can be built of ashlar, a finely finished, uniform stone, or of rough-hewn rubble. Rubble walls can be either bonded with mortar or dry-laid. Mortared walls require coping, a top finishing layer that prevents rain-water from penetrating the wall and gradually weakening the mortar. Once mortared walls are in place, they require little maintenance. If you prefer a more informal, natural-looking wall, consider a dry-stone structure; it is excellent for marking property boundaries, and tumbled stones are easily replaced.

A stone retaining wall must be constructed carefully to support the considerable weight of the earth behind it. The retaining wall should be built atop a gravel-filled trench that will allow water to seep away. It also should have buttresses, or "deadmen," set into the hillside at right angles to the wall in order to anchor it.

Instead of stone, you can use pressure-treated landscape timbers or recycled railroad ties to hold a series of stepped raised beds on a slope. The face of each short retaining wall will make an attractive backdrop for a border.

Wooden fences range in price and style, from ornamentally carved hardwood palings to picket fencing to simple post and split-rail assemblies. You can build a fence from scratch, purchasing your own lumber, or you can buy it in ready-made sections from a hardware supplier or a fence company, and install it yourself to save money.

When choosing wood for building your fence, you might select Southern yellow pine that has been pressure-treated with preservative chemicals to make it resistant to rot and insect damage; this pine is popular due to its relatively low cost. Use it especially for the posts. Although it is considered safe, there is a widespread opinion that pressure-treated wood should not be used where edible plants are situated. Check with your local lumber yard for up-to-date information on the safety of this product.

If you are planting a garden of herbs or other edible plants near your fence, you might prefer to use a naturally rot-resistant wood, such as cedar, redwood, or cypress. This wood is handsomer and more weather-resistant than pressure-treated wood, but it also costs more.

You can treat exposed wood yourself with a commercial wood preservative every few years. If you want to cover your fence with climbing

Trellis

A neat white trellis provides the perfect backdrop for a climbing rose. The rose subtly masks the grid of the trellis while the planting and backdrop combination creates a private and sheltered place for visitors entering or leaving the house.

Brick Wall

Soft, mounding perennials balance the heaviness of this handsome brick wall while the neatly trimmed shrubs reinforce its formality. Heat retained by the wall warms the soil early, bringing color to the border before any other part of the yard.

plants, be sure you choose a product that is not toxic to them.

Fence posts should be sunk well into the ground—to a depth at least twice their diameter. In areas where deep frost can be a problem, posts should be sunk at least 30 inches below ground level. Tall fences and closed-board fences that present a large surface to the wind should have their posts set in concrete footings. A fence that functions as a wind-screen should have an openwork rather than a solid surface design. The permeable surface of openwork will cut down the force of the wind, whereas a solid fence can cause the wind to backwash over the top, buffeting border plants on the lee side.

Cultivating a Stone Retaining Wall

Stone walls are an attractive way to retain terracing on a hilly lot, because the stones will look integral to the landscape. Building a series of stepped walls creates an excellent habitat for a fascinating variety of plants. Creepers will cascade over the top of a retaining wall. Alpines, rock garden plants—including various species of sedum

A Border of Drought-Tolerant Plants
This elegant white picket fence screens the house from the nearby road and serves as a backdrop for a casual border of Mexican sage, sea lavender, Peruvian lilies, and roses. These colorful, drought-tolerant plants thrive in the arid Del Mar, California, climate.

and saxifrage—and trailing plants such as *Aubrieta* are especially effective tucked into the crevices of a dry-laid stone wall. Herbs such as thyme and lavender also thrive in the well-drained conditions above a dry-laid stone wall. Just add a bit of soil between the rocks and these small charmers will thrive for years.

If you live in an area where native stone is easy to obtain, a low dry-laid stone wall is ideal for a country-style informal garden. But building a stone wall is not for everyone; it takes a strong back and some engineering instinct.

Fences to Fit Your Style

Various kinds of fencing have historical, regional, and stylistic associations that may influence your choice. A white picket fence is traditionally American. Its low height makes it a firm but friendly boundary that is well-suited to 18th- and 19th-century houses with colorful borders that abut the street. A Virginia rail fence, made of rough-hewn rails that zigzag across the landscape, creates planting pockets between the zigzags. A plain board fence, painted or unpainted, is an idea borrowed from horse country. It, too, looks right at home when backing up an informal border.

Where frequent exposure to desiccating winds and glaring sun can create difficult conditions for sensitive plants, an open board wooden fence

A Rock-Edged Terraced Border
Evergreens, perennials, and bulbs flourish in the perfect drainage supplied by this terraced Pennsylvania garden. Low-growing plants and the upright foliage of daffodils harmonize with the low, stepped-stone retaining walls.

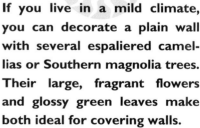

Tip

If you live in a mild climate, you can decorate a plain wall with several espaliered camellias or Southern magnolia trees. Their large, fragrant flowers and glossy green leaves make both ideal for covering walls.

may serve to solve the problem and add visual interest to the setting. Not only can the fence filter wind and light through its vertical gaps, it also can serve as a backdrop to wind-tolerant plants such as rock roses and wallflowers, or support tough climbers, including English ivy and trumpet creeper.

Hedges as Living Backdrops

You can substitute a hedge of evergreen or deciduous shrubs wherever you might use a wall or fence, except when you want to retain terraced earth. Evergreen hedges have the benefit of being a living part of the garden, and may produce fragrant flowers or attract wildlife. Forsythia and shrub roses make fine informal hedges; rose of Sharon does particularly well in western climates, and a tapestry hedge, combining desert sumac, Texas ranger, and quailbush, would be effective in a hot, dry climate. You can choose hedge plants in a variety of colors, ranging from shiny deep

Protection and Privacy
Golden candles of nettle-leaved mullein glow against a living wall of deep green hemlock that serves as both windbreak and privacy screen for this magnificent Pennsylvania perennial border.

When to Trim a Shrub

Timing and techniques for trimming shrubs vary with the type of plant and your goal in pruning. Deciduous shrubs usually can be pruned anytime during the growing season. But young, flowering, and evergreen shrubs need special attention, as shown here. New shrubs need light pruning from the start. Flowering shrubs benefit from occasional hard pruning to promote bloom. To avoid unsightly gaps in evergreens, do not cut back hard at one time.

▲ **Young Shrubs.** Container-grown plants need only minimal pruning at planting time. Shear half of the first year's growth at the end of the first season. Continue shearing half of each year's new growth in midsummer until the shrub has reached the desired size; then trim occasionally during the growing season to keep it neat.

▼ **Flowering Shrubs.** In addition to annual shearing, bushes such as forsythia that produce multiple branches from the ground will need thinning—the removal of about one-third of the old or non-productive branches—each year. Spring-flowering shrubs should be thinned after flowering, and summer-flowering shrubs during the dormant season. If your flowering shrubs produce berries, prune after the berries drop.

green to muted gray-green to variegated. You also could create a single hedgerow by combining different plants. Generally, hedges are less expensive to put in than walls or fences, and they are easier to modify if you should later change your mind.

Because they are living backdrops, hedges require some extra attention. First, they might take several seasons to become fully established. In harsh winter climates, they also could require protection from snow loads. Where space or water is limited, vigorous hedges may compete with border plants, thereby defeating their purpose.

Some of the best and most densely growing evergreens for hedges are boxwood, cotoneaster, cherry laurel, euonymus, osmanthus, and pittosporum. Some conifers work well, too, including Lawson cypress, yew, hemlock, arborvitae, and western red cedar. Suitable deciduous hedge plants include barberry, buckthorn, Russian olive, forsythia, hawthorn, flowering quince, and shrub roses, especially the rugosas and gallicas.

Hedges lend themselves to many forms of garden expression. Fine-textured shrubs that take well to shearing are the best choice for formal gardens. Flowering and deciduous shrubs are a better choice for informal settings. Whatever variety you choose, make sure its mature size and shape will suit the dimensions of your border.

▲ **Evergreen Hedges.** Shear occasionally during summer to maintain size. Do not cut back to leafless wood because most evergreens will not produce new growth on old wood. To rejuvenate, remove larger dead or damaged branches in late summer or fall, when the plants have finished growing actively for the season.

Establishing and Maintaining a Formal Hedge

Pruning a formal hedge is done primarily to increase its density and restrict its size and shape. Some young hedges need hand-pruning; older ones respond well to shearing. The general rule of established hedge maintenance is to cut off all but about a half-inch of each year's growth once the hedge reaches maturity. If the hedge is composed of fast-growing plants, you may need to prune it several times a year; if slow-growing, prune every other year.

▲ **1. Decide how wide** you want the bottom of the hedge and how much you want it to taper in at the top. Clip the top, front, and back starting from the bottom up, to create the proper angle. Do not clip sides that abut adjacent plants, as you will want the gap between plants to fill in over time. Step back periodically to check hedge form.

▶ **2. Shear a flat plane across** the top and sides of an established hedge. After you have finished shearing, remove clippings that have not fallen to the ground by running a leaf rake over the surface of the hedge. Finally, clean your shearing tool, making sure to remove encrusted sap or resin.

Passages and Pauses Amid Beds and Borders

Imaginative design can make a garden into more than a mere plot of favorite flowers. By thoughtfully laying out a palette of plant colors, textures, and shapes, you can create a bed, a border, or a combination of both that will transform your garden, like the ones shown here and on the following pages, into a serene journey or an enchanting destination.

A Shaded Place for Quiet Contemplation
Girded by borders of lush flowering shrubs in a tranquil woodland setting, this raised bed edged in mortared brick imparts a gratifying sense of constancy to any visitor fortunate enough to come upon it.

A. *Rhododendron* 'Daybreak' (3)
B. *Hosta fortunei* 'Aurea Marginata' (4)
C. *Hosta undulata var. univittata* (1)
D. *Hosta sieboldiana* 'Frances Williams' (2)
E. *Impatiens wallerana* (12)
F. *Viola x wittrockiana* (30)
G. *Hedera helix* (4)
H. *Ajuga reptans* (6)
I. *Rhododendron kaempferi* (1)
J. *Rhododendron* 'Blue Danube' (1)

NOTE: The key lists each plant type and the total quantity needed to replicate the garden shown. The diagram's letters and numbers refer to the type of plant and the number sited in an area.

A Parade of Color Ready for Review

Neatly framed by a low hedge of boxwood, this Long Island, New York, border presents the passing viewer with a billowing swath of flowers in many colors. Successful and dynamic borders like this one sometimes rely on both softscape, such as the hedge plants in front and trees in back, and hardscape, in this case the white picket fence, to define the space. Shades of pink, including blooms of Queen-of-the-prairie, yarrow, and astilbe, repeat throughout the length of the border to establish a pleasing sense of rhythm. The tidy boxwood serves as a soothing counterpoint to the complexity and planned unruliness of the plantings it contains.

A. Filipendula rubra (2)
B. Cephalaria gigantea (1)
C. Delphinium sp. (3)
D. Nicotiana langsdorfii (6)
E. Lysimachia clethroides (1)
F. Hemerocallis 'Stella d'Oro' (2)
G. Caryopteris x clandonensis 'Longwood Blue' (1)
H. Coreopsis verticillata 'Zagreb' (1)
I. Crocosmia 'Firebird' (3)
J. Hydrangea sp. (1)
K. Echinacea purpurea 'Alba' (1)
L. Rudbeckia laciniata (1)
M. Astilbe chinensis 'Superba' (1)
N. Sidalcea 'Party Girl' (2)

O. Lavatera 'Barnsley' (4)
P. Achillea 'Summer Shades' (3)
Q. Alchemilla mollis (1)
R. Campanula lactiflora (2)
S. Malva alcea (2)
T. Buxus sp. (12)

NOTE: The key lists each plant type and the total quantity needed to replicate the garden shown. The diagram's letters and numbers refer to the type of plant and the number sited in an area.

The Charm of Checkerboard

The soft interplay of green and gray gives this checkerboard bed of two different species of santolina in Santa Monica, California, an almost hypnotic visual appeal abetted by a pleasing fragrance. Although planted in a formal arrangement, the santolina grows out in a billowing habit that keeps the bed from appearing rigid. The border of mixed perennials enlivens the scene with an array of colors and complements the casual elegance of the bed, while the wrought-iron bench framed with potted hibiscus solidifies the setting as a marvelous place to stop and indulge the senses.

A. *Santolina virens* (44)
B. *Santolina chamaecyparissus* (40)
C. *Sium sisarum* (1)
D. *Convolvulus cneorum* (8)
E. *Rosa bracteata* 'Mermaid' (2)
F. *Penstemon* 'Flame' (3)
G. *Digitalis purpurea* (10)
H. *Hibiscus syriacus* 'Diana' (2)
I. *Pelargonium x hortorum* (2)
J. *Chilopsis linearis* (1)

NOTE: The key lists each plant type and the total quantity needed to replicate the garden shown. The diagram's letters and numbers refer to the type of plant and the number sited in an area.

Delightful Double Borders

An informal planting scheme imposed on what is traditionally a formal arrangement—the double border—makes an irresistible enticement to visitors to stroll through this Santa Monica, California, garden. The board-and-lattice fence provides an elegant backdrop for one of the borders, forming a starting point for the gradual descent of plant heights. The resulting cascade of color, made up mostly of hardy and tender perennials and two cultivars of roses, eventually spills out onto the path.

A. *Alyssum maritimum* 'Little Dorrit' (24)
B. *Dianthus chinensis* (1)
C. *Iris × germanica* 'Florentina' (6)
D. *Papaver nudicaule* (8)
E. *Viola tricolor* (4)
F. *Pelargonium × hortorum* (3)
G. *Rosa* 'The Fairy' (1)
H. *Rosa* 'Voodoo' (1)
I. *Foeniculum vulgare* (3)
J. *Antirrhinum majus* (8)
K. *Phlox drummondii* (6)
L. *Helichrysum bracteatum* (4)
M. *Campanula rapunculoides* (1)
N. *Aquilegia vulgaris* (1)
O. *Nicotiana alata* (12)

NOTE: The key lists each plant type and the total quantity needed to replicate the garden shown. The diagram's letters and numbers refer to the type of plant and the number sited in an area.

Setting the Scene for Relaxation

This border in the yard of an East Hampton, New York, home fronts a wooden deck that serves family and guests as a delightful place to commune with nature at its most appealing. The arrangement features a profusion of perennials and shrubs that offer up bloom from April through October. Then, throughout winter, evergreen shrubs provide a strong sense of structure and a splash of green. A tall hedge of arborvitae forms the backdrop for the border, focuses attention on the colorful plantings, and stands as a privacy barrier, screening the deck from the neighboring yard.

A. *Buddleia* 'White Bouquet' (1)
B. *Cephalaria gigantea* (2)
C. *Erysimum variegata* (3)
D. *Rosa* 'Grüss an Aachen' (2)
E. *Lavandula angustifolia* 'Hidcote' (1)
F. *Geranium macrorrhizum* (2)
G. *Salvia* x *superba* 'May Night' (9)
H. *Papaver* sp. (3)
I. *Filipendula vulgaris* 'Flore Pleno' (3)
J. *Helianthemum* 'Wisley Pink' (6)
K. *Erysimum* 'Bowles Mauve' (8)
L. *Geranium* 'New Hampshire' (1)

M. *Digitalis purpurea* (5)
N. *Paeonia* sp. (2)
O. *Rosa rubrifolia* (2)
P. *Dianthus* x *allwoodii* 'Lace Romero' (2)
Q. *Stachys byzantina* (1)
R. *Aster novae-angliae* 'Purple Dome' (3)
S. *Penstemon* 'Husker Red' (1)
T. *Aster novae-angliae* 'Harrington's Pink' (3)
U. *Crambe cordifolia* (1)
V. *Thuja* sp. (15)

NOTE: *The key lists the plant type and total quantity needed to replicate the garden shown. The diagram's letters and numbers refer to the plant type and the number sited in an area.*

The Precise Beauty of a Formal Layout

A place for stopping as well as passing through, this elegant variation on a knot garden in Athens, Georgia, shows the symmetry, straight lines, and simple curves that are the cornerstone of formal garden design. Its beds and borders also include all of the other elements of a classic formal plan: a limited palette of plants, a simple color scheme, and clearly defined axes. The varying pinks of the sedum, petunias, and geraniums add touches of color that pick up the warm tint of the brick walks. Neatly clipped boxwood and yew provide a living framework for the beds, while the white picket fence backs up the encircling borders.

A. *Buxus sempervirens* (240)
B. *Pelargonium x domesticum* (96)
C. *Sedum x* 'Autumn Joy' (24)
D. *Petunia x hybrida* 'Pink Satin' (36)
E. *Taxus* sp. (8)
F. *Hemerocallis* sp. (8)
G. *Phlox drummondii* (60)
H. *Aegopodium podagraria* 'Variegata' (24)

NOTE: The key lists each plant type and the total quantity needed to replicate the garden shown. The diagram's letters and numbers refer to the type of plant and the number sited in an area.

Plant Selection and Plans

A garden bed or border may be filled with a symphony of flowers selected to excite, soothe, or inspire visitors with their beauty. Start with a carefully considered plan, then select plants to create a rewarding garden. Plants translate your ideas about space and color into living, three-dimensional compositions. Carry a notepad to record pleasing plants and particular combinations that strike your fancy so you can re-create them in your own garden.

A Place of Serenity
Poised at the top of a sloping lawn, this simple bed of pink and white peonies and purple Iris sibirica puts on an early summer show in northern Virginia. Long after the flowers are gone, the foliage will continue to look appealing from all sides.

Perennials, annuals, and bulbs complement each other's bloom and growth cycles, so planning a garden that makes use of all three is a masterful way to extend color, fragrance, and beauty across the seasons. You can combine different types of plants to mask fading foliage, add an extra season of bloom, or fill gaps in your design as other plants become established or finish blooming. The plans at the end of this section present you with artful plant combinations that blend the assets of different types of plants for changing images of beauty throughout the growing season.

Combining Annuals, Perennials, Bulbs, and Ground Covers

When you start designing with plants, it helps to know and understand their different life cycles and uses. Annuals, as implied by their name, will provide color and interest for one growing season only, while bulbs and perennials will come back year after year. Annuals offer you the flexibility to alter color, texture, and height in your design,

while you can depend on bulbs and perennials to provide the same color and structure each year. Of course, you also can expect that bulbs and perennials will spread and grow until they reach maturity and will need to be divided eventually, unlike annuals, which you simply remove when they are finished blooming.

Annuals add splashes of color whenever and wherever you plant them. Properly tended, they can bloom for months. If planted in the foreground of your garden, they will screen the brown or yellowing foliage of spring bulbs and spring-to-summer perennials that have finished blooming. You will find annuals especially welcome as cover-ups for daffodils and tulips, whose

A Carefree Mix
Mid-spring in this Eugene, Oregon, border finds fresh tendrils of clematis drifting over the fence to join purple and gold bearded iris and a splendid coral-hued deciduous azalea in full bloom. The weathered silvery gray of the fence helps make a graceful link between these warm colors.

leaves and stems must be left undisturbed for several weeks to replenish the bulbs' store of energy for next season. Early-blooming tulips and daffodils finish their season just as the majority of flowering perennials are sending up their shoots. Instead of enduring a fallow period, overplant early-blooming bulbs with some annual phlox or pansies until the perennials can take over.

If you prefer to mix perennials with bulbs, plant spring-flowering bulbs near late emerging perennials. As the earlier-blooming bulbs die back, the foliage and flowers of the perennials will gracefully fill out over the wilting foliage.

Bulbs can be an integral part of a season-extending strategy, as shown in the plan on page 76. Groups of low-growing snowdrops, hyacinths, and daffodils and slightly taller tulips bloom from early to late spring. If positioned at the front of your border, they can work in tandem with later-peaking ground covers such as *Campanula elatines garganica* and perennials such as campion and sea lavender. As the growing season begins to wind down, *Lycoris squamigera* displays colorful flowers amid fading ground cover

such as lantana, while a bold burst of autumn crocus illuminates the border near the end of the flowering season.

Low-Maintenance Plants

Another way to approach plant selection—particularly if you have only weekend time to devote to keeping your garden in shape—is to concentrate on plants that require minimal care. Much as you may love the form, fragrance, or color of a particular plant, learn what it takes to keep the plant thriving before you buy it and incorporate it into your garden. If your time in the garden is limited, concentrate on plants that are adaptable to a wide range of climate and soil conditions, resist common pests and diseases, and require little

Silver and Gold Treasures
Gray slate pathways define these Malvern, Pennsylvania, beds filled with silver-leaved and golden-flowered plants, including lamb's ears, artemisia, yarrow, and butterfly weed, set off by the cool flowers of catmint and lavender.

Cool Colors for Sunny Sites

Ageratum houstonianum (flossflower)

Alcea rosea Powder Puffs Mixed (hollyhock)

Aquilegia flabellata (columbine)

Aster x *frikartii* 'Mönch' (aster)

Astilbe chinensis 'Pumila' (false spirea)

Boltonia asteroides 'Snowbank' (boltonia)

Buddleia alternifolia 'Argentea' (butterfly bush)

Campanula persicifolia 'Telham Beauty' (bellflower)

Caryopteris x *clandonensis* 'Blue Mist' (bluebeard)

Cleome hasslerana 'Helen Campbell' (spider flower)

Clethra barbinervis (summer-sweet)

Cosmos bipinnatus (cosmos)

Cynara cardunculus (cardoon)

Delphinium 'Blue Fountains' (delphinium)

Exochorda x *macrantha* 'The Bride' (pearlbush)

Hibiscus x 'Diana' (mallow)

Lavandula angustifolia (lavender)

Lobelia siphilitica (lobelia)

Platycodon grandiflorus 'Apoyama' (balloon flower)

67

or no staking and only infrequent dividing. Plants that can survive reasonable spells of excess rain or drought without long-term damage are a good choice.

If most of your plants are low maintenance, you might consider adding two or three species—hybrid tea roses, for example—that you love in spite of the considerable care they require. The low maintenance alternative is to select shrub roses that produce the flowers you want without the extra work.

Classic Combinations

Certain groupings of perennials, annuals, and bulbs have been used together long enough to be considered classics. One such association, suitable for a border in partial sun, is shown in the plan on page 76. This garden design combines classic spring bulbs (daffodils, snowdrops, and tulips) with traditional perennials (bleeding hearts, peonies, and lilies) and fills in the gaps with tried-and-true annuals (impatiens).

If you want to extend a particular color across the season, you'll find several combinations that will yield the desired results. In the range of blue to blue-purple, consider combinations from among the following: spring crocus, iris, ceanothus, and anemone; early summer convolvulus, gentian, and catmint; summer delphinium, lavender, and lobelia; and late summer aconitum, ageratum, and Michaelmas daisies.

Many annual and perennial layouts incorporate remarkable foliage plants as backgrounds or fillers. One interesting choice is the annual castor bean, which grows rather quickly to become an 8- to 10-inch-tall plant with prominent, handsome, sharply lobed, dark green leaves. Acanthus is a 2- to 3-inch-tall perennial with coarse, bold green leaves. The plan on page 74 incorporates

Colorful Bulbs to Brighten Any Season

The bulbs pictured below offer a diverse palette of heights, planting depths, and flower color. Use the chart to help you position plants for best visibility and to decide how you want to overplant the various bulbs with perennials and annuals.

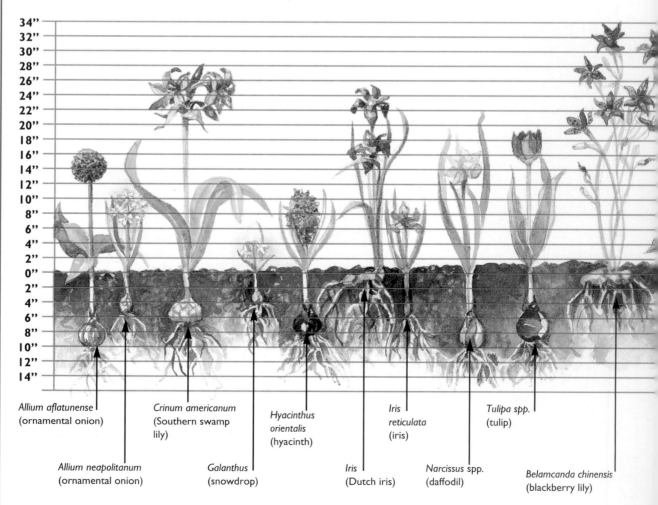

Allium aflatunense
(ornamental onion)

Allium neapolitanum
(ornamental onion)

Crinum americanum
(Southern swamp lily)

Galanthus
(snowdrop)

Hyacinthus orientalis
(hyacinth)

Iris
(Dutch iris)

Iris reticulata
(iris)

Narcissus spp.
(daffodil)

Tulipa spp.
(tulip)

Belamcanda chinensis
(blackberry lily)

A Rich Mix for Shade

Receiving only early morning sun, these foliage plants thrive in the afternoon shade of this Eugene, Oregon, border. Miscanthus sinensis 'Morning Light' glows amid pink coral bells, ferns, hostas, and a dwarf hemlock.

coleus, an annual, with artemisia and hosta, both perennials, in an island bed of continuous color. Coleus hybrids are available with a wide variety of brilliant leaves and make wonderful, fast-growing fillers. The soft, silvery leaves of artemisia species can smooth transitions between bolder colors. Taller varieties make a great foil for dark, vibrant flowers, while shorter ones are useful as edgings.

Hostas are among the most self-sufficient and ornamental shade-tolerant perennials available. Hosta leaves range from smooth to deeply ribbed and from small to very large. They come in a wide range of solid colors, including chartreuse,

Deceptively delicate snowdrops are among the earliest and hardiest of spring blooms. For a splash of bold, tropical summer color, choose caladiums for their foliage or cannas for their flowers and stature. Or, if hungry rodents are a problem, plant some foul-tasting crown-imperials.

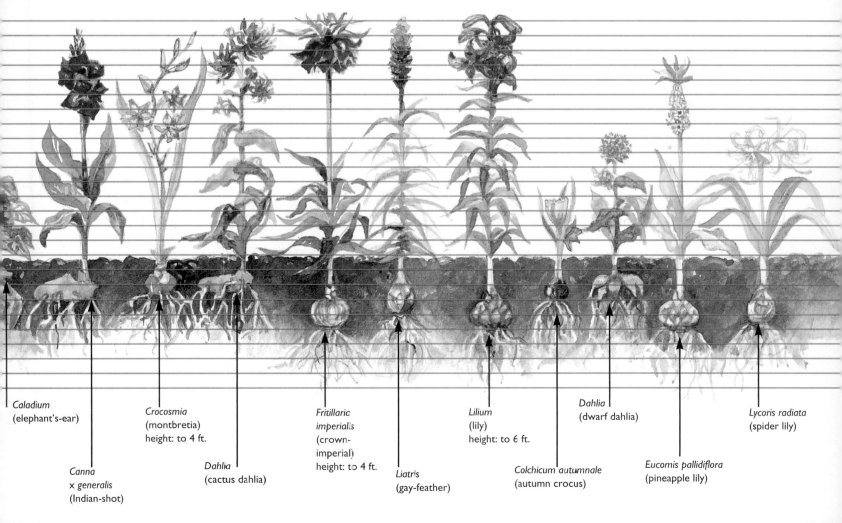

Caladium
(elephant's-ear)

Canna
x generalis
(Indian-shot)

Crocosmia
(montbretia)
height: to 4 ft.

Dahlia
(cactus dahlia)

Fritillaria
imperialis
(crown-imperial)
height: to 4 ft.

Liatris
(gay-feather)

Lilium
(lily)
height: to 6 ft.

Colchicum autumnale
(autumn crocus)

Dahlia
(dwarf dahlia)

Eucomis pallidiflora
(pineapple lily)

Lycoris radiata
(spider lily)

Broadleaf (coarse texture)

Digitalis
(foxglove)

Hibiscus moscheutos
(mallow)

Hosta
(plantain lily)

Hydrangea
(hydrangea)

Mahonia
(holly grape)

Nicotiana
(flowering tobacco)

Rhododendron
(rhododendron)

Ricinus
(castor-oil plant)

Verbascum
(mullein)

Viburnum
(viburnum)

Yucca
(yucca)

Delicate (fine texture)

Achillea
(yarrow)

Adiantum
(maidenhair fern)

Artemisia
(wormwood)

Boltonia asteroides
'Snowbank'
(boltonia)

Chrysanthemum coccineum
(chrysanthemum)

Coreopsis rosea
(tickseed)

Cosmos
(cosmos)

Dianthus
(pink)

Nigella damascena
(love-in-a-mist)

Pennisetum
(fountain grass)

Santolina
(lavender cotton)

Spiraea
(spirea)

Patterns for Success
Spikes of red feather grass and mounds of bush marigold and pink twinspur weave among this massed planting of purple Mexican bush sage and white trailing lantana. This Clayton, California, summer border is framed by a plain-board fence.

blue, and green, as well as with figured markings. Most hostas also produce lavender-blue or white lilylike flowers, some of which emit delightfully sweet fragrances.

Bulbs also can be used to add foliage interest and contrast to a bed or border composition. Their long, slender, generally smooth leaves are distinctly different from those of most annuals and perennials in texture and in their erect or arching forms. The swordlike blades of iris and crocosmia, for example, make attractive complements to clumping perennials such as hostas.

Basic Care of Established Plants

Every bed or border benefits from some degree of tending throughout the year. The work begins with a general cleanup in early spring. If you live in a cold winter climate, you will need to replace mulch to a depth of 2 to 3 inches. You also will need to remove any dead or damaged plant parts and add them to your compost pile. But if you suspect that a disease is present, do not add those pieces to your compost.

Your perennials, whether new transplants or established residents, will grow more quickly and develop a healthier root system if you work the earth around them with a hand-held cultivator to a depth of an inch or two. Avoid damaging tender new growth by cultivating only the soil around the edges of each plant's mature spread. Use the chart on page 71 to help you determine the spread of some commonly used garden plants as well as to figure out the correct number and type of plants for particular areas in your garden.

Periodic, regular watering is important in every garden, but it's crucial in hot, arid, or windy areas. It's better to water infrequently but thoroughly to encourage roots to grow deeply in their search for moisture. After watering, use a trowel to determine whether the soil is moist at least 3 or 4 inches down. If it's not, you will need to run your irrigation system for a longer period—and possibly more often, if the soil drains quickly.

Soaker hoses and drip irrigation systems release water directly onto the soil, reducing runoff and evaporation. They can be operated at any time of day—morning or night. If you opt for an overhead sprinkler system, the best time to water is early in the morning so that leaves have a chance to dry off during the day. Continually damp leaves, especially those of roses and phlox, are susceptible to fungal diseases. A simple timer can be set to maintain your watering schedule when you are away or at any other time you choose. With a little practice and observation, you will be able to tell just by looking at your plants whether they need water.

Dividing in Order to Multiply

For many perennials, division supplies new plants for colonizing elsewhere, controls their size, and rejuvenates old stock where overcrowding is harming the health of plants or reducing the number of blooms. Unless you live in an area where winters are severe, fall is the best time to divide spring- and summer-flowering perennials, and spring is preferred for fall-blooming plants. If winters in your area are severe, divide them in the

Is there an easy way to tell when my flower beds need water?

Garden phlox speaks clearly about the water conditions around it; drooping leaves on the lower stems are a sign to water this plant, and the surrounding plants, well.

Size and Growth Habit of Popular Bed and Border Plants

		Height	Spread	Shape
ANNUALS	*Calendula officinalis* (pot marigold)	2 feet	2 feet	sprawling
	Consolida ambigua (larkspur)	4 feet	1 foot	upright branching
	Helianthus annuus (sunflower)	3-10 feet	1-1½ feet	upright
	Nemesia strumosa (nemesia)	8 inches-1½ feet	6 inches	bushy
	Nigella damascena (love-in-a-mist)	2 feet	8 inches	slender upright
	Papaver rhoeas (corn poppy)	2 feet	1 foot	slender upright
PERENNIALS	*Digitalis grandiflora* (foxglove)	2½ feet	1 foot	clump-forming
	Gypsophila paniculata (baby's-breath)	2-2½ feet	3 feet	wiry, branching stems
	Heuchera sanguinea (coral bells)	1-2½ feet	1-1½ feet	mounding
	Mertensia virginica (Virginia bluebells)	1-2 feet	1-1½ feet	upright
	Primula japonica (primrose)	6 inches-2 feet	1 foot	tall stalks
	Sanguisorba canadensis (Canadian burnet)	4-6 feet	2 feet	clump-forming
GRASSES	*Festuca cinerea* (blue fescue)	6 inches-1 foot	6 inches-1 foot	tufted
	Helictotrichon sempervirens (blue oat grass)	1½ feet	1½ feet	mounded
	Miscanthus sinensis (Japanese silver grass)	1-6 feet	6 inches-3 feet	upright arching
	Pennisetum alopecuroides (fountain grass)	2-3 feet	2-3 feet	mounded

71

spring. This strategy gives plants an entire growing season to recover before they flower again.

Divide a plant only when the leaves have been cut back for winter or before the plant has sprouted in early spring. Dig around the root ball to free the anchored plant, then cut or break apart the roots to divide it. Some shallow-rooted plants, such as primrose and lily-of-the-valley, simply come apart when lifted out of the earth. Others, such as phlox, may need moderate prying to pull their whiskery roots apart. Still others, such as daylily, become so entwined that they require a bit of force. Drive two spading forks back-to-back into the center of the root mass and press the handles together so that the tines leverage outward to force the clump apart. Trim off damaged roots and, after enriching the soil with organic matter, replant the newly divided clumps. Give the remaining pieces to a friend, plant them elsewhere in your garden, or discard them.

Supporting Taller Plants

Staking is necessary for those bed and border plants that cannot support their large heads (peonies, asters, and chrysanthemums, for exam-

ple) and for some plants with single, tall stalks (such as hollyhocks). In the spring, before the plants become too tall and top-heavy, circle them with green-painted bamboo stakes driven securely into the ground. Weave a cat's cradle with gardener's twine, going across and around the circle of stakes at various heights, and let the plant stems grow up naturally through the supports; they will be nearly invisible in the foliage.

Another natural-looking staking method is to use 16- to 20-inch-long forked branches that have been pruned from fruit trees earlier in the spring. Stick the branches into the ground to form a circle when the plant is about 8 inches high. They will provide an informal cage for the plant as it grows.

You also can buy prefabricated staking systems. Ring stakes and link stakes, constructed of heavy wire, are available from most garden supply stores and catalogs.

Summer Sentinels
Discreetly supported with green bamboo stakes and ties, a stand of bright blue delphiniums adds height, interesting flower form, and vivid color to these beds in Princeton, New Jersey.

To stake a single stalk, place the support an inch or so from the stem, drive it in, and loosely tie the plant at a few locations, allowing room for movement. An alternative to staking is to use sturdy, low-growing hedge plants to contain and support their more weak-kneed bedfellows.

Pinching Plants for Better Bloom and Form

Pinching is a method that encourages plants that bloom in the fall, such as hardy asters, boltonias, and chrysanthemums, to bear more flowers on a more compact plant. When the plant is about 6 inches tall, pinch off the tip of each stem along with its top bracket of leaves. This forces additional shoots to grow at lower leaf joints. If you repeat this technique after each additional 6 inches of growth until midsummer, you will be rewarded with a bushier plant that produces two to three times more flowers.

Disbudding, a related technique, involves removing side buds along a stem to channel the flower's energy into the top bud, which then may grow to tremendous proportions. Deadheading, or snipping off spent blossoms, keeps bulbs vital and extends the flowering life of some annuals (energy is redirected to the flowers, foliage, or roots rather than to making seed). It also helps to keep your bed or border looking neat and improves air circulation for healthier plants.

The following pages contain a series of inspiring bed and border plans. Choose from among designs based on four-season interest (An Island of Continuous Color), site specifications (Late Spring Splendor Along a Walkway), flower color (A Serene Border of Soft Summer Hues), function (A Cutting Bed of Bold Color and Form), or style (A Perennial Bed with Herbs).

Tip

Snails and slugs can devastate a garden, but using commercial insecticides to kill them can endanger children and pets. Try placing small piles of orange peels around your favorite plants. The pests will be feasting on the peels in the morning, and you can scoop them up and dispose of them easily.

Edible Plants in Beds and Borders

Adding herbs, vegetables, and edible flowers to beds and borders gives them yet another dimension of beauty and usefulness. Plan your garden so that you can easily harvest its bounty and perform maintenance chores, including watering and fertilizing. Herbs blend readily with annuals and perennials, but don't fill your border with only one type of herb. For example, if you plant only basil in a mixed border of other annuals and perennials, harvesting the basil will leave unsightly gaps. Let vegetables become design accents in their season. Tomatoes or scarlet runner beans on a trellis, for example, give instant summer height.

If you grow flowers to eat, do not use pesticides on any plants in the same bed or border. Edible flowers make a tasty, and in the case of nasturtiums, tangy, addition to salads or stir-fry dishes. For a milder flavor, try pansies, chive flowers, or pot marigolds. Other flowers, such as the delicate petals of roses and sweet violets, either fresh or candied, make an elegant decoration for frosted cakes.

▶ Lovely but inedible Lathyrus (sweet pea) backs a neat row of compact globe basil that fronts larger green-and-purple sweet basil. Marjoram, tarragon, parsley, chives, and sage visually anchor the end of the bed.

Edible Foliage

Allium schoenoprasum (chives)

Ocimum basilicum (basil)

Origanum vulgare (oregano)

Petroselinium crispum (parsley)

Salvia officinalis (garden sage)

Tropaeolum majus (nasturtium)

Edible Flowers

Agastache foeniculum (anise hyssop)

Begonia x *tuberhybrida* (tuberous begonia)

Bellis perennis (English daisy)

Calendula (pot marigold)

Chrysanthemum (chrysanthemum)

Dianthus (pink)

Hemerocallis (daylily)

Hibiscus rosa-sinensis (hibiscus)

Monarda (bee balm)

Rosa (rose)

Sambucus canadensis, Sambucus caerulea (elderberry)

Syringa vulgaris (lilac)

Viola (pansy, Johnny-jump-up, violet)

An Island of Continuous Color

If you want bright, abundant flowers throughout the spring and summer, consider planting this colorful island bed. Although replacement of its annual plants each year will mean a bit more work, the results will be worth it. From early spring to first frost, this diverse bed will abound with colors and shapes pleasing from every angle. These plants will perform best in light shade to full sun and well-drained, fertile soil.

In cold-winter climates, plant perennials after the last frost in spring. In milder climates, fall also is a good time to plant. Dahlias, lantanas, begonias, petunias, and coleus are seasonal bedding plants usually purchased from commercial growers. Other annuals (musk mallow, cosmos, love-in-a-mist) can be grown from seeds sown in place. The continuous color display begins with the early spring bloomers, bleeding hearts and petunias. These soon are joined by poppies, campanulas, and astilbes. As spring draws to a close, tall spires of delphinium, iris, airy heuchera, and papery cosmos blooms emerge and add to the display. Of these, only astilbe, poppies, and bellflowers fade in the summer months.

The bed is at its best in early summer, as shown below. Position it within view of a porch or deck to enjoy the highlights of this season, including the blooms of rose, hibiscus, dahlia, lantana, and coreopsis. Other plants that are sure to delight you with flowers in early- to midsummer months include dianthus, veronica, lily, salvia, nigella, and begonia. In summer, the silvery leaves of artemisia and variegated foliage of hosta and coleus provide interest. Snip off coleus blooms to focus attention on their showy leaves.

As daylight shortens in late summer and early fall, the splendor of many plants begins to wane. Emerging chrysanthemum, sedum, and musk mallow, however, will more than compensate, brightening this island bed with color up to the first hard frost.

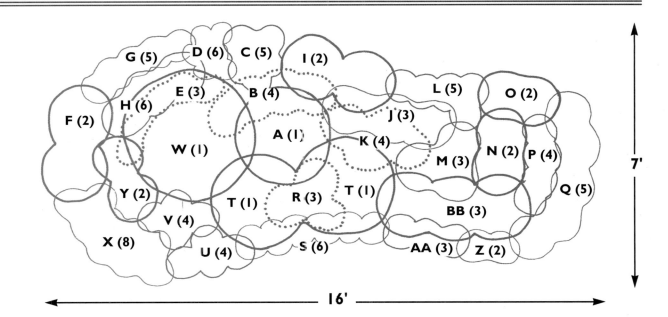

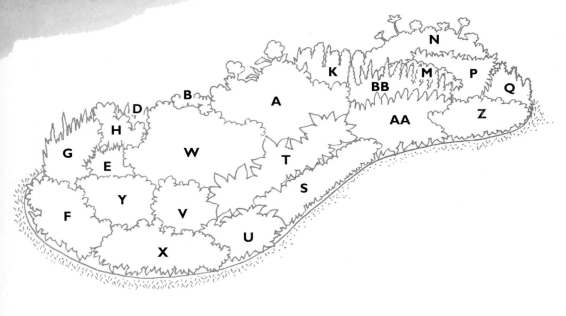

Plant List

A. *Hibiscus moscheutos* 'Satan' (1)

B. *Papaver orientale* 'Raspberry Queen' (4)

C. *Petunia* x *hybrida* 'Dazzler White' (5)

D. *Dianthus* x *allwoodii* 'Helen' (6)

E. *Artemisia ludoviciana* 'Silver King' (3)

F. *Lantana camara* 'Dazzler' (2)

G. *Veronica* 'Sunny Border Blue' (5)

H. *Iris* 'Navy Strut' (6)

I. *Sedum spectabile* 'Brilliant' (2)

J. *Chrysanthemum* x *morifolium* (3)

K. *Delphinium* 'Blue Fountains' (4)

L. *Abelmoschus moschatus* (5)

M. *Chrysanthemum* x *superbum* 'Alaska' (3)

N. *Cosmos sulphureus* (2)

O. *Coreopsis grandiflora* 'Sunray' (2)

P. *Lilium* 'Golden Splendor' (4)

Q. *Salvia coccinea* (5)

R. *Dicentra spectabilis* 'Alba' (3)

S. *Impatiens wallerana* (6)

T. *Hosta fortunei* 'Aurea Marginata' (2)

U. *Coleus* x *hybridus* 'Dragon Series' (4)

V. *Campanula glomerata* 'Superba' (4)

W. *Rosa* 'The Fairy' (1)

X. *Dahlia* 'Irene V.D. Zwet', 'Murillo', 'Red Riding Hood' (8)

Y. *Nigella damascena* (2)

Z. *Begonia* x *semperflorens-cultorum* (2)

AA. *Heuchera* x *brizoides* 'June Bride' (3)

BB. *Astilbe* x *arendsii* 'Deutschland' (3)

Late Spring Splendor Along a Walkway

This vivid border enlivens an otherwise ordinary walkway in front of a white picket fence. Fertile, but not overly rich soil in a partial shade setting is ideal for this plan.

The pickets on the fence echo the tall, spiky forms of astilbe and iris, and provide some back support to the peonies. Furnish additional support to the peonies early in the season so that their heavy blooms are held up for easy viewing. Peonies don't like being moved, so place them exactly where you want them. Accommodate their deep roots by digging the soil as deep as 2 feet when planting, then mulch annually.

Remember that the annual impatiens should be planted only after the last frost. This applies as well to the tender perennial caladium, which is best treated as an annual. The other plants in this garden are a bit less particular. Only the impatiens and bleeding hearts may demand extra watering during the bloom season. Steppingstones, shown in the overhead plan on page 77, have been placed across the back of the border

and throughout the interior to provide access to all the plants for necessary watering, weeding, and deadheading.

When the blooms of tulips and narcissus have gone, leave their foliage until it turns yellow, nourishing bulbs for the coming year. In colder climates, annual mulching each fall provides needed winter protection for the rose.

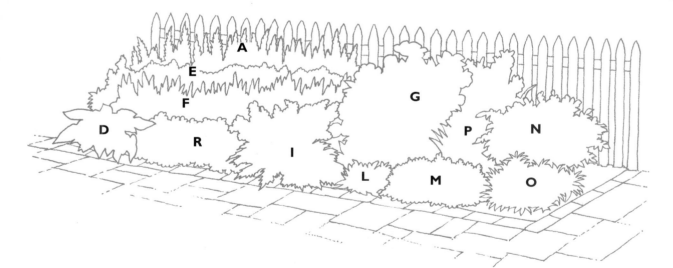

Plant List

A. *Astilbe* x *arendsii* 'Feuer' ('Fire') (6)

B. *Lilium* 'Sorbet' (28)

C. *Narcissus* (mixed) (33)

D. *Caladium bicolor* 'Little Miss Muffet' (4)

E. *Heuchera* 'Pluie de Feu' (5)

F. *Veronica spicata* 'Snow White' (8)

G. *Paeonia lactiflora* 'Sea Shell' (3)

H. *Tulipa* 'Angelique' (18)

I. *Dicentra eximia* 'Luxuriant' (4)

J. *Narcissus* 'February Gold' (17)

K. *Pulmonaria saccharata* 'Mrs. Moon' (2)

L. *Galanthus elwesii* (100)

M. *Artemisia stellerana*

'Silver Brocade' (6)

N. *Rosa* 'Purple Tiger' (1)

O. *Lilium* 'Stargazer' (10)

P. *Iris sibirica* 'Caesar's Brother' (4)

Q. *Lycoris squamigera* (4)

R. *Impatiens wallerana* (5)

S. *Lilium* 'Black Dragon' (22)

T. *Geranium endressii* 'Wargrave Pink' (3)

A (6)   S (22)   Q (4)

T (3)   B (28)   E (5)   G (3)   P (4)   N (1)
                            H (18)

C (33)   F (8)

D (4)   R (5)   I (4)   J (17)   K (2)   L (100)   M (6)   O (10)

5'

20'

A Serene Border of Soft Summer Hues

Set this border against a section of an informal-looking split-rail fence and enjoy a soft medley of blooms from spring until fall. All of these plants will thrive in full sun with fertile, well-drained soil. The fence defines the border while it supports the taller plants at the back. Some leaners, such as delphiniums, may need extra staking to keep them from tumbling over.

Early blooming peonies and poppies lead off in the spring with the shooting stars of pink columbines. A few weeks later, the bed will be diversified by spires of delphiniums, irises, and spidery mountain bluet (*Centaurea*). These soon will be joined by phlox, yarrow, geranium, coral bells, and astilbe for a gentle sweep of color.

By midsummer, the bed will fill with color as upright spikes of hollyhock and foxglove fill out the middle rear, while painted daisies brighten the right-hand corner. Across the middle of the bed, lupine, veronica, coneflower, daylily, lavender, bugbane, 'Silver Queen' artemisia, and pincushion flower spread in purple, pink, white, and peach. At the front edge of the bed, masking the bases of these midsized growers, are short spikes of salvia, bright-eyed pink, 'Silver Brocade' artemisia, bellflower, hosta, and a riot of impatiens.

As the daylight hours of summer grow shorter, blue asters, anemones, dahlias, and heliotropes arrive to perk up the color scheme. Be sure to deadhead throughout the summer to help direct each plant's energy toward producing more blooms, rather than seeds, into early autumn. Keep vigorous 'Silver Queen' artemisia under control by dividing it each spring.

Plant List

A. *Veronica spicata* 'Blue Peter' (4)

B. *Phlox paniculata* 'Fairest One' (4)

C. *Papaver rhoeas* (4)

D. *Echinacea purpurea* 'White Swan' (1)

E. *Delphinium hybridum* 'Summer Skies' (6)

F. *Hemerocallis* 'Ruffled Apricot' (5)

G. *Alcea rosea* Powder Puffs Mixed (1)

H. *Lavandula angustifolia* 'Munstead' (2)

I. *Iris* 'Victoria Falls' (4)

J. *Digitalis purpurea* 'Excelsior Hybrids' (3)

K. *Paeonia lactiflora* 'Raspberry Sundae' (2)

L. *Salvia x superba* 'May Night' (3)

M. *Artemisia ludoviciana* 'Silver Queen' (4)

N. *Cimicifuga racemosa* (1)

O. *Scabiosa caucasica* 'House's Hybrids' (1)

P. *Aster novi-belgii* 'Blue Lake' (7)

Q. *Dahlia* (1)

R. *Centaurea montana* (3)

S. *Heliotropium arborescens* 'Black Beauty' (3)

T. *Artemisia stellerana* 'Silver Brocade' (3)

U. *Dianthus x allwoodii* (2)

V. *Achillea* 'Hoffnung' (3)

W. *Lupinus* 'Russell Hybrids' (4)

X. *Geranium* 'Johnson's Blue' (4)

Y. *Heuchera brizoides* 'June Bride' (2)

Z. *Campanula carpatica* 'Blue Chips' (6)

AA. *Astilbe chinensis* (4)

BB. *Aquilegia caerulea* (4)

CC. *Lilium* 'Sorbet' (11)

DD. *Hosta ventricosa* (2)

EE. *Impatiens* x 'New Guinea' (6)

FF. *Tanacetum* 'Helen' (5)

GG. *Anemone hupehensis* 'September Charm' (3)

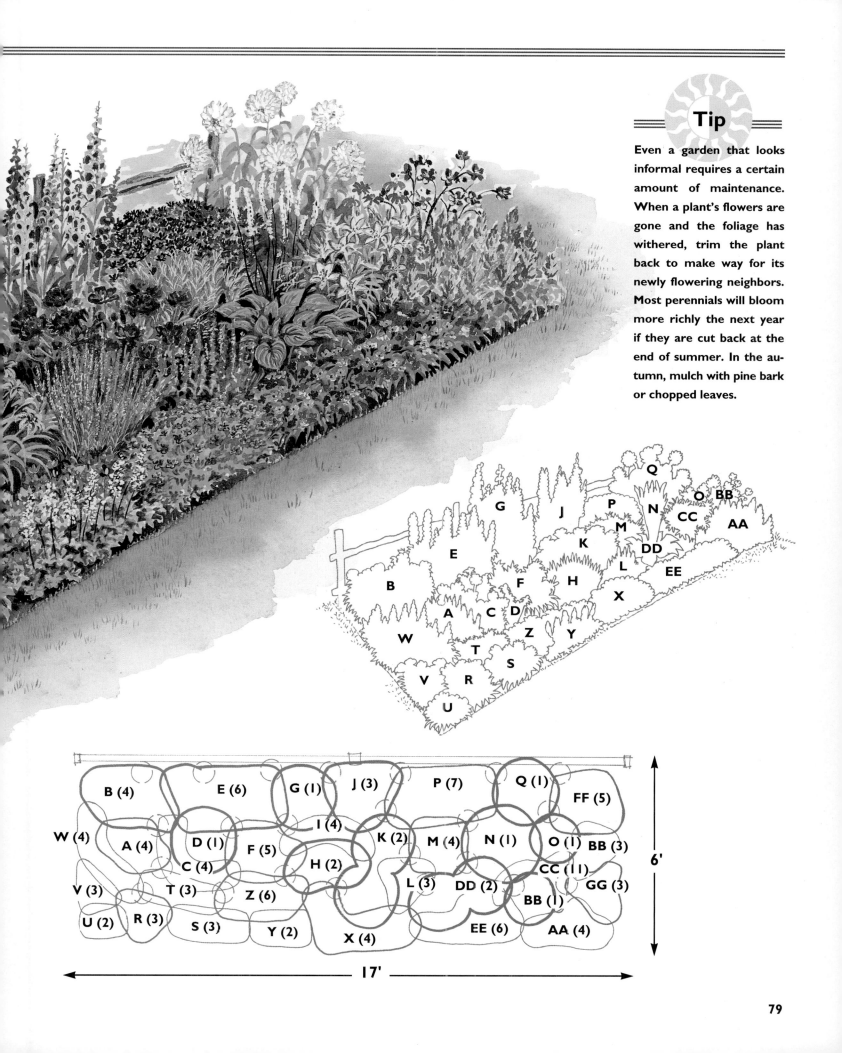

Even a garden that looks informal requires a certain amount of maintenance. When a plant's flowers are gone and the foliage has withered, trim the plant back to make way for its newly flowering neighbors. Most perennials will bloom more richly the next year if they are cut back at the end of summer. In the autumn, mulch with pine bark or chopped leaves.

G J P Q
O BB
E K N CC AA
M
B F H L DD
A C D X EE
W Z Y
T
S
V R
U

B (4) E (6) G (1) J (3) P (7) Q (1) FF (5)

W (4) A (4) D (1) F (5) I (4) K (2) M (4) N (1) O (1) BB (3)
C (4) CC (11)
H (2)
V (3) T (3) L (3) DD (2) GG (3)
Z (6) BB (1)
U (2) R (3) S (3) Y (2) X (4) EE (6) AA (4)

6'

17'

A Cutting Bed of Bold Color and Form

If you enjoy bringing your garden indoors, consider creating this cutting garden full of plants with striking color, long-lasting blooms, and upright stems. The curving island form was designed so that all plants are within reach for easy picking and maintenance.

This bed, shown in its full summer splendor, yields flowers in a variety of shapes and sizes designed to make both the garden and your indoor arrangements look their best. Purple coneflower, rudbeckia, aster, cosmos, and helenium all produce daisylike flowers. More rounded blooms are found on chrysanthemums, dahlias, pinks, roses, pincushion flowers, marigolds, and zinnias. Spiky blooms of gay-feather, salvia, celosia, and snapdragon add contrasting form and, often, color. Trumpet-shaped lilies and daylilies, along with tightly packed flattop bouquets of heliotropium and yarrow complete the scene.

Offer these plants full sun and you will be rewarded with bouquets of blooms throughout the late days of summer and into fall.

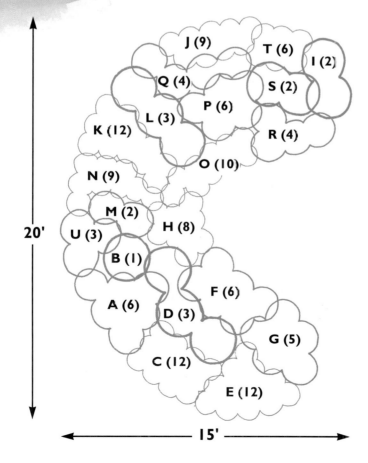

Plant List

A. *Salvia* x *superba* 'Blue Queen' (6)

B. *Echinacea purpurea* (1)

C. *Zinnia elegans* (12)

D. *Rudbeckia hirta* (3)

E. *Heliotropium arborescens* 'Black Beauty' (12)

F. *Chrysanthemum* x *morifolium* (6)

G. *Dianthus barbatus* 'Scarlet Beauty' (5)

H. *Liatris spicata* 'Kobold' (8)

I. *Rosa* 'French Lace' (2)

J. *Celosia cristata* (9)

K. *Salvia nemorosa* 'East Friesland' (12)

L. *Helenium autumnale* (3)

M. *Chrysanthemum* x *superbum* 'Alaska' (2)

N. *Tagetes erecta* (9)

O. *Hemerocallis lilioasphodelus* (10)

P. *Cosmos bipinnatus* (6)

Q. *Scabiosa fama* (4)

R. *Achillea* 'Hoffnung' (4)

S. *Aster novae-angliae* 'Harrington's Pink' (2)

T. *Antirrhinum majus* 'Black Prince' (6)

U. *Dahlia* 'Double Pompon Mix' (3)

A Perennial Bed with Herbs

A formal garden can be both colorful and useful, as shown in this circular bed *(see page 29 for instructions for laying out a circular bed)* planted with perennials and herbs. The circular shape was designed to allow for viewing from all sides as well as from the symmetrical interior paths.

Whether you prefer to walk along a path of brick, pea gravel, or bark mulch, you may want to make it wide enough for two people to stroll along side by side. This also will enable you to roll a garden cart through the bed for easy harvesting and maintenance of the herbs and flowers.

While formal, bisecting pathways lead you through the garden, a central ornament such as an urn, as shown, or a piece of classical sculpture will tend to draw your eye to the center of the bed, even from a distance. A less formal path material like bark mulch or more cottagey plants might call for more casual ornamentation, perhaps a sundial or a wooden sculpture.

Although not all of these plants are scented, if you brush against the lavender while on a summer afternoon stroll, you will be rewarded with the pungency of this useful herb. Dried lavender added as a sachet to bathwater has a relaxing effect. And it makes a good moth repellent, too.

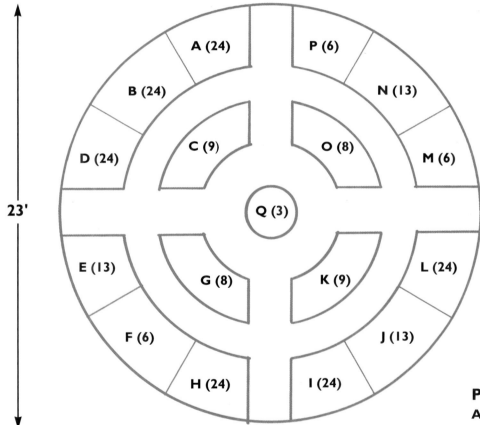

23'

Plant List

A. *Salvia* x *superba* 'Blue Queen' (24)

B. *Campanula carpatica* 'White Chips' (24)

C. *Echinacea purpurea* 'Bright Star' (9)

D. *Liatrus spicata* 'Kobold' (24)

E. *Dianthus barbatus* 'Newport Pink' (13)

F. *Verbascum* x 'Pink Domino' (6)

G. *Alcea rosea* 'Chater's Double' (8)

H. *Veronica spicata* 'Blue Queen' (24)

I. *Achillea* 'Paprika' (24)

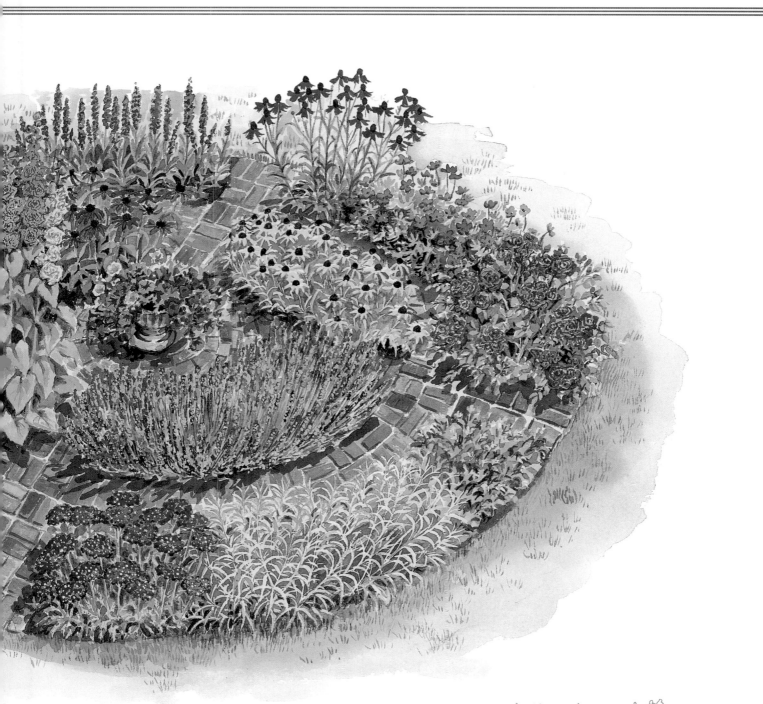

J. *Artemisia ludoviciana* 'Silver King' (13)

K. *Lavandula angustifolia* 'Munstead' (9)

L. *Aquilegia* x *hybrida* 'Biedermier Mixed' (24)

M. *Rosa* 'Canterbury' (6)

N. *Geranium* 'Johnson's Blue' (13)

O. *Rudbeckia fulgida* 'Goldsturm' (8)

P. *Helenium autumnale* 'Bruno' (6)

Q. *Petunia integrifolia* (3)

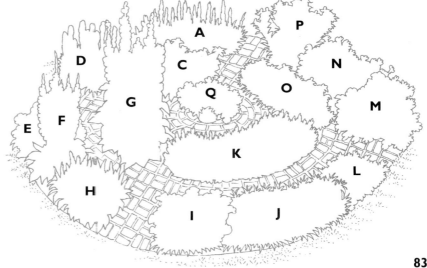

Using Shrubs in Mixed Beds and Borders

Shrubs can serve as more than just backdrops. Their varied sizes and shapes, the colors of their flowers, foliage, and berries, and the distinctive textures and tones of their bark offer many choices in terms of selection and application. Such diversity makes them a natural choice for use in mixed beds and borders *(page 90)* and just as effective as single plantings *(page 86)*.

Evergreen shrubs provide greenery and mass to a garden framework, while the bare branches of deciduous specimens create graceful patterns above a winter-bound bed. Forethought is important in selection and placement because most shrubs are long-lived and can grow quite large. Once established, they are difficult to move.

Selection and Siting of Shrubs

Shrubs, especially the sizable container-grown specimens, can be expensive, so make your choices wisely. Chances are good that the most popular varieties of shrubs grown in your area are hardy and disease-resistant. If you prefer to select a less familiar or more exotic shrub, you may need to devote more time than you wish to its care. As with any plant, consider the soil, sun, and moisture requirements, as well as the wind tolerance of a particular shrub before you buy it. Also think about whether you really want to spend the time needed to provide winter protection for marginally hardy shrubs or whether you prefer a more easy-care approach. If your conditions are a questionable match for a plant, or if your gardening time is limited, err on the side of conservatism and choose a shrub that is hardy to one zone colder than where you live.

Be sure to consider what the mature size of the shrub will be compared to the scale of your bed or border. Choosing the right size shrub for your garden means you should need only to prune lightly to maintain shape, to remove dead or damaged branches, or to increase flowering.

Manicured Boxwood
Boxwood displays its adaptability to pruning in this immaculately trimmed formal South Carolina shade garden. White wax begonias flourish in the center of each bed.

Smaller shrubs such as smoke tree (*Cotinus coggygria*), 'Blue Mound' ceanothus, and several varieties of spirea would, for example, be good choices for smaller beds or borders.

You can use shrubs to add color interest, as in the plan based on fruiting shrubs on page 86, or year-round structure, as in the evergreen bed shown on page 88. Many deciduous shrubs, including witch hazel and hydrangea species, offer a vivid display of showy blooms during the growing season as well as a blaze of fall foliage color before going completely dormant. Over winter, nothing adds sparkle to the garden scene like shrubs with jewel-toned bark. Consider the striking crimson bark of Tartarian dogwood, the yellow-green of Japanese rose, or the rich purple of violet willow (*Salix daphnoides*).

If you are more interested in form than in color, look for deciduous shrubs with intriguing branch shapes. Possibilities include Harry Lauder's walking stick (*Corylus avellana* 'Contorta'), whose corkscrew branches are bedecked with catkins that decorate the plant all winter, and double file viburnum (*Viburnum plicatum* var. *tomentosum*), with its layer upon layer of horizontal tiered branches.

Planting and Caring for Shrubs

The key to establishing healthy shrubs, and all plants, is getting them off to a good start. When planting shrubs, dig holes that are no deeper than the diameter of the root ball, mixing the soil from the planting hole with a generous helping of compost. The roots of shrubs tend to grow near the surface, so loosen the soil for several feet around the planting hole. Add enough compost to extend out to where the leaf canopy ends.

In general, shrubs need little fertilizing, unless the soil in your garden is very poor. Mulch around the base of shrubs and, during the first season, water to keep the soil evenly moist.

Pruning Flowering Shrubs

Ornamental shrubs need little pruning beyond removal of broken or diseased branches whenever they appear. Timing is more important, however, when you are pruning to improve flowering. Shrubs generally fall into one of two categories: They bloom either on year-old wood or on the current season's growth. Prune shrubs that flower on old wood right after blooms have faded, giving them time to produce growth for next year's flowers. Generally, spring-flowering plants such as azalea bloom on old wood. Prune shrubs that flower on new wood while they are dormant, either in very early spring or in late fall, so they will have a chance to set buds. Later-flowering shrubs, such as the hydrangea shown here, usually bloom on new wood.

Prune when Dormant

Artemisia (wormwood)

Buddleia (butterfly bush)

Callicarpa japonica (beautyberry)

Calluna vulgaris (heather)

Fatsia japonica (Japanese fatsia)

Hamamelis virginiana (witch hazel)

Hibiscus syriacus (rose of Sharon)

Holodiscus discolor (ocean-spray)

Hydrangea macrophylla (hydrangea)

Hypericum (St.-John's-wort)

Lagerstroemia indica (crape myrtle)

Nandina domestica (sacred bamboo)

Potentilla (cinquefoil)

Spiraea japonica (Japanese spirea)

Symphoricarpos (snowberry)

Vitex agnus-castus (chaste tree)

Prune after Blooming

Buddleia alternifolia (butterfly bush)

Cotinus coggygria (smoke tree)

Daphne (daphne)

Deutzia (deutzia)

Forsythia (forsythia)

Jasminum (jasmine)

Kerria japonica (Japanese rose)

Kolkwitzia (beautybush)

Lonicera (honeysuckle)

Philadelphus (mock orange)

Physocarpus (ninebark)

Pieris japonica (lily-of-the-valley bush)

Spiraea prunifolia (bridal-wreath)

Syringa (lilac)

Weigela (weigela)

▶ *Summer-blooming hydrangeas, like the large-leafed type in this New York garden, flower on the current season's growth, and should be pruned in early spring, before new growth begins. Cut back each cane by half to get masses of medium-sized blooms; more rigorous pruning may produce blossoms too large for the canes to support.*

A Border Showcase of Fruiting Shrubs

This border, set against a backdrop of small evergreens, offers three seasons of interest with a diverse collection of blossoms, berries, and foliage. The shrubs, interspersed with perennials and annuals in this plan, will flourish in partial shade with average to moist soil. Plant the shrubs and perennials in spring, or, if you garden in a warmer climate, in fall. The impatiens can be planted in spring after the last frost.

The fruits of the various shrubs in this plan will attract a number of birds, such as cedar waxwings, chickadees, titmice, and nuthatches. The birdbath, reachable by the stone pathway, also will draw them to this garden.

Spring offers blooms of dogwood, fothergilla, serviceberry *(Amelanchier)*, and andromeda. Next to bloom are aromatic lilac and viburnum.

Summer-sweet, enkianthus, spirea, and, later, the rose and beautyberry, will burst forth with summer color. After blooming, all the shrubs in this bed will produce a vivid display of fruit, starting in late summer. If not eaten by birds, the berries will persist into fall, while the decidous shrubs will blaze with color.

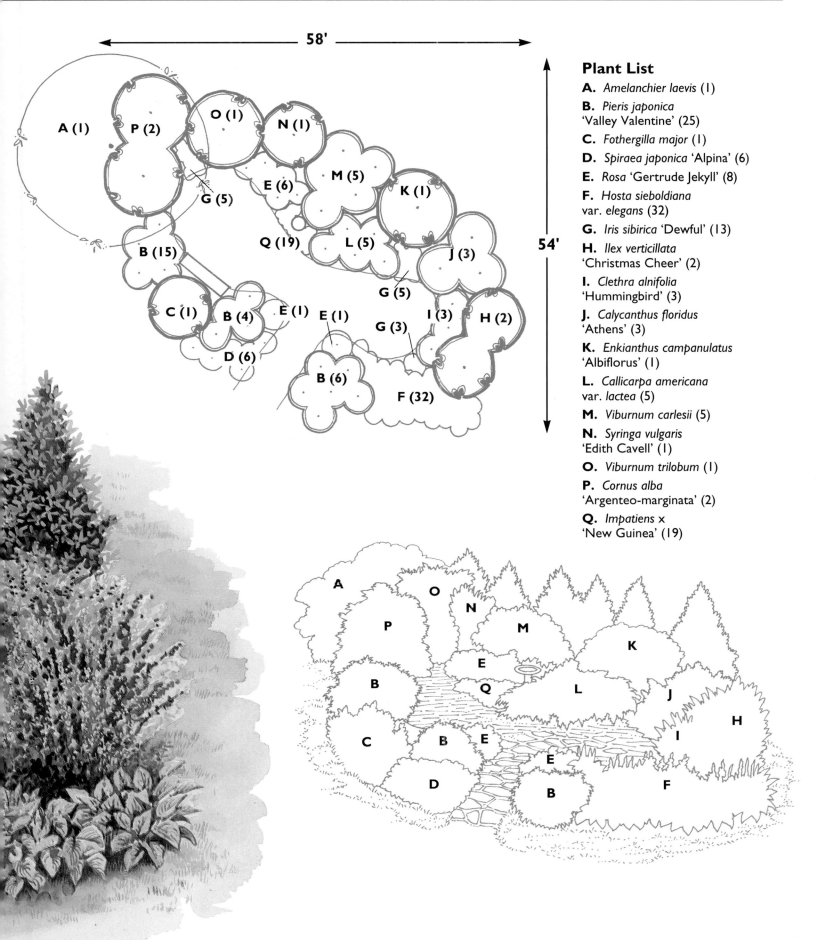

58'

A (1)

P (2)

O (1)

N (1)

M (5)

G (5)

E (6)

K (1)

B (15)

Q (19)

L (5)

J (3)

G (5)

C (1)

B (4)

E (1)

E (1)

I (3)

H (2)

D (6)

G (3)

B (6)

F (32)

54'

Plant List

A. *Amelanchier laevis* (1)

B. *Pieris japonica* 'Valley Valentine' (25)

C. *Fothergilla major* (1)

D. *Spiraea japonica* 'Alpina' (6)

E. *Rosa* 'Gertrude Jekyll' (8)

F. *Hosta sieboldiana* var. *elegans* (32)

G. *Iris sibirica* 'Dewful' (13)

H. *Ilex verticillata* 'Christmas Cheer' (2)

I. *Clethra alnifolia* 'Hummingbird' (3)

J. *Calycanthus floridus* 'Athens' (3)

K. *Enkianthus campanulatus* 'Albiflorus' (1)

L. *Callicarpa americana* var. *lactea* (5)

M. *Viburnum carlesii* (5)

N. *Syringa vulgaris* 'Edith Cavell' (1)

O. *Viburnum trilobum* (1)

P. *Cornus alba* 'Argenteo-marginata' (2)

Q. *Impatiens* x 'New Guinea' (19)

A

O

N

P

M

K

E

B

Q

L

J

C

B

E

H

I

D

E

F

B

An Evergreen All-Season Bed

Careful plant and site selection will ensure that this bed of shrubs will be visually appealing year-round. Situated in a partial shade setting with acid soil, this bed requires minimal care to perpetuate its beauty. Plant the bed in spring and consider using a mulch of pine needles. As the needles break down, they will contribute slightly to the acidity of the soil.

Shown here in late spring, the bed is alive with the colorful blooms of the rhododendron, mahonia, mountain laurel *(Kalmia)*, fetterbush *(Leucothoe)*, and pieris. As these blooms fade, white cup-shaped flowers will open on the yucca, while more delicate, airy white flowers will hover atop the heuchera. Deadhead old flow-ers, except those of the holly, to promote next year's blooms. All summer long, the shiny, deep green leaves of the holly, the variegated foliage of the fetterbush, and the flat needles of the yew will remain constant in both form and color.

As fall and winter approach, bright red berries will emerge on the holly, providing a dash of color in this otherwise deep green winter bed. Be sure to plant both male and female holly plants so they can cross-pollinate, a prerequisite for pro-duction of the berries.

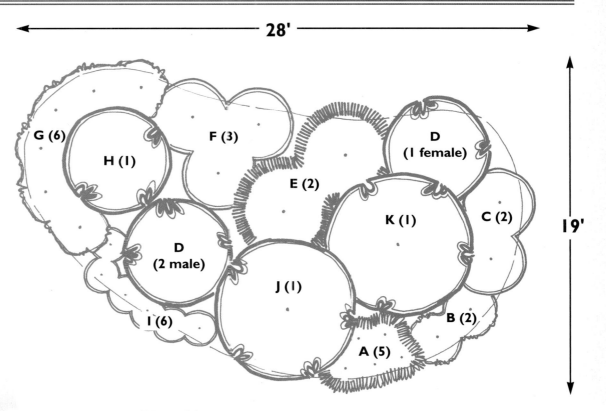

Plant List

A. *Yucca filamentosa* 'Bright Edge' (5)

B. *Mahonia aquifolium* 'Mayan Strain' (2)

C. *Rhododendron* 'Yaku Princess' (2)

D. *Ilex glabra* 'Compacta' (3)

E. *Taxus cuspidata* 'Nana' (2)

F. *Pieris japonica* 'Dorothy Wycoff' (3)

G. *Leucothoe fortanesiana* 'Girard's Rainbow' (6)

H. *Rhododendron catawbiense* (1)

I. *Heuchera* 'Purple Palace' (6)

J. *Rhododendron maximum* (1)

K. *Kalmia latifolia* 'Olympic Fire' (1)

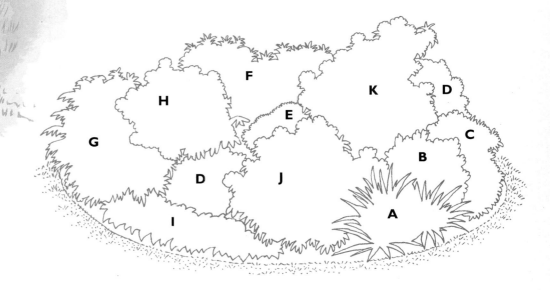

A Mixed Border for Masking Foundations

Whether at the base of a house, deck, or garage, a foundation presents an interesting challenge and an opportunity for creative border design. The curved front edge of this border, for example, softens the horizontal seam between the latticework base of the deck and the lawn. It's important to leave enough room at the back of the border so that air can circulate among all the plants, and to make a pleasing transition between the vertical backdrop and the horizontal foreground.

Suited to full sun and well-drained soil, the strongly colored plants featured in this border will establish a festive mood wherever you site the planting. Put in the shrubs and perennials in spring, or in fall in warm-winter climates.

After installing all the plants, place the steppingstones to create access for maintenance. Once the plants reach their mature sizes, the pavers will be almost completely hidden. Tuck the annuals in among the other plants after the last frost of spring. Mulch the entire bed to keep weeds down while the plants get established.

The annuals will provide color right up to the first frost if they are deadheaded regularly. Deadhead all other plants throughout the season to increase blooms and to keep plants compact. The 'Annabelle' hydrangea will produce flowers up to 12 inches in size, but the shrub itself will never get too large for this attractive border.

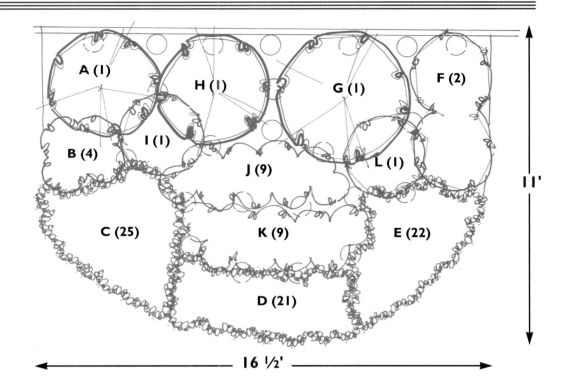

Tip

When planting along a foundation, resist the temptation to build up the soil to mask the concrete base. The concrete keeps pests and vermin from burrowing into the house. An elevated soil level will just provide them with better access to the wooden clapboards or shingles, which are much easier to penetrate.

A (1)
H (1)
G (1)
F (2)
I (1)
B (4)
J (9)
L (1)
C (25)
K (9)
E (22)
D (21)

11'

16 ½'

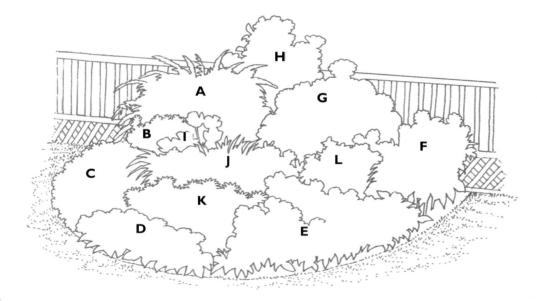

H

A

G

B

I

F

C

J

L

K

E

D

Plant List

A. *Buddleia davidii* 'Nanho Blue' (1)

B. *Coreopsis verticillata* 'Moonbeam' (4)

C. *Begonia* x *semperflorens-cultorum* (25)

D. *Ageratum* (21)

E. *Zinnia elegans* (22)

F. *Dahlia* (2)

G. *Hydrangea arborescens* 'Annabelle' (1)

H. *Rosa* 'Graham Thomas' (1)

I. *Papaver orientale* (1)

J. *Hemerocallis* 'Stella d'Oro' (9)

K. *Chrysanthemum* x *superbum* 'Marconi' (9)

L. *Helenium autumnale* 'Butterpat' (1)

Troubleshooting Guide

Even the most carefully tended beds and borders can fall prey to pests and diseases. To keep them in check, regularly inspect your plants for warning signs. Lack of nutrients, improper pH levels, and other environmental conditions may cause symptoms that could be confused with disease. If wilting or yellowing appears on neighboring plants, the source is probably environmental; pest and disease damage is usually more random.

This guide is intended to help identify and solve most of your pest and disease problems. In general, proper drainage,

fertile soil, and good air circulation help prevent diseases. To aid in controlling pests, consider using any of the common beneficial insects, such as ladybugs and lacewings, that prey on pests. Natural solutions to garden problems are best. For persistent infestations, use horticultural oils, insecticidal soaps, and neem tree-based insecticides; these products are the least disruptive to beneficial insects and will not destroy the soil balance that is the foundation of a healthy garden. If you must use chemicals, treat only the affected plant.

PESTS

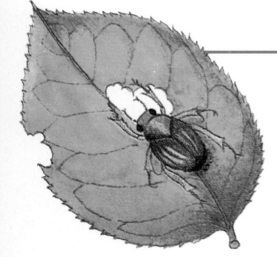

Problem: Leaves curl, are distorted, and may be sticky and have a black, sooty appearance. Buds and flowers are deformed, new growth is stunted, and leaves and flowers may drop.

Cause: Aphids are pear-shaped, semitransparent, sucking insects about ⅛ inch long, and range in color from green to red, pink, black, or gray. Aphids suck plant sap, and in doing so may spread viral disease. Infestations are most severe in spring and early summer, when the pests cluster on new shoots, undersides of leaves, and around flower buds. Winged forms appear when colonies become overcrowded. Aphids secrete a sticky substance known as honeydew onto leaves. This substance fosters the growth of a black fungus called sooty mold.

Solution: Spray plants frequently with a steady stream of water from a garden hose to knock aphids off plants and discourage them from returning. In severe cases, prune infested areas, and use a diluted insecticidal soap solution or a recommended insecticide. Ladybugs or lacewings, which eat aphids, may be introduced into the garden.
Susceptible plants: many perennials, including Asiatic lily, chrysanthemum, columbine, delphinium, globe thistle, hollyhock, iris, lupine, poppy, primrose, rose, and sunflower.

Problem: Ragged or neat, round holes are eaten into leaves, leaf edges, and flowers. Leaves may be reduced to skeletons with only veins remaining.

Cause: Japanese beetles, iridescent blue-green with bronze wing covers, are the most destructive of a large family of hard-shelled chewing insects ranging in size from ¼ to ¾ inch long. Other genera include Asiatic garden beetles (brown), northern masked chafers (brown with dark band on head), and Fuller rose beetles (gray), as well as blister beetles (metallic black, blue, purple, or brown) and flea beetles (shiny dark blue, brown, black, or bronze). Adult beetles are voracious in summer. Larvae (white grubs) feed on plant roots from midsummer through the next spring, when they emerge as adults.

Solution: Handpick small colonies (*Caution:* Use gloves when picking blister beetles), placing them in a can filled with soapy water. Japanese beetles can be caught in baited traps. Place traps in an area away from susceptible plants so as not to attract more beetles into the garden. The larval stage can be controlled with milky spore disease, which can be applied to the whole yard. For heavy infestations, contact your local Cooperative Extension Service.
Susceptible plants: astilbe, foxglove, hollyhock, rose, New York aster, purple coneflower, rose mallow.

Problem: Holes appear in leaves, buds, and flowers; entire leaves and stems also may be eaten.

Cause: Caterpillars, including the larvae of violet sawfly, verbena bud moth, sunflower moth, and painted lady butterfly, come in a variety of shapes and colors, and can be smooth, hairy, or spiny. These voracious pests are found in gardens in spring and summer.

Solution: Handpick to control small populations. The bacterial pesticide *Bacillus thuringiensis* (Bt) kills many types without harming beneficial insects. If caterpillars return to your garden every spring, spray Bt as a preventive measure. Identify the caterpillar species to determine the control options and timing of spray applications. Introduce beneficial insects that prey on caterpillars, including spined soldier bugs, assassin bugs, minute pirate bugs, and lacewings. Keep garden clear of debris and cultivate frequently. Destroy all visible cocoons and nests.
Susceptible plants: annuals and perennials, especially tender new shoots.

Problem: White or light green tunnels are bored through leaves; older tunnels turn black. Leaves may lose color, dry up, and die. Seedlings may be stunted or die.

Cause: Leaf miners, minute (1/16 to 1/8 inch long), translucent, pale green larvae of certain flies, moths, or beetles, are hatched from eggs laid on plant leaves. During spring and summer, the larvae eat the tender interior below the surface of the leaf, leaving behind serpentine trails of blistered tissue known as mines.

Solution: Damage may be unsightly but is usually not lethal. Pick off and destroy infested leaves as they appear. In the fall, cut the plant to the ground and discard stalks. Do not compost. Remove and destroy leaves with egg clusters. Keep the garden well weeded. Inspect plants before purchase and do not buy any with trails in leaves.
Susceptible plants: many annuals and perennials, especially columbine; many shrubs, including American holly.

Problem: Leaves become stippled or flecked, then discolor, turning yellow or nearly white with brown edges; the leaves of some shrubs become speckled with gray. Entire leaves may turn yellow or bronze and curl. Flowers and buds discolor or dry up. Webbing may be seen on undersides of leaves and on the branches of shrubs. Growth is stunted; leaves may drop.

Cause: Mites are pinhead-size, spider-like sucking pests that can be reddish, pale green, or yellow. These insects can become a major problem in hot, dry weather when several generations of mites may occur in a single season. Adults of some species hibernate over the winter in sod, in bark, and on weeds and plants that retain their foliage.

Solution: Damage is worst to plants in full sunlight and hot areas. Detect by gently shaking branch or leaf over paper; if dust moves, it's mites. Keep plants watered and mulched. Regularly spray the undersides of leaves, where mites feed and lay eggs, using water or a diluted soap solution. Horticultural oils also may be applied to undersides. Insecticidal soaps control nymphs and adults but not eggs. Introduce natural predators such as green lacewing larvae.
Susceptible plants: many perennials including rose, daylily, garden phlox and iris; annuals such as zinnia and salvia; shrubs such as azalea, boxwood, and juniper; elm, holly, fir, and pine trees.

Problem: Ragged holes appear in leaves, especially those near the ground. New leaves and entire young seedlings may be eaten. Telltale shiny silver streaks appear on leaves and garden paths.

Cause: Slugs and snails are serious pests in the shade garden, favoring such an environment over hot, sunny conditions. They prefer damp, cool locations and are most damaging in summer, especially in wet regions or during rainy years.

Solution: Keep the garden clean to minimize hiding places. Handpick, or trap them by placing saucers of beer near plants. Slugs also will collect under citrus or melon rinds. Salt kills slugs and snails but may damage plants. Strips of coarse sand, cinders, or copper garden edging placed around beds or small amounts of diatomaceous earth worked in around new transplants will deter both slugs and snails. Spading in spring destroys dormant slugs and eggs. *Susceptible plants: virtually all, particularly those with young or tender foliage. Hosta is especially susceptible.*
Note: Choose less susceptible plants, including artemisia and other perennials with silver leaves.

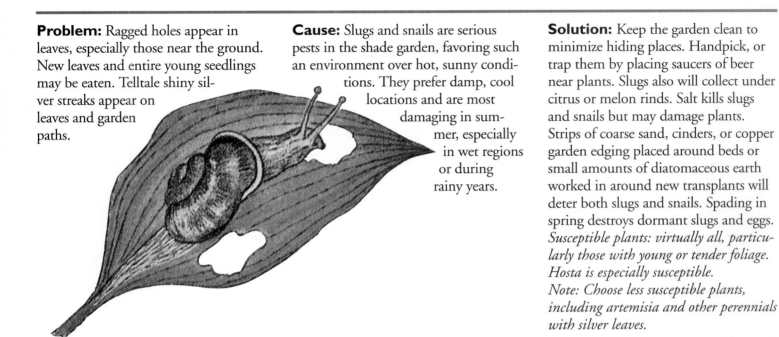

DISEASES

Problem: Circular black spots that are ¼ inch in diameter and surrounded by a yellow halo appear on upper leaf surfaces of rose plants. The spots enlarge and coalesce until the entire leaf is yellow and falls from the plant.

Cause: Black spot, a fungus disease, is most often found under humid and rainy conditions because fungus spores germinate in water. Once rose plants are infected, the fungus will remain on the canes through the winter and reappear on the next season's growth.

Solution: Choose less susceptible roses and plant them in sunny locations. Water early in the day. Avoid splashing leaves. Clean up all refuse after pruning. Prune canes of infected plants farther back than normal to eliminate fungus that survives over the winter, and apply a lime-sulfur spray before leaves open. If symptoms appear, remove and destroy all infected leaves, including those on the ground. Spray leaves with fungicide to keep fungus from spreading.
Susceptible plants: rose, especially hybrid perpetual, hybrid tea, polyantha, and tea rose.

Problem: A brownish gray moldy growth appears on flowers and foliage. Stalks are weak and flowers and foliage droop. Buds may not open. Discolored blotches appear on leaves, stems, and flowers. Stem bases rot. Plant parts eventually turn brown and dry up. Flowering plants are most affected.

Cause: Botrytis blight, known as gray mold, thrives in moist air and cool temperatures, survives winter in the soil or on dead plants and spreads on wind or water.

Solution: Limit watering to early in the day and avoid overhead watering. Place plants in well-drained soil, and thin to provide more light and air. Cut and destroy all infected plant parts and leaves. Spray plants with Bordeaux mixture.
Susceptible plants: flowering plants are most at risk, including rhododendron, lily, rose, and tulip.

Problem: Leaves develop small yellow, brown, or black spots that are surrounded by a rim of discolored tissue. Spots often join to produce large, irregular blotches. Entire leaf may turn yellow, wilt, and drop. Spotting usually starts on lower leaves and moves upward.

Cause: The many leaf-spot diseases are caused by a number of fungi or bacteria. All are particularly severe in wet weather because they are spread by splashing water.

Solution: Clean up all fallen leaves before winter. Water overhead only in the morning, as damp foliage in cool night air encourages spreading of the diseases. Prune and destroy infected leaves of perennials and shrubs. A fungicide can protect healthy foliage but will not destroy fungus on infected leaves. *Susceptible plants: all types of plants.*

Problem: Leaves are covered with spots or a thin layer of grayish white powdery material. Infected parts may distort and curl, then turn yellow or purplish; leaves may finally drop off. Badly infected buds will not open properly.

Cause: Powdery mildews are fungus diseases that thrive when nights are cool and days are hot and humid. The diseases are most noticeable in late summer and fall, and at times when plant growth is vigorous.

Solution: Plant mildew-resistant varieties. Susceptible plants should receive full sun with good air circulation. Water overhead only in the early morning. In the fall, cut infected perennials to the ground and discard. Do not compost. Spray a solution of 1 teaspoon baking soda and ¼ teaspoon summer horticultural oil to 1 gallon water every 5 to 7 days until symptoms disappear. *Susceptible plants: many perennials; young growth of many woody plants, especially rose, lilac, and euonymus.*

Problem: Leaves turn yellow, red, or brown and are stunted and wilted; the entire plant may wilt and die. Flowers may not develop. Roots are discolored dark brown or black, are soft and wet, and carry a mushroomlike odor. Trees have rotting bark at the base, followed by a white, fibrous fungus.

Cause: Root rot is caused by a variety of fungi, many of which thrive in heavy, wet soil conditions.

Solution: Remove and destroy infected plant parts; if infection is severe, remove plant and the surrounding soil. Improve soil drainage. Water early in the day and allow the soil to dry between waterings. A fungicide can be applied to the soil before replanting. *Susceptible plants: all types of plants.*

Problem: Upper leaf surfaces have pale yellow or white spots, and undersides are covered with orange or yellow pustules. Leaves wilt or shrivel and hang down along the stem, but do not drop off. Pustules may become more numerous, destroying leaves and occasionally the entire plant. Plants may be stunted.

Cause: Rust, a fungus disease, is a problem in late summer and early fall and is most prevalent when nights are cool and humid. Rust spores are spread easily by wind and splashing water and overwinter on infected plant parts.

Solution: Buy rust-resistant varieties whenever possible. Water early in the day and avoid wetting leaves. Remove and destroy infected plant parts in the fall and again in the spring. Do not compost. Spray with sulfur, lime sulfur, or Bordeaux mixture—a traditional antifungal treatment originally used in vineyards. *Susceptible plants: virtually all.*

Color Guide to Herbaceous Plants

Organized by plant color, this chart provides information needed to select species and varieties that will thrive in your garden's conditions. For additional information on each plant, refer to the encyclopedia that begins on page 104.

Color	Plant	Zones	Dry	Well-drained	Moist	Full sun	Partial shade	Shade	Spring	Summer	Fall	Winter	Under 1 ft.	1-3 ft.	3-6 ft.	6-10 ft.	Over 10 ft.	Foliage	Flowers	Fragrance	Fruit/seeds
WHITE	Acanthus mollis	7-10	✔	✔		✔	✔			✔					✔			✔	✔		
	Antirrhinum majus 'White Sonnet' [4]	8-9		✔		✔	✔		✔	✔	✔			✔					✔		
	Boltonia asteroides 'Snowbank'	4-8		✔	✔	✔				✔	✔				✔				✔		
	Capsicum annuum 'Holiday Cheer' [4]	10-11		✔	✔	✔				✔			✔					✔	✔		✔
	Chrysanthemum x superbum	3-9		✔		✔				✔	✔			✔				✔	✔		
	Cimicifuga racemosa	3-9		✔	✔	✔	✔			✔					✔	✔		✔	✔		
	Cosmos bipinnatus 'Sonata' [1]		✔	✔		✔	✔			✔	✔								✔		
	Crinum asiaticum	7-11		✔	✔	✔	✔			✔				✔				✔	✔	✔	
	Dicentra spectabilis 'Alba'	3-8		✔	✔		✔		✔					✔				✔	✔		
	Epimedium x youngianum 'Niveum'	4-8		✔	✔		✔	✔	✔				✔					✔	✔		
	Eucomis comosa	8-10		✔		✔	✔			✔				✔				✔	✔	✔	
	Galanthus nivalis	3-8		✔	✔	✔	✔		✔			✔	✔						✔		
	Heuchera micrantha 'Chocolate Ruffles'	3-9		✔	✔	✔	✔			✔				✔				✔	✔		
	Hosta x tardiana 'Royal Standard'	3-9		✔	✔		✔	✔		✔	✔			✔				✔	✔	✔	
	Iris cristata 'Alba'	3-8		✔	✔	✔	✔		✔				✔					✔	✔		
	Nicotiana sylvestris [4]	9-10		✔	✔	✔	✔			✔					✔				✔		
	Paeonia lactiflora 'Elsa Sass'	3-8		✔		✔	✔		✔	✔				✔				✔	✔	✔	
	Primula japonica 'Postford White'	6-8		✔	✔		✔		✔	✔				✔					✔		
YELLOW	Abelmoschus manihot [4]	9-10		✔	✔	✔				✔						✔		✔	✔		
	Achillea x 'Coronation Gold'	4-8	✔	✔		✔				✔	✔			✔				✔	✔		
	Aquilegia canadensis 'Corbett'	3-8		✔	✔	✔	✔		✔	✔				✔				✔	✔		
	Belamcanda flabellata	5-10		✔	✔	✔				✔				✔					✔		✔
	Coreopsis verticillata	4-9	✔	✔		✔				✔	✔			✔				✔	✔		
	Epimedium x versicolor 'Sulphureum'	4-8		✔	✔		✔	✔	✔				✔					✔	✔		
	Eremurus stenophyllus	4-8		✔		✔			✔	✔					✔			✔	✔		
	Hemerocallis citrina	3-9		✔	✔	✔	✔			✔	✔			✔				✔	✔	✔	
	Ligularia stenocephala 'The Rocket'	5-8			✔	✔	✔			✔					✔			✔	✔		
	Lilium 'Golden Splendor'	3-9		✔	✔	✔	✔			✔					✔				✔	✔	

[1] Tender annual   [2] Half-hardy annual   [3] Hardy annual   [4] Perennial, but grown as an annual in colder zones

	ZONES	SOIL			LIGHT			BLOOM SEASON				PLANT HEIGHT					NOTED FOR			
		Dry	Well-drained	Moist	Full sun	Partial shade	Shade	Spring	Summer	Fall	Winter	Under 1 ft.	1-3 ft.	3-6 ft.	6-10 ft.	Over 10 ft.	Foliage	Flowers	Fragrance	Fruit/seeds
YELLOW																				
Narcissus 'Carlton'	3-10		✔		✔	✔		✔					✔					✔	✔	
Narcissus jonquilla	3-10		✔		✔	✔		✔				✔						✔		
Rudbeckia maxima	4-9		✔		✔	✔			✔	✔				✔	✔			✔		
Santolina chamaecyparissus	6-8	✔	✔		✔				✔				✔				✔	✔	✔	
Tagetes erecta [1]			✔		✔				✔	✔		✔	✔				✔	✔		
Verbascum chaixii	4-9		✔		✔				✔					✔			✔	✔		
ORANGE																				
Asclepias tuberosa	3-9	✔	✔	✔	✔				✔	✔			✔					✔		✔
Belamcanda chinensis	5-10		✔	✔	✔	✔			✔				✔	✔				✔		✔
Canna x generalis 'Pretoria' [4]	7-10		✔	✔	✔				✔	✔				✔			✔	✔		
Fritillaria imperialis 'Aurora'	4-7		✔	✔	✔	✔		✔					✔					✔		
Hemerocallis fulva 'Kwanso'	3-9		✔	✔	✔	✔			✔				✔				✔	✔		
Zinnia angustifolia [1]			✔		✔				✔	✔		✔					✔	✔		
RED																				
Acanthus dioscorides var. perringii	8-10	✔	✔		✔	✔			✔				✔					✔		
Aster novi-belgii 'Royal Ruby'	3-8		✔	✔	✔				✔	✔			✔					✔		
Astilbe x arendsii 'Fanal'	4-8		✔	✔	✔	✔			✔				✔				✔	✔		
Crocosmia 'Lucifer'	5-9		✔	✔	✔				✔				✔					✔		
Dianthus deltoides 'Brilliant'	4-7		✔	✔	✔	✔		✔				✔					✔	✔		
Gomphrena globosa 'Strawberry Fields' [1]			✔		✔				✔	✔		✔						✔		
Lobelia cardinalis	3-9		✔	✔	✔				✔	✔			✔	✔				✔		
Lycoris radiata	5-10		✔		✔	✔				✔			✔					✔		
Paeonia tenuifolia	3-8		✔		✔	✔		✔					✔				✔	✔		
Phlox paniculata 'Starfire'	3-8		✔	✔	✔	✔	✔		✔	✔				✔				✔		
Primula japonica 'Miller's Crimson'	6-8		✔	✔		✔	✔	✔					✔					✔		
Tulipa 'Plaisir'	3-8		✔		✔			✔				✔						✔		
PINK																				
Achillea 'Paprika'	4-8	✔	✔		✔				✔	✔			✔				✔	✔		
Allium cernuum	4-10		✔	✔	✔	✔		✔	✔			✔	✔					✔		
Anemone hupehensis	6-8		✔	✔	✔	✔			✔	✔			✔				✔			
Astilbe chinensis 'Pumila'	4-8		✔	✔	✔	✔			✔	✔		✔	✔				✔	✔		
Begonia grandis	6-10		✔			✔	✔		✔	✔			✔				✔	✔		
Chrysanthemum coccineum 'Roseum'	3-9		✔		✔				✔	✔			✔				✔	✔		
Dianthus x allwoodii 'Doris'	3-9		✔	✔	✔	✔		✔	✔				✔				✔	✔	✔	
Dicentra eximia	3-8		✔	✔		✔			✔				✔				✔	✔		

[1] Tender annual   [2] Half-hardy annual   [3] Hardy annual   [4] Perennial, but grown as an annual in colder zones

Color	Plant	ZONES	Dry	Well-drained	Moist	Full sun	Partial shade	Shade	Spring	Summer	Fall	Winter	Under 1 ft.	1-3 ft.	3-6 ft.	6-10 ft.	Over 10 ft.	Foliage	Flowers	Fragrance	Fruit/seeds
PINK	Echinacea purpurea 'Bright Star'	3-9	✔	✔		✔	✔			✔				✔					✔		
PINK	Epimedium grandiflorum 'Rose Queen'	4-8		✔	✔		✔	✔	✔				✔					✔	✔		
PINK	Eustoma grandiflorum 'Echo Pink' [4]	9-10		✔	✔	✔	✔			✔				✔					✔		
PINK	Lycoris squamigera	5-10		✔		✔	✔			✔				✔					✔	✔	
PINK	Petunia integrifolia [1]			✔		✔				✔			✔						✔		
PINK	Pulmonaria saccharata 'Janet Fisk'	4-8		✔	✔		✔	✔	✔				✔					✔	✔		
PINK	Sedum sieboldii	3-8	✔	✔		✔					✔		✔					✔	✔		
PINK	Tulipa 'Angelique'	3-8		✔		✔			✔					✔					✔		
PURPLE/LAVENDER	Allium christophii	4-8		✔	✔	✔	✔			✔				✔					✔		
PURPLE/LAVENDER	Campanula glomerata 'Joan Elliott'	3-8		✔	✔	✔	✔			✔				✔				✔	✔		
PURPLE/LAVENDER	Cleome hasslerana 'Violet Queen' [1]			✔	✔	✔	✔			✔	✔				✔			✔	✔		✔
PURPLE/LAVENDER	Colchicum speciosum 'Lilac Wonder'	4-9		✔	✔	✔					✔	✔						✔			
PURPLE/LAVENDER	Cynara cardunculus	8-9		✔	✔	✔				✔	✔				✔			✔	✔		
PURPLE/LAVENDER	Dictamnus albus 'Purpureus'	3-8		✔	✔	✔	✔			✔				✔				✔	✔	✔	✔
PURPLE/LAVENDER	Echinacea pallida	3-9	✔	✔		✔	✔			✔					✔				✔		✔
PURPLE/LAVENDER	Heliotropium arborescens [4]	9-10		✔		✔	✔			✔				✔					✔	✔	
PURPLE/LAVENDER	Hosta sieboldiana	3-9		✔	✔		✔	✔		✔	✔			✔				✔	✔		
PURPLE/LAVENDER	Lavandula angustifolia 'Hidcote'	5-8		✔		✔				✔				✔				✔	✔	✔	
PURPLE/LAVENDER	Lavandula stoechas	7-9		✔		✔				✔				✔				✔	✔	✔	
PURPLE/LAVENDER	Liatris spicata 'Kobold'	3-10		✔		✔	✔			✔				✔					✔		
PURPLE/LAVENDER	Petunia x hybrida 'Heavenly Lavender' [1]			✔		✔				✔	✔	✔							✔		
PURPLE/LAVENDER	Salvia x superba 'East Friesland'	5-8		✔		✔	✔		✔	✔				✔					✔		
PURPLE/LAVENDER	Verbena 'Homestead Purple'	6-9		✔	✔	✔				✔	✔		✔					✔	✔		
BLUE	Ageratum houstonianum 'Blue Horizon' [1]			✔	✔	✔				✔	✔		✔	✔				✔	✔		
BLUE	Anemone blanda	6-8		✔	✔	✔	✔		✔				✔					✔	✔		
BLUE	Aquilegia flabellata	3-9		✔	✔	✔	✔		✔	✔			✔					✔	✔		
BLUE	Aster amellus 'Joseph Lakin'	5-8		✔	✔	✔				✔	✔			✔					✔		
BLUE	Campanula carpatica 'Blue Chips'	3-8		✔	✔	✔	✔		✔	✔			✔					✔	✔		
BLUE	Ceratostigma plumbaginoides	5-10		✔		✔	✔			✔	✔		✔					✔	✔		
BLUE	Delphinium x belladonna 'Bellamosa'	3-7		✔	✔					✔					✔				✔		
BLUE	Geranium 'Johnson's Blue'	5-8	✔	✔	✔	✔	✔		✔	✔				✔				✔	✔		
BLUE	Hyacinthus orientalis 'Blue Jacket'	3-7		✔	✔	✔			✔				✔						✔	✔	

[1] Tender annual   [2] Half-hardy annual   [3] Hardy annual   [4] Perennial, but grown as an annual in colder zones

	ZONES	SOIL			LIGHT			BLOOM SEASON				PLANT HEIGHT					NOTED FOR			
		Dry	Well-drained	Moist	Full sun	Partial shade	Shade	Spring	Summer	Fall	Winter	Under 1 ft.	1-3 ft.	3-6 ft.	6-10 ft.	Over 10 ft.	Foliage	Flowers	Fragrance	Fruit/seeds
BLUE																				
Iris sibirica 'Dewful'	4-8		✔	✔	✔	✔		✔					✔					✔	✔	
Lobelia siphilitica	4-7		✔	✔	✔	✔			✔	✔			✔					✔		
Perovskia atriplicifolia 'Longin'	5-9		✔		✔				✔					✔			✔	✔	✔	
Phlox divaricata	4-9		✔	✔	✔	✔	✔	✔	✔			✔	✔					✔	✔	
Platycodon grandiflorus 'Mariesii'	4-9		✔		✔	✔			✔				✔					✔		
Pulmonaria longifolia	4-8		✔	✔		✔	✔	✔				✔						✔	✔	
Salvia farinacea [4]	8-10		✔		✔	✔			✔	✔			✔					✔	✔	✔
Veronica spicata 'Blue Peter'	4-8		✔		✔	✔		✔	✔				✔					✔		
MULTICOLOR																				
Alcea rosea 'Country Garden Mix'	3-9		✔		✔				✔	✔				✔				✔		
Anemone blanda 'de Caen'	6-8		✔	✔	✔	✔		✔				✔					✔	✔		
Begonia x semperflorens-cultorum [4]	9-10		✔	✔		✔	✔	✔	✔	✔		✔					✔	✔		
Caladium bicolor 'Aaron' [4]	10		✔	✔		✔	✔		✔				✔				✔			
Caladium bicolor 'Little Miss Muffet' [4]	10		✔	✔		✔	✔					✔					✔			
Celosia cristata [1]		✔	✔	✔	✔				✔	✔		✔	✔				✔	✔		
Coleus x hybridus 'Fiji' [4]	10-11		✔	✔		✔			✔				✔				✔			
Dahlia x hybrida [4]	9-11		✔	✔	✔				✔	✔		✔	✔	✔			✔			
Gaillardia x grandiflora 'Monarch Strain' [2]	3-8	✔	✔		✔				✔	✔			✔					✔		
Impatiens wallerana [1]			✔	✔		✔	✔		✔	✔		✔	✔					✔	✔	
Lantana camara 'Confetti' [4]	9-10		✔		✔				✔				✔	✔			✔	✔	✔	
Lupinus 'Russell Hybrids'	4-6		✔	✔	✔	✔			✔					✔			✔	✔		
Nigella damascena [1]			✔		✔				✔				✔					✔		✔
Papaver nudicaule	3-8	✔	✔		✔	✔		✔					✔					✔		
GREEN																				
Adiantum pedatum	2-8		✔	✔		✔	✔	✔					✔				✔			
Adiantum venustum	5-8		✔	✔		✔	✔	✔				✔					✔			
Artemisia lactiflora	5-9	✔	✔		✔								✔				✔			
Athyrium filix-femina	4-7		✔	✔		✔	✔						✔				✔			
Athyrium nipponicum 'Pictum'	4-7		✔	✔		✔	✔						✔				✔			
Miscanthus sinensis 'Morning Light'	5-9	✔	✔		✔				✔	✔	✔			✔			✔	✔		✔
Miscanthus sinensis var. condensatus 'Silberpfeil'	5-9	✔	✔		✔				✔	✔	✔			✔			✔	✔		✔
Ocimum basilicum 'Purple Ruffles' [1]			✔	✔	✔				✔				✔				✔	✔	✔	
Pennisetum orientale	5-9		✔	✔	✔				✔				✔				✔	✔	✔	
Ricinus communis [1]			✔		✔				✔	✔						✔		✔		

[1] Tender annual   [2] Half-hardy annual   [3] Hardy annual   [4] Perennial, but grown as an annual in colder zones

Guide to Woody Plants

Organized by plant type, this chart provides information needed to select species and varieties that will thrive in the particular conditions of your garden. For additional information on each plant, refer to the encyclopedia that begins on page 104.

	ZONES	SOIL			LIGHT			BLOOM SEASON				PLANT HEIGHT				NOTED FOR				
		Dry	Well-drained	Moist	Full sun	Partial shade	Shade	Spring	Summer	Fall	Winter	Under 3 ft.	3-6 ft.	6-10 ft.	Over 10 ft.	Foliage	Flowers	Fragrance	Fruit/seeds	Form
EVERGREEN SHRUBS																				
Aucuba japonica	7-10		✔	✔		✔	✔	✔						✔		✔			✔	
Berberis julianae	6-8		✔	✔	✔	✔			✔					✔		✔	✔		✔	
Berberis verruculosa	5-9		✔	✔	✔	✔			✔				✔			✔	✔		✔	
Buxus microphylla var. koreana	4-9		✔		✔	✔						✔				✔				✔
Buxus microphylla 'Wintergreen'	6-9		✔		✔	✔										✔				✔
Camellia japonica	7-9		✔	✔		✔				✔	✔				✔	✔	✔			
Camellia sasanqua	7-9		✔	✔		✔				✔	✔			✔		✔	✔			
Euonymus japonica	7-9		✔		✔	✔	✔		✔						✔	✔				
Gardenia augusta 'August Beauty'	8-10		✔	✔	✔	✔			✔	✔			✔			✔	✔	✔		
Gardenia augusta 'Radicans'	8-10		✔	✔	✔	✔			✔	✔		✔				✔	✔	✔		
Hypericum patulum 'Sungold'	6-9	✔	✔		✔	✔			✔			✔				✔	✔			
Ilex cornuta 'Burfordii'	6-9		✔	✔	✔				✔					✔		✔			✔	
Kalmia latifolia	4-9		✔	✔	✔	✔	✔		✔					✔	✔	✔	✔			
Leucothoe fontanesiana	5-9		✔	✔		✔	✔	✔						✔		✔	✔	✔		✔
Mahonia aquifolium	4-9		✔	✔		✔	✔	✔						✔		✔	✔		✔	
Mahonia bealei	6-9		✔	✔		✔	✔	✔						✔	✔	✔	✔	✔	✔	
Pieris floribunda	5-8		✔	✔	✔	✔			✔			✔	✔			✔	✔	✔		✔
Rhododendron maximum	3-9		✔	✔	✔	✔			✔				✔	✔	✔	✔	✔			
Taxus baccata 'Repandens'	4-7		✔			✔	✔					✔				✔				
Taxus x media 'Densiformis'	5-7		✔			✔	✔						✔			✔				
Yucca glauca	4-8	✔	✔		✔				✔				✔			✔	✔			✔
DECIDUOUS SHRUBS																				
Aronia arbutifolia 'Brilliantissima'	4-9		✔		✔	✔		✔						✔		✔	✔		✔	
Buddleia alternifolia 'Argentea'	5-9		✔		✔			✔	✔					✔		✔	✔	✔		✔
Buddleia davidii	5-9		✔		✔				✔	✔			✔			✔	✔	✔		
Callicarpa japonica	5-8		✔		✔	✔			✔				✔			✔	✔		✔	
Calycanthus floridus	4-9		✔	✔	✔	✔		✔	✔					✔		✔	✔	✔		
Caryopteris x clandonensis	5-8		✔		✔				✔	✔			✔			✔	✔			
Ceratostigma willmottianum	5-10		✔		✔	✔			✔	✔		✔				✔	✔			

DECIDUOUS SHRUBS

	ZONES	SOIL			LIGHT			BLOOM SEASON				PLANT HEIGHT				NOTED FOR				
		Dry	Well-drained	Moist	Full sun	Partial shade	Shade	Spring	Summer	Fall	Winter	Under 3 ft.	3-6 ft.	6-10 ft.	Over 10 ft.	Foliage	Flowers	Fragrance	Fruit/seeds	Form
Clethra alnifolia 'Hummingbird'	3-9			✔	✔	✔	✔		✔				✔			✔	✔	✔		
Clethra barbinervis	3-9	✔	✔	✔	✔	✔	✔		✔					✔		✔	✔	✔		
Cornus alba 'Sibirica'	3-8		✔	✔	✔	✔		✔					✔			✔	✔		✔	
Cornus mas	5-8		✔	✔	✔	✔		✔						✔		✔	✔		✔	
Cornus sericea 'Flaviramea'	2-8		✔	✔	✔	✔		✔					✔			✔	✔		✔	
Cotinus coggygria	5-8		✔		✔				✔						✔	✔	✔		✔	
Cytisus x praecox	5-10	✔	✔		✔			✔					✔			✔	✔			✔
Enkianthus campanulatus	4-7		✔	✔	✔	✔		✔						✔	✔	✔	✔			
Euonymus alata 'Compacta'	3-8		✔		✔	✔	✔		✔					✔	✔	✔			✔	
Exochorda x macrantha 'The Bride'	5-9		✔		✔	✔		✔					✔			✔	✔			
Exochorda racemosa	5-9		✔		✔	✔		✔						✔		✔	✔			
Fothergilla gardenii	6-8		✔	✔	✔	✔		✔				✔				✔	✔	✔		
Fothergilla major	4-8		✔	✔	✔	✔		✔					✔			✔	✔	✔		
Hibiscus syriacus 'Diana'	5-8		✔	✔	✔	✔			✔	✔			✔	✔		✔				
Hydrangea arborescens 'Annabelle'	3-9		✔	✔	✔	✔			✔				✔			✔	✔			
Hydrangea quercifolia 'Snow Queen'	5-9		✔	✔	✔	✔			✔	✔				✔		✔	✔			
Ilex 'Sparkleberry'	4-8		✔	✔	✔	✔		✔							✔	✔			✔	
Kerria japonica	4-9		✔		✔		✔						✔			✔	✔			
Lespedeza bicolor	4-8	✔	✔		✔				✔					✔		✔	✔			
Nandina domestica	6-9		✔	✔	✔	✔		✔						✔		✔			✔	✔
Potentilla fruticosa 'Abbotswood'	3-7	✔	✔		✔	✔			✔	✔	✔	✔				✔	✔			
Punica granatum	8-10	✔	✔		✔				✔				✔			✔	✔		✔	✔
Rhododendron schlippenbachii	4-7		✔	✔	✔	✔		✔					✔			✔	✔			
Rhododendron vaseyi 'White Find'	4-8		✔	✔	✔	✔		✔					✔			✔	✔			
Rosa rugosa hybrids	3-10		✔		✔				✔	✔			✔			✔	✔	✔	✔	
Spiraea japonica	4-8		✔		✔	✔			✔				✔			✔	✔			
Spiraea prunifolia	3-8		✔		✔	✔		✔						✔		✔	✔			
Syringa x laciniata	4-8		✔	✔	✔			✔					✔			✔	✔	✔		
Syringa vulgaris	3-7		✔	✔	✔			✔						✔	✔	✔	✔	✔		
Viburnum x carlcephalum	5-8		✔	✔	✔	✔		✔						✔		✔	✔	✔		
Viburnum carlesii	4-8		✔	✔	✔	✔		✔						✔		✔	✔	✔		
Vitex agnus-castus	7-10		✔		✔				✔	✔			✔	✔		✔	✔	✔		

A Zone Map of the U.S. and Canada

A plant's winter hardiness and tolerance of summer heat are critical in deciding whether it is suitable for your garden. The map below divides the United States and Canada into 11 climatic zones based on average minimum temperatures, as compiled by the U.S. Department of Agriculture. Find your zone and check the zone information in the plant selection guide *(pages 96-101)* or the encyclopedia *(pages 104-151)* to help you choose the plants most likely to flourish in your climate.

Zone 1: Below -50° F

Zone 2: -50° to -40°

Zone 3: -40° to -30°

Zone 4: -30° to -20°

Zone 5: -20° to -10°

Zone 6: -10° to 0°

Zone 7: 0° to 10°

Zone 8: 10° to 20°

Zone 9: 20° to 30°

Zone 10: 30° to 40°

Zone 11: Above 40°

Cross-Reference Guide to Plant Names

Adam's-needle—*Yucca filamentosa*

Alumroot—*Heuchera*

Andromeda—*Pieris japonica*

Autumn crocus—*Colchicum*

Azalea—*Rhododendron*

Balloon flower—*Platycodon*

Barberry—*Berberis*

Barrenwort—*Epimedium*

Bear's-breech—*Acanthus*

Beautyberry—*Callicarpa*

Bee larkspur—*Delphinium elatum*

Bellflower—*Campanula*

Bethlehem sage—*Pulmonaria saccharata*

Blackberry lily—*Belamcanda*

Black-eyed Susan—*Rudbeckia hirta*

Black widow—*Geranium phaeum*

Blanket-flower—*Gaillardia*

Bleeding heart—*Dicentra*

Bluebeard—*Caryopteris*

Boxwood—*Buxus*

Broom—*Cytisus*

Bugbane—*Cimicifuga*

Burning bush—*Euonymus alata*

Bush clover—*Lespedeza*

Butterfly bush—*Buddleia*

Butterfly weed—*Asclepias tuberosa*

Cardinal flower—*Lobelia cardinalis*

Cardoon—*Cynara*

Carolina allspice—*Calycanthus*

Castor-oil plant—*Ricinus*

Chaste tree—*Vitex*

Chokeberry—*Aronia*

Cinquefoil—*Potentilla*

Columbine—*Aquilegia*

Common basil—*Ocimum*

Coneflower—*Rudbeckia*

Cornelian cherry—*Cornus mas*

Cranesbill—*Geranium*

Crown-imperial—*Fritillaria imperialis*

Daylily—*Hemerocallis*

Desert-candle—*Eremurus*

Dittany—*Dictamnus*

Dogwood—*Cornus*

Dusty-miller—*Artemisia stellerana*

Dwarf inkberry—*Ilex glabra* 'Compacta'

Elephant's-ear—*Caladium*

Eulalia—*Miscanthus*

False spirea—*Astilbe*

Fetterbush—*Leucothoe*

Fetterbush—*Pieris floribunda*

Flowering tobacco—*Nicotiana alata*

Flossflower—*Ageratum*

Fountain grass—*Pennisetum*

Foxglove—*Digitalis*

Foxtail lily—*Eremurus*

Gas plant—*Dictamnus*

Gay-feather—*Liatris*

Globe amaranth—*Gomphrena*

Golden hurricane lily—*Lycoris aurea*

Golden-ray—*Ligularia*

Harry Lauder's walking stick—*Corylus avellana* 'Contorta'

Heavenly bamboo—*Nandina*

Heliotrope—*Heliotropium*

Hellebore—*Helleborus*

Holly—*Ilex*

Holly grape—*Mahonia*

Hollyhock—*Alcea*

Hyacinth—*Hyacinthus*

Indian-shot—*Canna*

Japanese laurel—*Aucuba japonica*

Japanese painted fern—*Athyrium nipponicum*

Japanese rose—*Kerria*

Jewelweed—*Impatiens*

Lady fern—*Athyrium filix-femina*

Lavender—*Lavandula*

Lavender cotton—*Santolina*

Larkspur—*Delphinium*

Leadwort—*Ceratostigma*

Lenten rose—*Helleborus orientalis*

Leopard lily—*Belamcanda chinensis*

Lilac—*Syringa*

Love-in-a-mist—*Nigella*

Lungwort—*Pulmonaria*

Lupine—*Lupinus*

Maidenhair fern—*Adiantum*

Mallow—*Hibiscus*

Marigold—*Tagetes*

Milkweed—*Asclepias*

Montbretia—*Crocosmia*

Mountain laurel—*Kalmia*

Mullein—*Verbascum*

Musk mallow—*Abelmoschus*

October daphne—*Sedum sieboldii*

Onion—*Allium*

Oregon grape—*Mahonia aquifolium*

Painted daisy—*Chrysanthemum coccineum*

Pearlbush—*Exochorda*

Peony—*Paeonia*

Pepper—*Capsicum*

Pineapple lily—*Eucomis*

Pink—*Dianthus*

Plantain lily—*Hosta*

Plumbago—*Ceratostigma*

Pomegranate—*Punica*

Poppy—*Papaver*

Powell's swamp lily—*Crinum* x *powellii* 'Album'

Prairie gentian—*Eustoma*

Primrose—*Primula*

Purple coneflower—*Echinacea*

Resurrection lily—*Lycoris squamigera*

Rock geranium—*Heuchera americana*

Rose of Sharon—*Hibiscus syriacus*

Rose mallow—*Hibiscus*

Russian sage—*Perovskia*

Sage—*Salvia*

Shasta daisy—*Chrysanthemum* x *superbum*

Smoke tree—*Cotinus*

Snapdragon—*Antirrhinum*

Sneezeweed—*Helenium*

Snowdrop—*Galanthus*

Soapweed—*Yucca glauca*

Speedwell—*Veronica*

Spider flower—*Cleome*

Spider lily—*Crinum*

Spider lily—*Lycoris*

Spindle tree—*Euonymus*

Spirea—*Spiraea*

Spotted laurel—*Aucuba japonica*

Stars-of-Persia—*Allium christophii*

St.-John's-wort—*Hypericum*

Stonecrop—*Sedum*

Summer lilac—*Buddleia davidii*

Summer-sweet—*Clethra*

Sweet basil—*Ocimum*

Sweet shrub—*Calycanthus*

Sweet William—*Dianthus barbatus*

Tickseed—*Coreopsis*

Vervain—*Verbena*

White sage—*Artemisia ludoviciana*

Windflower—*Anemone*

Witch alder—*Fothergilla gardenii*

Wormwood—*Artemisia*

Yarrow—*Achillea*

Yellow flag—*Iris pseudacorus*

Yellow sage—*Lantana camara*

Yew—*Taxus*

Encyclopedia of Plants

The plants mentioned in this volume are listed alphabetically by genus. The Latin botanical name is followed by its pronunciation and, in bold type, its common name. If you know only the common name, refer to the cross-reference chart on page 103 or to the index.

A botanical name consists of the genus and a species, both usually printed in italics. Species also may have common names, which appear in parentheses, and many species contain one or more cultivars, whose names appear between single quotation marks. An "x" preceding the name indicates a hybrid.

"Hardiness" refers to the zones described on the USDA Hardiness Zone Map for the U.S. and Canada (page 102). For annuals, hardiness refers to their ability to withstand frost. Hardy annuals, as small seedlings, can survive all but extreme cold; half-hardy can tolerate a light frost; tender annuals should be planted after the frost.

Abelmoschus
(a-bel-MOS-kus)
MUSK MALLOW

Abelmoschus moschatus 'Oriental Pink'

Hardiness:	Zones 9-10
Plant type:	annual or tender perennial
Height:	15 inches to 6 feet
Interest:	flowers, foliage
Soil:	moist, well-drained, fertile
Light:	full sun to partial shade

The hibiscus-like flowers and deeply lobed leaves of musk mallow provide a bold texture and exotic appearance to borders. Taller types work well in the back of the border or as a fast-growing hedge, while shorter types, with their neat, mounded habit, are best sited near the front of the border.

Selected species and varieties: *A. manihot*—to 6 feet tall or more, 3- to 5-inch sulfur yellow flowers. *A. moschatus* (musk mallow, tropic jewel hibiscus)—15 to 24 inches tall with a mounded habit and showy, 3- to 4-inch blooms that appear continuously from midsummer until frost, in colors ranging from yellow to scarlet with blends of pink and orange that fade to white near the center; 'Oriental Pink' bears pink flowers with white centers.

Growing conditions and maintenance: Plants thrive in hot weather and are usually grown as an annual from seed, performing well up to Zone 6. Space *A. moschatus* 12 to 18 inches apart.

Acanthus
(a-KAN-thus)
BEAR'S-BREECH

Acanthus spinosissimus

Hardiness:	Zones 7-10
Plant type:	perennial
Height:	1½ to 4 feet
Interest:	flowers, foliage
Soil:	well-drained to dry acid loam
Light:	full sun to partial shade

The broad, deeply lobed evergreen leaves of acanthus are borne in spreading clumps. Each stiffly arching leaf is glossy and up to 2 feet long, with a bold appearance useful as an accent or border backdrop. Dense, cylindrical spikes of tubular flowers unfold atop 3- to 4-foot stalks.

Selected species and varieties: *A. dioscorides* var. *perringii*—to 18 inches, rose red flowers on compact spikes; Zones 8-10. *A. mollis*—to 5 feet with shallow lobed to deeply cut shiny, dark green leaves and purplish flowers on dense spikes; Zones 8-10. *A. spinosissimus* (spiny bear's-breech)—to 4 feet with leathery, deep green spiny leaves and profuse rose to mauve and sometimes white flowers; Zones 7-10.

Growing conditions and maintenance: Plants need light shade where summers are hot. Space at least 3 feet apart to allow adequate room for arching leaves to develop. Propagate from seed or by division in spring.

Achillea
(ak-il-EE-a)
YARROW

Achillea x 'Coronation Gold'

Hardiness: Zones 4-8

Plant type: perennial

Height: 1 to 3 feet

Interest: flowers, foliage

Soil: dry, poor to average, well-drained

Light: full sun

Broad, flat clusters of tiny flowers rise on sturdy stems above yarrow's graceful, ferny, aromatic gray-green foliage. The soft-textured clumps are especially effective in masses in a sunny border or wildflower bed.

Selected species and varieties: *A.* x 'Coronation Gold'—bright yellow summer-to-fall flowers on sturdy 30- to 36-inch stems above fernlike, gray-green leaves; 'Galaxy Series' produces summer-to-fall blooms in many shades of pink and salmon on 12- to 36-inch stems; 'Moonshine', to 2 feet with pale yellow flowers that are good for cutting and gray leaves; 'Paprika', to 1½ feet with hot-pink flowers that fade to creamy yellow.

Growing conditions and maintenance: Space yarrows 1½ to 2 feet apart in average soil. Tall varieties may require staking. They tolerate drought and infertile soil. When grown in rich, moist soil, they are weak-stemmed and produce poor-quality flowers. Divide in spring or fall; many self-seed.

Adiantum
(ad-ee-AN-tum)
MAIDENHAIR FERN

Adiantum pedatum

Hardiness: Zones 2-8

Plant type: perennial

Height: 8 inches to 3 feet

Interest: foliage

Soil: moist, well-drained, fertile

Light: full to light shade

Maidenhair ferns add fine texture to shady woodland borders and naturalized beds. Borne on reddish brown to black stems, delicate leaflets form gracefully arching mounds. Slowly creeping on rhizomes, these ferns form colonies.

Selected species and varieties: *A. pedatum* (northern maidenhair)—one of the earliest ferns to leaf out with deep red fiddleheads in early spring, developing into light green fronds that are slightly arching, branched, and fan-shaped, 12 to 18 inches tall with chestnut brown stems, spreading slowly; Zones 2-8. *A. venustum* (evergreen maidenhair)—graceful, lacy, arching fronds 8 to 12 inches long; Zones 5-8.

Growing conditions and maintenance: Ferns do best in sites that mimic the moisture and shade of their native woodland settings. Amend soil with leaf mold or peat moss before planting, and top-dress with bone meal every year. Space plants 2 feet apart; divide rhizomes in early spring.

Ageratum
(aj-er-AY-tum)
FLOSSFLOWER

Ageratum houstonianum

Hardiness: tender

Plant type: annual

Height: 6 to 30 inches

Interest: flowers, foliage

Soil: moist, well-drained

Light: full sun

A profusion of fluffy flowers with threadlike petals crowns ageratum's clumps of heart-shaped leaves. With soft colors and a compact, mounding habit, dwarf varieties create excellent edgings. Taller varieties combine well with other flowers in the middle or back of a border, and are good candidates for indoor arrangements.

Selected species and varieties: *A. houstonianum*—tiny blue or bluish purple flowers in dense, fuzzy clusters from summer through fall, white- and pink-flowered varieties are available; 'Blue Horizon' grows to 30 inches with deep blue flowers that are excellent for cutting; 'Summer Snow', 6 to 8 inches tall with pure white flowers that begin early and continue until frost.

Growing conditions and maintenance: Sow seed indoors 6 to 8 weeks before the last expected frost. Space plants 6 to 12 inches apart. Pinching early growth will promote compactness, and removing spent blooms will encourage continuous production of flowers.

Alcea
(al-SEE-a)
HOLLYHOCK

Alcea rosea

Hardiness: Zones 3-9

Plant type: perennial or biennial

Height: 2 to 9 feet

Interest: flower

Soil: well-drained, fertile

Light: full sun

The bell-shaped flowers of hollyhock are borne on sturdy, erect stems. The lower flowers open first, with new blossoms appearing from midsummer to early fall. This old-fashioned favorite provides both height and a long season of color for the back of a mixed border.

Selected species and varieties: *A. rosea*—to 9 feet with 2- to 4-inch flowers in shades of white, pink, red, and yellow; 'Country Garden Mix' grows 4 to 6 feet with large, single flowers in shades of deep mahogany, rose, pink, and ivory; 'Majorette', 2 feet with early double flowers in a wide range of colors, may be grown as an annual; Powder Puffs Mixed, double flowers in pastel shades.

Growing conditions and maintenance: Plant seed indoors in winter for spring transplanting; some will bloom their first summer. Seed sown outdoors in spring will usually bloom its second year. Space plants 1 to 1½ feet apart. Once they become established, hollyhocks will self-seed in Zones 3 to 9.

Allium
(AL-lee-um)
ONION

Allium sphaerocephalum

Hardiness: Zones 3-9

Plant type: bulb

Height: 8 inches to 5 feet

Interest: flowers

Soil: moist, well-drained, sandy

Light: full sun to light shade

Flowering onions produce showy flower clusters composed of hundreds of tiny blooms. Mass smaller types for effect in spring and summer beds or borders, or interplant with ground covers; strategically site larger types as garden accents.

Selected species and varieties: *A. giganteum*—to 6 feet, with 5-inch umbel and 50 or more star-shaped purple flowers. *A. sphaerocephalum*—to 2 feet with very dense umbel and up to 40 bell-shaped pinkish purple flowers. *A. ursinum*—to 1½ feet with lance-like flowers at base of plants, flowers white in umbels.

Growing conditions and maintenance: Plant bulbs in fall in northern zones, in spring or fall in warmer areas. Set bulbs at a depth two to three times their diameter. Space smaller bulbs 4 to 6 inches apart, larger ones 12 to 18 inches apart. Cut flowers after they fade, but allow foliage to die back before removing it.

Anemone
(a-NEM-o-nee)
WINDFLOWER

Anemone x hybrida 'Honorine Jobert'

Hardiness: Zones 4-9

Plant type: perennial

Height: 3 inches to 4 feet

Interest: flowers, foliage

Soil: moist, well-drained, fertile

Light: full sun to partial shade

Windflowers' open-faced blooms rise above clumps of finely cut leaves. Low-growing types are useful as border edgings; tall selections are well suited for the back of the border.

Selected species and varieties: *A. blanda* (Grecian windflower)—2-inch-wide blue flowers in midspring on 3- to 8-inch stems; 'de Caen' blooms vary in color from white through red to blue; Zones 6-8. *A. hupehensis* (dwarf Japanese anemone)—1½ to 3 feet tall with summer-to-fall pink flowers; 'September Charm' [sometimes attributed to *A. x hybrida*] grows to 30 inches with silvery pink blooms; Zones 6-8. *A. x hybrida* (Japanese anemone)—1 to 4 feet with 2- to 3-inch flowers from late summer to midfall; 'Honorine Jobert' has white flowers; 'Queen Charlotte' has semidouble pink blooms; Zones 4-8.

Growing conditions and maintenance: Space anemones 1 to 2 feet apart and protect them from wind and hot sun. Propagate by seed or division.

Antirrhinum
(an-tir-RYE-num)
SNAPDRAGON

Antirrhinum majus

Hardiness: Zones 8-9

Plant type: annual or tender perennial

Height: 6 inches to 4 feet

Interest: flowers

Soil: well-drained, fertile

Light: full sun to partial shade

Snapdragons' popularity is easily understood given their wide range of heights and flower colors, and their long season of bloom. Short varieties make perfect edgings; taller ones are well suited to the middle and rear of mixed borders. Though perennial in warm climates, they are usually grown as annuals.

Selected species and varieties: *A. majus*—terminal clusters of flowers that open from the bottom up, each bloom has five lobes, divided into an upper and lower lip. Varieties are classified by height—small, 6 to 9 inches; intermediate, 12 to 24 inches; tall, 2 to 4 feet. 'Black Prince' grows to 18 inches with crimson flowers and bronze foliage; 'White Sonnet', 2 inches with white flowers that are superb for cutting.

Growing conditions and maintenance: Start seed indoors in early spring; space plants 6 to 18 inches apart. Deadhead to encourage continuous flowering. Taller types may need staking. Some are susceptible to rust.

Aquilegia
(ak-wil-EE-jee-a)
COLUMBINE

Aquilegia x hybrida 'Biedermier Mixed'

Hardiness: Zones 3-9

Plant type: perennial

Height: 8 inches to 3 feet

Interest: flowers, foliage

Soil: moist, well-drained

Light: full sun to partial shade

Columbines are dainty plants bearing unusual spurred flowers and fernlike leaves. They provide color in mixed borders and naturalized beds in spring and early summer.

Selected species and varieties: *A. canadensis* (wild columbine)—1 to 3 feet tall with nodding yellow and red flowers in late spring and early summer; 'Corbett' has yellow flowers; Zones 3-8. *A. flabellata* (fan columbine)—compact plants with lilac blue flowers; 'Nana Alba' is a dwarf with white flowers; Zones 3-9. *A. x hybrida* (hybrid columbine)—1 to 3 feet tall with spring flowers; 'Biedermier Mixed' has white-tipped petals on 12-inch plants; 'McKana Hybrids', large blooms in many shades; Zones 3-9.

Growing conditions and maintenance: Space columbines 1½ to 2 feet apart. They do not tolerate dry soil, and benefit from organic matter mixed into the soil prior to planting. Propagate by seed or careful division. Plants may be short-lived but often self-sow.

Aronia
(a-RO-nee-a)
CHOKEBERRY

Aronia melanocarpa

Hardiness: Zones 4-9

Plant type: shrub

Height: 3 to 10 feet

Interest: fruit, foliage, flowers

Soil: well-drained

Light: full sun to partial shade

Chokeberry produces a profusion of tiny white flowers that develop into shiny black or red berries in hanging clusters that persist into winter. Glossy, dark green oval leaves turn bright scarlet in autumn. Chokeberry's upright colonies look best when massed.

Selected species and varieties: *A. arbutifolia* 'Brilliantissima'—6 to 10 feet tall and 3 to 5 feet wide with an upright habit and 1- to 1½-inch clusters of white to reddish spring flowers, followed by abundant clusters of dark red ¼-inch berries in fall. *A. melanocarpa* (black chokeberry)—3 to 5 feet tall with similar spread, white spring flowers followed by purplish black berries; suckers profusely.

Growing conditions and maintenance: Easy to transplant and tolerant of almost any soil, it flowers and fruits more heavily and produces better fall color in full sun than in shade. Base suckers may become a nuisance. Propagate by digging up suckers, taking softwood cuttings, or layering.

Artemisia (ar-tem-IS-ee-a) **WORMWOOD**	*Asclepias* (as-KLEE-pee-as) **MILKWEED**	*Aster* (AS-ter) **ASTER**

Artemisia absinthium	*Asclepias tuberosa*	*Aster x frikartii 'Mönch'*

Hardiness: Zones 3-9

Plant type: perennial

Height: 4 inches to 5 feet

Interest: foliage

Soil: poor, well-drained to dry

Light: full sun

Wormwood's finely textured green or silvery gray leaves complement more dramatic hues in a border. Its form ranges from low and mounding to tall and erect, in most cases with inconspicuous flowers.

Selected species and varieties: *A. abrotanum* (southernwood)—4 to 5 feet tall with feathery, light gray-green leaves that give off a camphorlike scent; Zones 4-8. *A. absinthium*—to 4 feet tall with silvery, silky stems and finely divided leaves; used in making absinthe; Zones 4-8. *A. ludoviciana* 'Silver King'—2 to 3 feet tall, silvery gray stems and foliage. *A. schmidtiana* (silvermound artemisia)—compact, 2-foot mounds of filigreed silvery leaves; 'Nana' grows 4 inches tall; Zones 3-7.

Growing conditions and maintenance: Space smaller artemisias 1 foot apart, taller types 2 feet apart. Hot, humid weather can cause them to rot. Prune plants back hard if they become overgrown. Propagate by seed or division.

Hardiness: Zones 3-10

Plant type: perennial

Height: 2 to 6 feet

Interest: flowers, seedpods

Soil: moist to dry

Light: full sun

Milkweeds are well suited to the middle or rear of a herbaceous border and put on a fine display from summer until frost. The flowers are followed by attractive seedpods that are useful in dried arrangements.

Selected species and varieties: *A. incarnata* (swamp milkweed)—sturdy stems 2 to 3 feet tall and narrow, lance-shaped leaves; small, tight umbels of bright pink flowers followed by typical pods; Zones 3-10. *A. tuberosa* (butterfly weed)—stems erect to 3 feet with thin, pointed leaves and terminal clusters of orange, yellow, or red flowers late spring through summer followed by attractive pods; Zones 3-9.

Growing conditions and maintenance: Space plants 1 to 2 feet apart. Since they emerge late in spring, mark their location to avoid planting on top of them. Swamp milkweed is useful for wet areas and is not as weedy as other species. Propagate from seed or root cuttings; plants resist transplanting.

Hardiness: Zones 3-8

Plant type: perennial

Height: 1 to 5 feet

Interest: flowers

Soil: moist, well-drained

Light: full sun

Versatile asters range from compact mounds to open branching clumps, all crowned with flowers composed of feathery fringes of petals surrounding colorful centers.

Selected species and varieties: *A. amellus* (Italian aster)—1½-inch purple summer-to-fall flowers with yellow centers on bushy plants 1 to 3 feet tall; 'Joseph Lakin' has blue flowers; Zones 5-8. *A. x frikartii* 'Mönch'—lavender-blue summer-to-fall flowers on 3-foot plants; Zones 5-8. *A. novae-angliae* (New England aster)—3 to 5 feet tall with 1- to 2-inch summer-to-fall flowers; 'Purple Dome' is an 18-inch dwarf with purple fall flowers; Zones 3-8. *A. novi-belgii* (New York aster)—10 inches to 4 feet tall with white, pink, red, blue, and violet blooms from late summer through fall; 'Royal Ruby' grows to 18 inches; Zones 3-8.

Growing conditions and maintenance: Space plants 2 to 3 feet apart. Propagate by division or from stem cuttings. Some species self-seed.

Astilbe
(a-STIL-bee)
FALSE SPIREA

Astilbe chinensis 'Pumila'

Hardiness: Zones 4-8

Plant type: perennial

Height: 8 inches to 4 feet

Interest: flowers, foliage

Soil: moist, well-drained, fertile

Light: partial shade to full sun

Astilbe's feathery spikes appear on stiff stems above mounds of glossy, fernlike foliage. Astilbes are excellent as a border filler or massed as a ground cover in a partly shaded bed.

Selected species and varieties: *A.* x *arendsii* (garden spirea)—2- to 4-foot-tall flower spikes in white, pink, rose, red, coral, and lilac over clumps of foliage; 'Fanal' is an early bloomer, 24 inches tall, with deep red flowers and bronze leaves, and produces the darkest red of astilbe flowers. *A. chinensis* 'Pumila' (dwarf Chinese astilbe)—8 to 15 inches tall with spreading habit and mauve pink flowers in mid- to late summer; *A.* var. *taquetii* 'Purple Lance' (fall astilbe)—4 feet tall with purple-red blooms.

Growing conditions and maintenance: Plant astilbes 1½ to 2 feet apart in moist soil, preferably in a cool location. Water well and mulch if in full sun. Propagate by division every 3 or 4 years in spring or early summer.

Athyrium
(a-THER-ee-am)
ATHYRIUM

Athyrium nipponicum 'Pictum'

Hardiness: Zones 4-7

Plant type: perennial

Height: 1 to 3 feet

Interest: foliage

Soil: moist, well-drained

Light: partial to full shade

Athyriums are deciduous woodland ferns that thrive in even the deepest shade. Arising in clumps, the light green fronds are finely divided and grow upright or gracefully arched. These delicately textured plants work well as accents, space fillers, background plants, or beside water. Late-summer foliage tends to look worn.

Selected species and varieties: *A. fil-ix-femina* (lady fern)—2 to 3 feet tall with an upright habit and reddish, brownish, or tan stalks and erect, twice-pinnate lacy fronds 6 to 9 inches wide. *A. nipponicum* 'Pictum' (Japanese painted lady fern)—12 to 18 inches tall forming large clumps with divided and strongly dissected gray-green foliage flushed with maroon only on the upper half of the maroon stems.

Growing conditions and maintenance: Lady ferns perform best in slightly acidic, rich loam, but will accept a wide range of soil types. Space plants 4 feet apart, keep moist, and locate out of wind. Propagate by root division.

Aucuba
(aw-KEW-ba)
AUCUBA

Aucuba japonica 'Picturata'

Hardiness: Zones 7-10

Plant type: shrub

Height: 5 to 10 feet

Interest: foliage, fruit

Soil: moist, well-drained, fertile

Light: full to light shade

Aucuba is a broad-leaved evergreen that thrives in shade. The lustrous, leathery leaves are from 3 to 8 inches long. Only female plants bear ½-inch-long scarlet berries that are often hidden by the foliage. Aucuba is useful as an accent, background planting, or a transition between the border and a woodland area.

Selected species and varieties: *A. japonica* (spotted laurel, Japanese laurel)—dark and lustrous leaves in all seasons on semiupright branches that reach 6 to 10 feet with a similar spread; 'Crotonifolia' leaves are large and finely sprinkled with pale yellow; 'Picturata' leaves are splashed with yellow in the center and have yellow specks elsewhere.

Growing conditions and maintenance: Aucuba grows best in sites with year-round shade and enriched soil. Young leaves blacken if exposed to strong sun. Pollination from male bush nearby is essential for females to set berries. Propagate by cuttings.

Begonia
(be-GO-nee-a)
BEGONIA

Begonia x semperflorens-cultorum

Hardiness: Zones 6-10

Plant type: annual or tender perennial

Height: 6 inches to 3 feet

Interest: flowers, foliage

Soil: moist, well-drained, fertile

Light: partial to bright full shade

Prized for continuous bloom from late spring or early summer to frost, begonias provide vivid color in borders and woodland beds.

Selected species and varieties: *B. grandis* (hardy begonia)—2- to 3-foot branching stems with clusters of pale pink blooms in late summer and large green leaves with red veins above and below; Zones 6-9; 'Alba' produces white flowers. *B.* x *semperflorens-cultorum* (wax begonia)—6 to 12 inches tall with a mounding habit and single or double flowers in shades of white, salmon, and red; the glossy, rounded leaves may be green, bronze, burgundy, or variegated; usually grown as annuals.

Growing conditions and maintenance: Space wax begonias 8 to 12 inches apart. Propagate from seed or cuttings. Hardy begonias form tiny tubers in leaf axils; tubers fall and sprout the following year. All prefer light, open shade.

Belamcanda
(bel-am-CAN-da)
BLACKBERRY LILY

Belamcanda chinensis

Hardiness: Zones 5-10

Plant type: perennial

Height: 1 to 4 feet

Interest: flowers, fruit

Soil: moist, well-drained

Light: full sun to light shade

Blackberry lilies carry sprays of flat, star-shaped flowers with narrow, pointed petals on zigzag-branching flower stalks above fans of swordlike leaves. Each flower lasts only a day, but new blossoms open over several weeks. Flowers are followed by attractive seedpods that burst open to reveal shiny, black, berrylike seeds. Use blackberry lilies in the midground of a sunny border or as cut flowers. Dried seedpods decorate the winter garden and can be used in dried arrangements.

Selected species and varieties: *B. chinensis*—2-inch orange flowers with pointed, curving petals spotted with red on 2- to 4-foot stalks. *B. flabellata* —light yellow flowers.

Growing conditions and maintenance: Plant blackberry lilies in spring or fall, setting rhizomes 1 inch deep and 6 to 8 inches apart. They grow tallest in moist, fertile soil, shorter in dry soil, and prefer full sun. Propagate by division in spring or fall; they often self-sow, producing flowers in 2 years.

Berberis
(BER-ber-is)
BARBERRY

Berberis thunbergii var. atropurpurea

Hardiness: Zones 5-8

Plant type: shrub

Height: 2 to 8 feet

Interest: foliage, flowers, fruit

Soil: moist, well-drained, slightly acid

Light: full sun to light shade

Barberries are dense, thorny shrubs with bright yellow flowers in spring and colorful berries that often persist into fall. They provide attractive backgrounds and accents in a border. Some species reseed freely.

Selected species and varieties: *B. julianae*—dense, evergreen growth to 6 feet tall and 10 feet wide; Zones 6-8. *B. thunbergii* 'Aurea'—deciduous, 3 to 4 feet tall with bright yellow leaves; *B. thunbergii* var. *atropurpurea*—burgundy foliage and red berries; 'Crimson Pygmy' grows to 2 feet tall and 3 to 5 feet wide with mounding habit; *B. verruculosa*—slow growth to 5 feet tall and 6 feet wide; Zones 6-8.

Growing conditions and maintenance: Barberries are tolerant of most soils that are well drained. Avoid planting evergreen types in windy locations. Propagate by cuttings.

Boltonia
(bowl-TO-nee-a)
BOLTONIA

Boltonia asteroides 'Snowbank'

Hardiness: Zones 4-8

Plant type: perennial

Height: 3 to 6 feet

Interest: flowers

Soil: moist, well-drained loam

Light: full sun

Boltonia's masses of small, daisylike flowers appear on tall, branching stems over an extended period in late summer and fall. Their height and airy texture make them suitable for use in the background of a border. They are attractive for fall bouquets.

Selected species and varieties: *B. asteroides* (white boltonia)—many white, pink, or lilac-to-purple flowers ¾ to 1 inch wide on branched stems to 6 feet with narrow gray-green leaves 1 to 3 inches long; 'Pink Beauty' grows 4 to 5 feet tall with pink blooms; 'Snowbank', 3 to 4 feet tall with graceful white flowers on sturdy stems that generally do not require staking.

Growing conditions and maintenance: Space boltonias 1 to 2 feet apart in full sun, where they will produce compact growth; partial shade produces lanky growth. They tolerate both wet and dry soils. Tall types may require staking. Propagate by division in spring or fall, or by tip cuttings in spring.

Buddleia
(BUD-lee-a)
BUTTERFLY BUSH

Buddleia davidii 'Black Knight'

Hardiness: Zones 5-9

Plant type: shrub

Height: 4 to 20 feet

Interest: flowers, foliage

Soil: well-drained, fertile

Light: full sun

The arching stems of the butterfly bush are lined with narrow gray-green leaves that emerge rather late in the spring. Tiny, fragrant flowers are densely arranged on elongated, drooping clusters. This large, graceful shrub makes a fine background or accent plant for the border.

Selected species and varieties: *B. alternifolia* 'Argentea' (fountain butterfly bush)—4-inch leaves with silky hairs and soft purple flowers in late spring and summer on plants to 20 feet tall with a similar spread. *B. davidii* (summer lilac)—leaves to 10 inches long on shrubs to 10 feet and equally wide, with flowers appearing from midsummer to frost; 'Black Knight' grows 4 to 5 feet tall with deep purple flowers.

Growing conditions and maintenance: Prune *B. alternifolia* after flowers fade; new flowers form on the previous season's growth. *B. davidii* should be cut back to live wood in late winter before growth begins; blooms on current season's wood. Propagate by cuttings.

Buxus
(BUKS-us)
BOXWOOD

Buxus microphylla 'Wintergreen'

Hardiness: Zones 4-9

Plant type: shrub

Height: 2 to 20 feet

Interest: foliage

Soil: well-drained

Light: full sun to light shade

Boxwood is an elegant, long-lived evergreen shrub whose tiny leaves impart a fine texture to any planting. It is well suited for use as a background hedge or border edging.

Selected species and varieties: *B. microphylla* var. *koreana* (Korean boxwood)—to 2½ feet and twice as wide, hardy to Zone 4; 'Wintergreen' grows to 2 feet tall and 4 feet wide, and retains its bright green foliage throughout winter when many other varieties turn brownish green, hardy to Zone 6. *B. sempervirens* (common boxwood)—to 20 feet with equal spread, hardy to Zone 5 or 6, depending on variety.

Growing conditions and maintenance: Plant boxwoods in well-drained location with protection from drying winds. Mulch to keep roots cool and moist. Shade helps protect boxwoods from leaf burn in winter. Boxwoods perform best in areas that do not have extreme heat or cold.

Caladium
(ka-LAY-dee-um)
ELEPHANT'S-EAR

Caladium bicolor 'Aaron'

Hardiness: Zones 10-11

Plant type: annual or tender bulb

Height: 8 inches to 2 feet

Interest: foliage

Soil: moist, well-drained

Light: partial to full shade

Caladium's large leaves, shaped like broad arrowheads and 6 to 18 inches long, are colorfully patterned in various combinations of red, pink, white, and green. Caladium is an excellent choice for massing in shady borders, or as an edging or accent plant.

Selected species and varieties: *C. bicolor*—shieldlike leaves either flat, wavy, or ruffled; 'Aaron' is green-edged with white leaves; 'Little Miss Muffet', miniature, 8 to 12 inches tall with red-speckled, lime green leaves.

Growing conditions and maintenance: Plant caladium tubers in spring when night temperatures are above 60° F; set 2 inches deep and 8 to 12 inches apart. They need ample water during the growing season and do poorly in areas with low humidity. Tender plants with tropical origins, they can be treated as perennials only in Zones 10 and 11. Elsewhere, lift and dry tubers in the fall to replant the next spring. Propagate by dividing tubers into sections having at least two buds each.

Callicarpa
(kal-i-KAR-pa)
BEAUTYBERRY

Callicarpa japonica 'Leucocarpa'

Hardiness: Zones 5-10

Plant type: shrub

Height: 3 to 8 feet

Interest: fruit

Soil: well-drained

Light: full sun to light shade

Beautyberry's colorful 1/8-inch berries appear in fall, densely clustered along arching stems. The berries persist for several weeks after the leaves fall. Oval, pointed leaves, arranged like ladders on either side of the stems, turn yellow, sometimes pinkish before dropping.

Selected species and varieties: *C. americana* (American beautyberry)—inconspicuous lavender summer flowers followed by magenta fruit in clusters encircling stems; var. *lactea*—white berries; Zones 7-10. *C. japonica* (Japanese beautyberry)—4 to 6 feet tall with equal spread, pink or white summer flowers and metallic purple berries in fall; 'Leucocarpa' produces white berries; Zones 5-8.

Growing conditions and maintenance: Beautyberries can be pruned within 4 to 6 inches of the ground in early spring to encourage fruit production. They can be propagated from softwood cuttings, layering, or seed, and are easily transplanted. Do not overfertilize or plants will become leggy.

Calycanthus
(kal-i-KAN-thus)
SWEET SHRUB

Calycanthus floridus

Hardiness: Zones 4-9

Plant type: shrub

Height: 6 to 9 feet

Interest: flowers, fragrance

Soil: moist, well-drained

Light: full sun to partial shade

Sweet shrub is an adaptable plant that blends well with other shrubs. Its unusual summer flowers add interest and a fruity fragrance to mixed shrub borders, and provide an attractive background for herbaceous plants in sunny or partially shaded beds.

Selected species and varieties: *C. floridus* (sweet shrub, Carolina allspice)—6 to 9 feet tall and 6 to 12 feet wide with long, dark green, aromatic leaves that are deciduous but persist late into fall, and rounded, fragrant, dark burgundy flowers with spreading, straplike petals blooming from late spring through early summer, and urn-shaped fruit persisting into winter; 'Athens' has highly fragrant yellow to yellow-green flowers.

Growing conditions and maintenance: Although it prefers moist, deep, well-drained soil, sweet shrub tolerates other soil conditions. It is easily transplanted, and new plants can be obtained from suckers around the plant's base.

Camellia
(kah-MEEL-ee-a)
CAMELLIA

Camellia sasanqua 'Snow Flurry'

Hardiness: Zones 7-9

Plant type: shrub

Height: 6 to 25 feet

Interest: flowers, foliage

Soil: moist, well-drained, acid

Light: light shade

Camellias are evergreens with dark, lustrous leaves that produce showy single, semidouble, or double flowers in shades of red, pink, rose, and white. Depending on the variety, flowers appear from early spring through early winter. They make an outstanding accent in the shrub border, and combine well with perennials.

Selected species and varieties: *C. japonica* (Japanese camellia)—10 to 25 feet tall, upright habit, and 3- to 5-inch flowers; 'Debutante' has 3-inch double pink blooms. *C. sasanqua* (sasanqua camellia)—6 to 10 feet tall with pyramidal habit and 2- to 3-inch flowers in fall and winter. *C. sasanqua* Ackerman Selections—6- to 10-foot plants with fall flowers and greater cold hardiness than the species; 'Snow Flurry' has double white flowers.

Growing conditions and maintenance: Plant camellias in organically rich soil, provide year-round mulch and protection from winter winds. Prune them after flowering.

Campanula
(kam-PAN-yew-la)
BELLFLOWER

Campanula glomerata 'Superba'

Hardiness: Zones 3-8

Plant type: perennial

Height: 4 inches to 5 feet

Interest: flowers, foliage

Soil: moist, well-drained

Light: full sun to partial shade

Bellflowers produce tubular or flaring summer flowers in clusters or spikes. Dwarf types are attractive as edgings, while taller types form neat clumps in a perennial border.

Selected species and varieties: *C. carpatica* (Carpathian bellflower)—compact plants under 1 foot tall with flowers up to 1½ inches across; 'Blue Chips' has blue flowers; 'White Chips', white blooms. *C. glomerata* (clustered bellflower)—stems topped with tight clusters of flowers; 'Joan Elliott' has exceptionally beautiful purple flowers on 18-inch stems; 'Superba', large, variable purple starry blooms atop 18-inch stems. *C. persicifolia* (peachleaf bellflower)—solitary deep blue to white blooms on 2- to 3-foot stems; 'Alba' has white flowers; 'Telham Beauty', light blue blooms.

Growing conditions and maintenance: Plant bellflowers 1 to 2 feet apart depending on their size. Dig and divide every 3 to 4 years to maintain vigor. Propagate by seed or division.

Canna
(CAN-ah)
INDIAN-SHOT

Canna x generalis 'Pretoria'

Hardiness: Zones 7-10

Plant type: tender perennial

Height: 18 inches to 6 feet

Interest: flowers, foliage

Soil: moist, well-drained, fertile

Light: full sun

Cannas produce 4- to 5-inch flowers with tousled stamens from summer through frost. Bold leaves provide a dramatic backdrop to the flowers. Standard varieties are well suited for the back of borders while dwarfs can be used in the mid- or foreground.

Selected species and varieties: *C. x generalis*—standard varieties to 6 feet tall, dwarfs less than 3 feet, leaves up to 24 inches long, usually a deep, glossy green but sometimes bronze or striped or veined in white or pink, flower colors include red, orange, salmon, yellow, pink, white, and bicolors; 'Pfitzer's Scarlet Beauty' has red flowers on 18-inch stems; 'Pretoria', a dwarf cultivar with green leaves striped with cream and orange-yellow flowers.

Growing conditions and maintenance: Start rhizomes indoors 4 weeks before night temperatures reach 60 degrees. Plant directly in garden in spring, space 1 to 2 feet apart. North of Zone 7, lift rhizomes in fall after frost and store in moist peat moss, or grow as annual.

Capsicum
(KAP-si-kum)
PEPPER

Capsicum annuum 'Treasure Red'

Hardiness: Zones 10-11

Plant type: annual or tender perennial

Height: 6 to 20 inches

Interest: foliage, fruit

Soil: moist, well-drained, fertile

Light: full sun

Pepper plants produce brightly colored fruit well displayed against dark green leaves. In their native tropical environment peppers are woody perennials, but in temperate climates are treated as annuals. They make tidy and colorful edgings for beds. Ornamental peppers are usually extremely hot.

Selected species and varieties: *C. annuum* (ornamental pepper)—leaves from 1 to 5 inches long and small white flowers followed by fruit from ¾ to 2 inches long, may be red, purple, yellow, green, black, cream, or variegated; 'Black Prince' grows 10 inches tall with black fruit that turns red when mature; 'Holiday Cheer', 8 inches with a compact habit and round, 1-inch fruit that turns from cream to red; 'Treasure Red', 8 inches with conical fruit that turns from white to red.

Growing conditions and maintenance: Start seed indoors in late winter to transplant into the garden after all danger of frost has passed. Space plants 8 to 15 inches apart.

Caryopteris
(kar-i-OP-ter-is)
BLUEBEARD

Caryopteris x clandonensis 'Blue Mist'

Hardiness: Zones 5-8

Plant type: perennial or shrub

Height: 1½ to 4 feet

Interest: flowers, foliage

Soil: light, well-drained

Light: full sun

Bluebeard is a small deciduous shrub with pleasantly aromatic flowers, stems, and leaves. The slender, upright stems form a rounded mound of gray-green foliage that is topped with clusters of misty blue flowers from midsummer to frost. They provide late-season color in the foreground of a mixed shrub border, or can be easily integrated into a perennial bed.

Selected species and varieties: *C.* x *clandonensis* (bluebeard, blue spirea)— 3 to 4 feet tall with a similar spread, slender 2- to 3-inch leaves and clusters of small flowers arising from the leaf axils on current season's growth; 'Blue Mist' grows 2 feet tall and produces powder blue flowers.

Growing conditions and maintenance: Best treated as a herbaceous perennial, cut it back to 4 inches in winter. When flower production slows in late summer, a light pruning will often stimulate a second flush of blooms. Propagate by cuttings taken in late spring or early summer.

Celosia
(sel-OH-see-a)
CELOSIA

Celosia cristata

Hardiness: tender

Plant type: annual

Height: 6 to 24 inches

Interest: flowers, foliage

Soil: moist to dry, well-drained

Light: full sun

These vibrantly colored annuals bear crested or plumed flowers that are extremely long-lasting, making them ideal for bedding and cutting for both fresh and dried arrangements.

Selected species and varieties: *C. cristata*—a range of heights and flower types; leaves may be green, purple, or variegated. Flowers appear from midsummer to fall and are usually deep shades of red, orange, yellow, or gold. The species is divided according to flower type: *Childsii* group (crested cockscomb)—elaborately crested or convoluted flower heads that resemble lumps of coral. *Plumosa* group (feather amaranth)—leathery 6- to 12-inch flower heads. *Spicata* group—flowers in slender spikes.

Growing conditions and maintenance: Transplant seedlings into the garden after all danger of frost is passed. In warm areas, sow directly outside. Space plants 6 to 18 inches apart. They thrive in warm weather and tolerate dry soils.

Ceratostigma
(ser-at-o-STIG-ma)
PLUMBAGO, LEADWORT

Ceratostigma plumbaginoides

Hardiness: Zones 5-10

Plant type: perennial or shrub

Height: 8 inches to 4 feet

Interest: foliage, flowers

Soil: well-drained

Light: full sun to partial shade

Plumbago develops shiny leaves and blue flowers that bloom late in the season. Low-growing species are effective as ground covers in shrub borders or for edging a bed. Taller types are well suited to the back of a mixed border. Masses of flat, 1-inch flowers cover the plant over a long season and are well displayed against the leaves, which often turn reddish bronze in the fall.

Selected species and varieties: *C. plumbaginoides* (common leadwort, dwarf plumbago)—gentian blue flowers from late summer through frost above 8- to 12-inch tufts of glossy, nearly evergreen 3-inch leaves that turn bronze in cooler climates.

Growing conditions and maintenance: Plant plumbago 12 to 24 inches apart. It does not tolerate soggy soil or competition from tree roots. Mulch over winter in Zones 5 and 6. Shear before new spring growth begins to promote flowering. Propagate by division in spring every 2 to 4 years.

Chrysanthemum
(kri-SAN-the-mum)
CHRYSANTHEMUM

Chrysanthemum x morifolium

Hardiness: Zones 3-9

Plant type: perennial

Height: 6 inches to 3 feet

Interest: flowers, foliage

Soil: well-drained, fertile

Light: full sun

Chrysanthemum flower forms vary widely, from daisylike to spider or football mums to tiny button mums. Their mounds of attractively lobed foliage blend well with other border plantings or can be massed for effect.

Selected species and varieties: *C. coccineum* (painted daisy)—wiry 2- to 3-foot stalks lined with ferny leaves support 2- to 3-inch, usually single flowers with yellow centers; 'Roseum' has soft, rose pink flowers. *C. x morifolium* (garden mum)—clusters of 1- to 6-inch summer-to-fall flowers in white, yellow, orange, red, bronze, and lavender on 1- to 3-foot plants. *C. x superbum* (Shasta daisy)—white flowers with yellow centers 3 to 6 inches across on 2½-foot stems.

Growing conditions and maintenance: Space chrysanthemums 1 to 2 feet apart in soil enriched with organic matter. Pinch fall-blooming plants twice before midsummer for profuse blooms. Propagate by division or spring cuttings.

Cimicifuga
(si-mi-SIFF-yew-ga)
BUGBANE

Cimicifuga racemosa

Hardiness: Zones 3-9

Plant type: perennial

Height: 2 to 8 feet

Interest: foliage, flowers, fruit

Soil: moist, well-drained, fertile

Light: full sun to partial shade

Bugbane is a graceful perennial for the rear of a shady border, with its tall spires of white flowers borne well above handsome dark green leaves. It lends itself to naturalizing in a woodland bed or at the edge of a pond.

Selected species and varieties: *C. americana* (American bugbane)—dense spikes of creamy blossoms on branched 2- to 6-foot flower stalks from late summer to fall; Zones 4-8. *C. racemosa* (cohosh bugbane)—4 to 8 feet tall with 3-foot wands of white flowers in midsummer; Zones 3-9. *C. simplex* (Kamchatka bugbane)—3 to 4 feet tall with attractive light green buds that open in fall to reveal 1- to 2-foot white flower spires; 'White Pearl' is free-flowering with a compact habit; Zones 4-8.

Growing conditions and maintenance: Plant bugbane in cooler areas of the garden in soil enriched with organic matter. Space plants 2 feet apart. Propagate by division in spring.

Cleome
(klee-O-me)
SPIDER FLOWER

Cleome hasslerana

Hardiness: tender

Plant type: annual

Height: 3 to 4 feet

Interest: flowers, seedpods

Soil: moist, well-drained

Light: full sun to light shade

Enormous clusters of 1-inch flowers top the stems of cleome continuously from summer until frost. The pink, lavender, or white flower petals surround 2- to 3-inch-long stamens that protrude from the center, creating a spiderlike effect, further enhanced by the conspicuous, slender seedpods that follow the flowers. They provide a graceful accent or border background.

Selected species and varieties: *C. hasslerana* [also listed as *C. spinosa*]—erect habit with dark green leaves and airy, ball-shaped flower heads. While individual flowers are short-lived, new flowers are produced continuously; 'Cherry Queen' bears rose red flowers; 'Helen Campbell', white blooms; 'Violet Queen', purple flowers.

Growing conditions and maintenance: Start seed indoors 4 to 6 weeks prior to the last frost, or plant directly in the garden in early spring. It often self-seeds. Space plants 12 inches apart. Cleome thrives in warm weather and responds well to abundant moisture.

Clethra
(KLETH-ra)
SUMMER-SWEET

Clethra barbinervis

Hardiness: Zones 3-9

Plant type: shrub

Height: 3 to 20 feet

Interest: flowers, fragrance, foliage, bark

Soil: moist, acid

Light: full sun to full shade

Summer-sweet's pink or white flowers appear in midsummer and are delightfully fragrant. This deciduous shrub can easily be sited in any mixed border or woodland bed.

Selected species and varieties: *C. alnifolia* (summer-sweet, sweet pepperbush)—3 to 8 feet tall and 4 to 6 feet wide, with deep green leaves that turn gold in fall, fragrant white flowers in 2- to 6-inch-long clusters; 'Hummingbird' reaches 4 feet with a dense habit. *C. barbinervis* (Japanese clethra)—10 to 20 feet tall with an upright habit and dark green leaves in clusters at branch tips, fragrant, white, late-summer flowers in 4- to 6-inch clusters and beautiful, smooth, exfoliating bark; Zones 5-8.

Growing conditions and maintenance: Tolerates most soil types as well as coastal conditions. Thrives in both sun and shade. Add organic matter to soil prior to planting. Prune in early spring. Propagate by seed or summer cuttings. Clump-forming types can be divided.

Colchicum
(KOL-chi-kum)
AUTUMN CROCUS

Colchicum autumnale

Hardiness: Zones 4-9

Plant type: bulb

Height: 4 to 12 inches

Interest: flowers

Soil: moist, well-drained, fertile

Light: full sun to light shade

Colchicum's flower stems appear in fall to provide 2 to 3 weeks of color. Each corm produces multiple blossoms, so flowers carpet the ground when planted thickly. The strap-shaped leaves appear in late winter or spring, after the flowers have faded. Colchicum fits easily in the foreground of beds or borders. All parts are poisonous if consumed.

Selected species and varieties: *C. autumnale* (common autumn crocus, mysteria)—to 8 inches tall with 4-inch pink to lilac flowers; 'Albo Plenum' is double-petaled; 'Album' has white flowers. *C. speciosum* (showy autumn crocus) —8 to 12 inches tall with 4- to 8-inch-wide rose to purple flowers with white throats; 'Lilac Wonder' bears 6-inch amethyst blooms.

Growing conditions and maintenance: Plant autumn crocus in summer, setting corms 3 to 4 inches deep and 6 to 9 inches apart. Propagate by removing cormels growing alongside larger corms in early summer after leaves wither.

Coleus
(KO-lee-us)
COLEUS

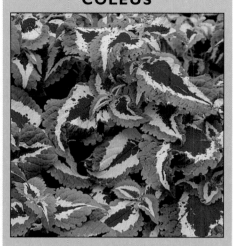

Coleus x hybrida 'Wizard Rose'

Hardiness: Zones 10-11

Plant type: annual or tender perennial

Height: 9 to 24 inches

Interest: foliage

Soil: moist, well-drained

Light: partial shade

The opposite, vibrantly colored, heart-shaped leaves of coleus grow on square stems and provide a long season of interest to borders in partially shaded sites. Leaves sport a wide variety of attractive patterns in colors that include chartreuse, green, orange, red, pink, bronze, and white.

Selected species and varieties: *C.* x *hybridus*—leaves usually 3 to 8 inches long with scalloped edges, upright pale blue flower spikes are often removed to encourage growth; 'Fiji' series has fringed leaf margins in bright colors; 'Wizard' series, to 10 inches with red, pink, and apricot shades all with cream or green edge, and resists flowering.

Growing conditions and maintenance: Start seed indoors or grow from leaf-stem cuttings overwintered indoors. Transplant outdoors after soil has warmed, allowing 8 to 12 inches between plants. Most grow best in partial shade, though some will do fine in full sun if adequate water is supplied. They are usually grown as annuals.

Coreopsis
(ko-ree-OP-sis)
TICKSEED

Coreopsis verticillata 'Zagreb'

Hardiness: Zones 4-9

Plant type: perennial

Height: 6 inches to 3 feet

Interest: flowers, foliage

Soil: well-drained to dry

Light: full sun

Coreopsis provides a long season of flowers atop mats or cushions of attractive foliage. The sturdy, dependable plant fits easily into casual borders.

Selected species and varieties: *C. auriculata* 'Nana' (eared tickseed)—6- to 9- inch mat of foliage with 1-inch yellow flowers in spring. *C. grandiflora*—yellow or orange 1- to 1½-inch single, semidouble, or double summer flowers on 2-foot stems. *C. rosea* (pink coreopsis)—inch-wide pink summer-to-fall flowers with yellow centers on 2-foot plants. *C. verticillata* (threadleaf coreopsis)—cushions of lacy leaves along 2- to 3-foot stems topped by yellow flowers from late spring to late summer; 'Golden Showers' has yellow blooms on 2- to 3-foot plants; 'Zagreb', yellow flowers on 8- to 18-inch plants.

Growing conditions and maintenance: Plant coreopsis 12 to 18 inches apart. Remove spent flowers to extend bloom period. Propagate by seed or division in early spring. Some species are invasive.

Cornus
(KOR-nus)
DOGWOOD

Cornus alba 'Elegantissima Variegata'

Hardiness: Zones 2-8

Plant type: tree or shrub

Height: 7 to 30 feet

Interest: flowers, foliage, berries, bark

Soil: moist, well-drained, acid

Light: full sun to light shade

Dogwoods offer year-round interest in woodland gardens and shrub borders. Flowers with petal-like bracts appear in spring. Their lustrous foliage persists through the summer, turning colors in fall as berries appear. Several species offer brightly colored bark.

Selected species and varieties: *C. alba* (Tartarian dogwood)—8 to 10 feet tall with equal spread, with stems that color blood-red in winter; 'Elegantissima Variegata' has creamy leaf margins. *C. mas*—height and spread to 15 feet, leaves turn reddish purple in fall, bright red fruits appear in spring. *C. sericea* 'Flaviramea'—to 10 feet tall and wide with 2½-inch white flower clusters on yellow stems; Zones 2-8.

Growing conditions and maintenance: Plant dogwoods in soil enriched with organic matter. Prune *C. alba* and *C. sericea* heavily in spring to promote new stem growth. Propagate by taking cuttings or by seed.

Cosmos
Cosmos
(KOS-mos)
COSMOS

Cosmos bipinnatus

Hardiness: tender

Plant type: annual

Height: 10 inches to 6 feet

Interest: flowers

Soil: well-drained to dry

Light: full sun to light shade

Daisylike flowers crown the wiry stems of this tropical American native. Its showy blooms appear singly or in long-stalked loose clusters from midsummer until frost. It makes a graceful addition to mixed borders where it will attract numerous butterflies, and is an excellent source of long-lasting cut flowers.

Selected species and varieties: *C. bipinnatus*—to 6 feet with finely cut leaves and flowers in shades of red, pink, and white; 'Sea Shells' grows 3 to 3½ feet with fluted petals of white, pink, or crimson surrounding a yellow center; 'Sonata', 24 inches tall with white flowers with crimson markings. *C. sulphureus*—18 to 36 inches tall with yellow, orange, or scarlet flowers.

Growing conditions and maintenance: Sow seed directly in the garden after the last frost in spring. Thin to allow 12 to 18 inches between plants. Do not fertilize. Taller types may require staking. They often self-seed.

Smoke Tree
Cotinus
(ko-TI-nus)
SMOKE TREE

Cotinus coggygria 'Royal Purple'

Hardiness: Zones 5-8

Plant type: tree or shrub

Height: 10 to 15 feet

Interest: foliage, flowers

Soil: well-drained

Light: full sun

The smoke tree is valued for its attractive foliage and the unusual, wispy flower stalks that create a smokelike appearance and which are effective throughout the summer. Leaves may be green or burgundy, depending on the variety. It provides both color and textural contrast in the shrub border.

Selected species and varieties: *C. coggygria*—10- to 15-foot shrub with a width equal to its height, or pruned to a multiple-stemmed, small tree, rounded, blue-green leaves up to 3 inches long and 8-inch clusters of fluffy blooms on wirelike stems from mid- to late summer; 'Flame' bears purple leaves and panicles, leaves usually fade to purple-green by the end of summer; 'Royal Purple', deep purple foliage and pink flower stalks.

Growing conditions and maintenance: The smoke tree prefers soil that is not too rich. It can be cut back to the ground in winter to encourage vigorous shoot growth. Propagate by softwood cuttings in mid- to late summer.

Spider Lily
Crinum
(KREE-num)
SPIDER LILY

Crinum x powellii 'Album'

Hardiness: Zones 7-11

Plant type: bulb

Height: 2 to 4 feet

Interest: flowers, fragrance, foliage

Soil: moist, well-drained, fertile

Light: full sun to light shade

Crinums produce whorls of lilylike flowers atop a stout stem rising from a clump of deep green, sword-shaped leaves. The blossoms are either funnel-shaped with thick, ridged petals curving backward, or lacy with narrow, straplike petals. They perform especially well at the edges of ponds or streams where there is constant moisture, slowly naturalizing into large clumps.

Selected species and varieties: *C. americanum* (Florida swamp lily)—up to six white flower funnels in late spring or summer on 2-foot stems before leaves appear. *C. asiaticum* (grand crinum)—up to 50 heavily scented white flowers with straplike petals in summer on stalks to 4 feet. *C. x powellii* 'Album' (Powell's swamp lily)—six to eight white flower trumpets on 2-foot stalks rising from evergreen leaves.

Growing conditions and maintenance: Plant crinums 2 to 3 feet apart so that the necks of the bulbs remain aboveground. Keep constantly moist. Propagate by seed or separating offsets.

Crocosmia
(kro-KOS-mee-a)
MONTBRETIA

Crocosmia 'Lucifer'

Hardiness: Zones 5-9

Plant type: bulb

Height: 2 to 4 feet

Interest: flowers

Soil: moist, well-drained, fertile

Light: full sun

Crocosmia's wiry stems are lined with 50 or more tightly clasped flower buds that unfurl from bottom to top revealing vividly colored tubular flowers up to 2 inches across. Emerging on either side of the stem, the combination of buds and open blooms provides interesting visual texture to any border.

Selected species and varieties: *C.* x *crocosmiiflora*—sturdy hybrids with 2- to 4-foot sprays of star-shaped flowers in yellow, salmon, red, maroon, and bicolors. *C.* 'Lucifer' has deep red summer flowers on 3-foot stems.

Growing conditions and maintenance: Plant in spring, setting corms 3 to 5 inches deep and 6 to 8 inches apart. Where conditions are particularly favorable, they can become invasive. Protect from frost with winter mulch, or lift corms in fall and store them in a cool, dry location until replanting in spring. Propagate by separating cormels from larger corms in spring or fall.

Cynara
(SIN-ah-ra)
CARDOON

Cynara cardunculus

Hardiness: Zones 8-9

Plant type: tender perennial

Height: 4 to 6 feet

Interest: flowers, foliage

Soil: moist, well-drained, fertile

Light: full sun

Cardoon forms clumps of thick stems lined with spiny, lacy, silver gray leaves with woolly undersides that provide a bold accent in a border, or a fast-growing summer hedge. Thistlelike flower globes tip each stem from summer through fall. Both leaves and flowers are prized by floral designers for fresh and dried arrangements.

Selected species and varieties: *C. cardunculus* (cardoon)—up to 6 feet tall in warm climates, but often only 4 feet in cooler regions, with leaves to 3 feet long, and purple flower heads surrounded by spiny bracts. *C. scolymus* (artichoke)—to 5 feet tall with coarse leaves and purple flower heads surrounded by bracts with edible bases.

Growing conditions and maintenance: Start seed indoors in late winter, transplanting to successively larger pots as needed before moving to the garden in midspring. Artichokes are best propagated by division. Allow 3 to 6 feet between plants. They can be grown as a perennial from Zone 8 south.

Cytisus
(SIT-is-us)
BROOM

Cytisus scoparius

Hardiness: Zones 5-10

Plant type: shrub

Height: 3 to 6 feet

Interest: foliage, flowers, stems

Soil: well-drained to dry

Light: full sun

Brooms are fast-growing shrubs that brighten the spring border with masses of pealike flowers that are typically yellow, but may be pink, red, purple, or white. Their small leaves line arching stems that remain green all year, adding interest during winter months.

Selected species and varieties: *C.* x *praecox* (Warminster broom)—3 to 6 feet tall with a similar spread and graceful, slender cascading stems that produce lemon yellow blooms in early spring; 'Albus' is slightly smaller with white flowers. *C. scoparius* (Scotch broom)—4 to 6 feet with a broad, rounded habit and erect green stems with distinct ridges and bright yellow, 1-inch blooms in late spring to early summer.

Growing conditions and maintenance: Brooms are most easily established in the garden by planting small container-grown specimens in spring. Prune immediately after flowering by cutting back stems by two-thirds. Propagate by cuttings or layering in spring.

Dahlia
(DAH-lee-a)
DAHLIA

Dahlia 'Smokey Orange'

Hardiness: Zones 9-11

Plant type: annual or tender perennial

Height: 12 inches to 8 feet

Interest: flowers

Soil: moist, well-drained, fertile

Light: full sun

Dahlias brighten the flower border over a long season with diverse blossoms whose sizes range from a few inches to more than a foot across. Tightly packed flowers are surrounded by one or more rows of petal-like ray flowers that may be doubled, curved, twisted, cupped, or rolled into tiny tubes. Colors range widely; some are bicolored or variegated. Dwarf dahlias are ideal in sunny beds or borders as low-growing, bushy edgings, standard dahlias work well as medium to tall fillers or as exhibition-size specimens. All dahlias make long-lasting cut flowers.

Selected species and varieties: *D.* x *hybrida* can be classified into the following groups: Anemone-flowered dahlias—a central disk obscured by a fluffy ball of short, tubular petals and rimmed by one or more rows of longer, flat petals; Cactus dahlias—straight or twisted petals rolled like quills to a pointed tip; Colarette dahlias—central disks surrounded by a collar of short, often ruffled or cupped petals, backed by a second collar of broad, flat petals; Peony-flowered dahlias—two or three overlapping layers of petals, often twisted or curled, surrounding a central disk; Formal decorative dahlias—double rows of flat, evenly spaced petals covering the central disk; Informal decorative dahlias—double rows of randomly spaced flat petals hiding the central disk; Ball dahlias—cupped, doubled petals crowding spirally into

Dahlia 'Elmira'

round domes or slightly flattened globes; Chrysanthemum-type dahlias—double rows of petals curving inward, hiding the central disk; Pompon dahlias—small, round balls of tightly rolled petals less than 2 inches in diameter; Semicactus dahlias—flat petals curling into tubes at their tips; Single dahlias—one or two rows of flat petals surrounding a central disk; Star dahlias—2 or 3 rows of short petals curving inward; Waterlily-flowered dahlias—short petals tightly clasped over a central disk, surrounded by several rows of broad, flat petals. Dahlias are further categorized by flower size.

Growing conditions and maintenance: Start seed indoors in early spring, or plant tubers directly in garden in spring. Plant tubers of tall types 6 to 8 inches deep and 3 to 4 feet apart. For shorter varieties, plant tubers 3 inches deep and 2 feet apart. Provide abundant water and mulch. Remove faded blooms to extend blooming. Taller types require staking.

Delphinium
(del-FIN-ee-um)
DELPHINIUM

Delphinium elatum 'Pacific Giants'

Hardiness: Zones 3-7

Plant type: perennial

Height: 2½ to 6 feet

Interest: flowers

Soil: moist, well-drained, fertile

Light: full sun

Enormous spikes of up to 2-inch flowers on stiff stalks bloom atop delphinium's clumps of finely cut, lobed leaves. The flowers often sport vividly contrasting centers known as bees. Delphiniums make impressive specimens in the flowering border.

Selected species and varieties: *D.* x *belladonna* (belladonna delphinium)—blue or white flowers on branching 3- to 5-foot-tall stems; 'Bellamosa' bears dark blue flowers. *D.* 'Blue Fountains' are dwarf delphiniums that grow 2½ to 3 feet tall with flowers in shades of blue. *D. elatum* (large-flowered delphinium, bee larkspur)—2-inch flowers in many colors on stalks up to 6 feet tall; 'Pacific Giants' include blue, violet, lavender, pink, or white mostly double-flowered varieties on stalks 4 to 6 and, rarely, 10 feet tall.

Growing conditions and maintenance: Plant delphiniums in slightly alkaline soil enriched with organic matter, spacing plants 2 feet apart. Propagate by seed. Stake tall varieties.

Dianthus
(dy-AN-thus)
PINK

Dianthus gratianopolitanus 'Tiny Rubies'

Hardiness: Zones 3-9

Plant type: perennial or biennial

Height: 3 to 20 inches

Interest: flowers, foliage, fragrance

Soil: moist, well-drained, slightly alkaline

Light: full sun to partial shade

Pinks form mats of grassy, sometimes evergreen foliage with single and bicolored flowers having fringed petals. Blooms are borne singly or in clusters, and most have a spicy fragrance reminiscent of cloves. Low-growing types make delightful edgings for beds or borders, and are attractive creeping among rocks or over walls. Taller selections are useful at the front or middle of a border.

Selected species and varieties: *D.* x *allwoodii* (Allwood pink)—12 to 24 inches tall with a compact, mounded habit, grassy gray-green leaves, and fragrant single or double flowers appearing two per stem in a wide range of colors over a 2-month period in late spring and early summer, and tolerating both heat and drought; 'Doris' grows pale pink semidouble blooms. *D. barbatus* (sweet William)—biennial that self-seeds so freely it performs like a perennial with flowers that are less scented than other species and borne in dense, flat-topped clusters from late

spring to early summer in shades of red, white, and pink, often with a contrasting eye or ring; 'Newport Pink' has coral pink blooms on stems to 2 feet; 'Scarlet Beauty', bright red flowers on 2-foot stems; Zones 4-7. *D. deltoides* (maiden pinks)—mats of gray-green leaves and ¾-inch red or pink flowers on stems to 12 inches; 'Albus' produces single white flowers on 10-inch stems; 'Brilliant', scarlet flowers; 'Zing Rose',

Dianthus barbatus 'Newport Pink'

deep rose pink blooms with a dark ring around the eye, often blooming all summer; Zones 4-7. *D. gratianopolitanus* (cheddar pinks)—compact habit with semiwoody stems 3 to 12 inches tall with masses of fragrant, late-spring, usually single flowers in shades of pink and white, above blue-green foliage; 'Tiny Rubies' produces double, deep pink flowers on 4-inch stems; Zones 3-9.

Growing conditions and maintenance: Plant dianthus 12 to 18 inches apart. Under appropriate conditions, mounds will increase quickly. Deadheading will often encourage flowering well into the summer. Cut back flowering stems completely after bloom, and shear mat-forming types in fall to promote dense growth. Maintain vigor by dividing every 2 to 3 years in early spring. Propagate by seed, cuttings, layering, or division. Some species will self-sow.

Dicentra
(dy-SEN-tra)
BLEEDING HEART

Dicentra spectabilis 'Alba'

Hardiness: Zones 3-8

Plant type: perennial

Height: 1 to 3 feet

Interest: flowers, foliage

Soil: moist, well-drained

Light: partial shade

Bleeding heart bears unusual, drooping flowers that resemble hearts along arching stems. The leaves are fernlike and their soft colors and mounded form add grace to any shady bed or border.

Selected species and varieties: *D. eximia* (fringed bleeding heart)—12 to 18 inches tall with blue-green leaves forming a neat mound and pink to purple teardrop-shaped blooms all summer; 'Alba' has white flowers; 'Adrian Bloom' has red flowers; 'Bountiful', deep pink flowers. *D. spectabilis* (common bleeding heart)—2 to 3 feet tall with blue-green leaves and large pink and white heart-shaped flowers in spring; 'Alba' has pure white flowers.

Growing conditions and maintenance: Plant fringed bleeding heart 1 to 2 feet apart, common bleeding heart 2 to 3 feet apart in soil enriched with organic matter. Propagate by seed or division.

Dictamnus
(dik-TAM-nus)
GAS PLANT, DITTANY

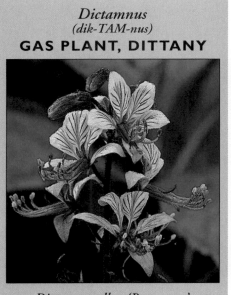

Dictamnus albus 'Purpureus'

Hardiness: Zones 3-8

Plant type: perennial

Height: 2 to 3 feet

Interest: flowers, foliage, seedpods

Soil: moist, well-drained

Light: full sun to light shade

Gas plant produces loose spikes of showy flowers followed by ornamental seedpods that are useful in dried arrangements. The common name refers to the lemon-scented, flammable oil secreted by the plant's leaves, stems, and roots.

Selected species and varieties: *D. albus*—mounds of leathery leaves spreading 2 to 3 feet wide and flower spikes consisting of many 1½- to 2-inch flowers held a foot above the foliage in early summer; 'Purpureus' has pale mauve-purple flowers with dark purple veins.

Growing conditions and maintenance: Select your site for gas plants carefully, because once planted, they do not like to be disturbed. Add organic matter to the soil prior to planting. Space plants 3 to 4 feet apart. It often takes a full season or more before plants bloom, but once established, they are reliable performers. Propagate by seed. Division is not recommended.

Digitalis
(di-ji-TAL-us)
FOXGLOVE

Digitalis purpurea 'Excelsior Hybrids'

Hardiness: Zones 3-9

Plant type: biennial or perennial

Height: 2 to 5 feet

Interest: flowers, foliage

Soil: moist, well-drained, acid

Light: partial shade

Foxglove's striking summer blooms line stiff stalks above clumps of coarse leaves, providing a vertical accent to borders and beds. Leaves contain digitalis, and are very poisonous.

Selected species and varieties: *D. grandiflora* (yellow foxglove)—perennial with brown-spotted yellow flowers on stems to 3 feet tall. *D. lutea* (straw foxglove)—perennial with white to pale yellow flowers on 2-foot stems. *D. x mertonensis* (strawberry foxglove)—perennial with strawberry red flowers with darker spots on 4-foot stems. *D. purpurea* (common foxglove)—biennial with purple, pink, white, rust, or yellow flowers often with spotted throats on stems to 5 feet; 'Excelsior Hybrids' reach 5 feet with blooms borne all around the stem, in a range of colors.

Growing conditions and maintenance: Space foxgloves 18 to 24 inches apart. Add compost to the soil prior to planting and mulch after the ground freezes in fall. Propagate by seed or division.

Echinacea
(ek-i-NAY-see-a)
PURPLE CONEFLOWER

Echinacea purpurea 'Magnus'

Hardiness: Zones 3-9

Plant type: perennial

Height: 1½ to 4 feet

Interest: flowers, seed heads

Soil: well-drained to dry

Light: full sun to light shade

Purple coneflowers form bold, stiff clumps of coarsely textured, hairy leaves. The durable, long-lasting, daisy-like flowers have drooping petals surrounding conical centers. They are reliable performers in beds, borders, or naturalized gardens.

Selected species and varieties: *E. angustifolia* (narrow-leaved purple coneflower)—18- to 30-inch stems topped with lavender-pink flowers with dark, spiny centers. *E. pallida* (pale coneflower)—3 to 4 feet tall with rosy purple to white flowers up to 3½ inches across. *E. purpurea*—2 to 4 feet tall with lavender-pink flowers up to 4 inches across with purplish brown centers; 'Bright Star' has bright pink flowers surrounding maroon centers on 2- to 3-foot stems.

Growing conditions and maintenance: Space coneflowers 2 feet apart. Plants tolerate both heat and drought. Propagate by seed or division.

Enkianthus
(en-kee-AN-thus)
ENKIANTHUS

Enkianthus campanulatus

Hardiness: Zones 4-7

Plant type: shrub

Height: 6 to 30 feet

Interest: flowers, foliage

Soil: moist, well-drained, acid, fertile

Light: partial shade to full sun

Enkianthus bears pendulous clusters of bell-shaped blossoms in spring. Its green leaves turn to brilliant shades of yellow, orange, and red in fall. This tall, erect shrub is an ideal companion to azaleas, rhododendrons, and other acid-loving plants in a shrub border.

Selected species and varieties: *E. campanulatus* (redvein enkianthus)—usually 8 to 12 feet tall, but may reach 30 feet in the South with open horizontal branching to 20 feet wide with tufts of 1- to 3-inch-long leaves clustered mostly at the ends of branches, and cream-colored, yellow, or orange ½-inch red-veined flowers in 3-inch clusters opening before the leaves appear, persisting for several weeks. *E. perulatus* (white enkianthus)—to more than 6 feet with white flowers.

Growing conditions and maintenance: Add liberal amounts of organic matter to the soil prior to planting enkianthus. Mulch to maintain even moisture. Pruning is rarely necessary. Propagate by stem cuttings or layering.

Epimedium
(ep-i-MEE-dee-um)
BARRENWORT

Epimedium grandiflorum 'Rose Queen'

Hardiness: Zones 4-8

Plant type: perennial

Height: 8 to 12 inches

Interest: flowers, foliage

Soil: moist, well-drained, fertile

Light: partial to full shade

The small, heart-shaped leaves of barrenwort are reddish bronze when they emerge in spring. They soon turn deep green, providing a lush ground cover for shady beds before turning bronze in fall. Sprays of flowers appear in spring.

Selected species and varieties: *E. grandiflorum* (longspur epimedium)—9 to 12 inches tall, forming dense clumps to 12 inches across with pink flowers in mid- to late spring; 'Rose Queen' bears pink and white flowers. *E.* x *versicolor* 'Sulphureum' (bicolored epimedium)—spreading mounds to 12 inches tall with yellow flowers in early spring. *E.* x *youngianum* 'Niveum'—slightly smaller than other species with nearly double white blossoms borne on 8-inch stems.

Growing conditions and maintenance: Barrenwort is a rugged plant that grows in a clump, increasing in size without becoming invasive. Space plants 8 to 12 inches apart and mulch well. Cut back old foliage before growth begins in spring. Propagate by division.

Eremurus
(e-ray-MEW-rus)
DESERT-CANDLE

Eremurus stenophyllus 'Shelford Hybrids'

Hardiness: Zones 4-9

Plant type: bulb

Height: 2 to 4 feet

Interest: flowers, foliage

Soil: well-drained, sandy, fertile

Light: full sun

Desert-candles carry hundreds of tiny, bell-shaped flowers in enormous spikes often 6 inches across above rosettes of fleshy leaves. Over several weeks, the flowers open from the bottom to the top so that each spike offers a range of tones. They are striking when grouped at the back of a border or in front of dark shrubs.

Selected species and varieties: *E. himalaicus* (Himalayan desert-candle)—white flower spikes on 3- to 4-foot stems above clumps of leaves. *E. stenophyllus* (Afghan desert-candle)—yellow or golden flowers covering the upper half of 3-foot stems; 'Shelford Hybrids' bear spikes of 1-inch flowers in shades of white, yellow, orange, pink, and rose on 4-foot stems; Zones 4-8.

Growing conditions and maintenance: Plant desert-candles in fall, 4 to 6 inches deep and 1½ to 3 feet apart. Provide a winter mulch. Propagate by seed or division, but best left undisturbed for 10 years or more.

Eucomis
(yew-KOME-is)
PINEAPPLE LILY

Eucomis comosa

Hardiness: Zones 8-10

Plant type: bulb

Height: 1 to 2 feet

Interest: flowers, foliage, fragrance

Soil: well-drained, sandy

Light: full sun to light shade

Pineapple lilies produce dense spikes of tiny flower stars topped by an arching tuft of leaflike bracts. The spikes rise in midsummer and persist for several weeks above rosettes of strap-shaped leaves. Group pineapple lilies at the front of borders or in patio beds. They make long-lasting cut flowers.

Selected species and varieties: *E. autumnalis*—spikes of ¾-inch greenish white flowers fading to yellow green on 1- to 2-foot stems. *E. comosa* (pineapple flower)—fragrant, ½-inch greenish white, sometimes creamy white blooms with purple throats on 2-foot stems with purple-spotted leaves.

Growing conditions and maintenance: Plant in spring, setting bulbs 5 to 6 inches deep and 1 foot apart. Mulch bulbs over winter in Zones 8 to 10. North of Zone 8, grow pineapple lilies in containers, setting bulbs just below the surface and allowing three to five bulbs per 12-inch pot. Propagate by removing bulb offsets that develop at the base of mature bulbs.

Euonymus
(yew-ON-i-mus)
SPINDLE TREE

Euonymus japonica 'Aureo-marginata'

Hardiness: Zones 3-9

Plant type: ground cover or shrub

Height: 4 inches to 20 feet

Interest: foliage, fruit

Soil: well-drained

Light: full sun to full shade

This genus includes deciduous shrubs with brilliant fall color and evergreen shrubs and ground covers with a nearly endless variety of white, cream, and yellow variegations. All are well suited to the shrub border.

Selected species and varieties: *E. alata* (winged euonymus, burning bush) —winged branches, red fruit, and flaming red fall leaf color on rounded, deciduous shrubs to 20 feet with similar spread; 'Compacta' grows to 10 feet; Zones 3-8. *E. japonica* (Japanese spindle tree)—rounded evergreen shrub with lustrous leaves and compact habit to 15 feet tall with similar spread; 'Aureo-marginata' leaves are edged with yellow; Zones 7-9.

Growing conditions and maintenance: Euonymus tolerates most soils, but does not like sogginess or drought. Plant winged euonymus in full sun for best fall color, others thrive in sun or shade. Propagate by cuttings.

Eustoma
(yew-STO-ma)
PRAIRIE GENTIAN

Eustoma grandiflorum 'Echo Pink'

Hardiness: Zones 9-10

Plant type: annual or perennial

Height: 2 to 3 feet

Interest: flowers

Soil: moist, well-drained

Light: full sun to partial shade

Prairie gentian produces waxy blue-green leaves on a thick stem with upturned flowers resembling small roses. Though exacting in their growth requirements, they are well worth the effort. When grown well, they are exquisite border plants and make superb cut flowers, lasting up to 2 weeks.

Selected species and varieties: *E. grandiflorum* [also listed as *Lisianthus russellianus*]—erect habit with sturdy stems and 3-inch oblong leaves, and single or double flowers, to 2 inches wide and usually purple, though pink, blue, and white varieties are available; 'Echo Pink' bears double pink blooms.

Growing conditions and maintenance: Prairie gentian can be grown as an annual by starting seed indoors 3 months prior to last frost. Or sow seed in fall and overwinter plants in a cold frame. Move them to the garden after the soil warms, spacing plants 6 to 10 inches apart. Keep soil evenly moist. They are slow growers and need a long growing season to perform well.

Exochorda
(ex-o-KORD-a)
PEARLBUSH

Exochorda x macrantha 'The Bride'

Hardiness: Zones 5-9

Plant type: shrub

Height: 3 to 15 feet

Interest: flowers, foliage

Soil: well-drained

Light: full sun to partial shade

The pearlbush derives its common name from the pearl-like chains of round flower buds that appear in clusters along the previous season's stems. Open in mid- to late spring, the 1½- to 2-inch white flowers cover the shrub in white for a period of 1 to 2 weeks. The attractive foliage provides a fine backdrop at other times.

Selected species and varieties: *E.* x *macrantha*—up to 10 feet high and wide and bearing snow white flowers; 'The Bride' is 3 to 6 feet tall with a mounded, compact habit and flowers to 2 inches across. *E. racemosa* (common pearlbush)—upright habit reaching 10 to 15 feet tall with an equal spread, and 1¼-inch flowers.

Growing conditions and maintenance: Pearlbush tolerates most soils as long as they are well drained. Plant in early spring. Prune immediately after flowering by removing old, twiggy branches. Propagate by cuttings taken in late spring or early summer, or by layering.

Fothergilla
(faw-ther-GIL-a)
FOTHERGILLA

Fothergilla major

Hardiness: Zones 4-8

Plant type: shrub

Height: 2 to 10 feet

Interest: flowers, fragrance, foliage

Soil: moist, well-drained, acid

Light: partial shade to full sun

Fothergilla is a deciduous shrub that is covered with small, fragrant, white spiky flowers in spring. In fall, the leaves turn shades of yellow, orange, and scarlet. It is an excellent choice for the shrub border or a mass planting, and makes an attractive companion to azaleas and rhododendrons.

Selected species and varieties: *F. gardenii* (witch alder, dwarf fothergilla)—a dense mound 2 to 3 feet tall with an equal or greater spread, dark blue-green leaves and petalless flowers with showy stamens in 1- to 2-inch-long clusters in spring. *F. major* (large fothergilla)—upright habit reaching 6 to 10 feet tall with slightly less spread and 2- to 4-inch white flower spikes tinged with pink, and oval dark green leaves.

Growing conditions and maintenance: Incorporate organic matter into soil prior to planting fothergilla. It is easy to grow, but the soil must be acidic. Propagate by softwood cuttings.

Fritillaria
(fri-ti-LAH-ree-a)
FRITILLARY

Fritillaria imperialis

Hardiness: Zones 4-7

Plant type: bulb

Height: 2½ to 3 feet

Interest: flowers

Soil: moist, well-drained, sandy

Light: full sun to light shade

Fritillarias produce a garland of nodding flower bells atop a stout stalk to provide a bold accent to spring flower beds. They are effectively massed in perennial borders and are best situated where later blooming plants will fill in when the fritillaria foliage dies down in early summer. They should be placed where their skunklike odor will not be objectionable.

Selected species and varieties: *F. imperialis* (crown-imperial)—bold stalks of 30 to 36 inches lined on the lower half with whorls of glossy, pointed leaves and topped by a tuft of leaves beneath which hangs a ring of nodding 2-inch red, white, yellow or purple-flowers; 'Aurora' grows to 2 feet high with orange flowers.

Growing conditions and maintenance: Plant in late summer or fall, setting bulbs 4 inches deep and 12 inches apart. Propagate by removing and replanting bulb offsets in fall to reach flowering size in 3 to 4 years.

Gaillardia
(gay-LAR-dee-a)
BLANKET-FLOWER

Gaillardia x grandiflora 'Goblin'

Hardiness:	Zones 3-8
Plant type:	perennial
Height:	1 to 3 feet
Interest:	flowers
Soil:	well-drained to dry
Light:	full sun

Gaillardia produce cheerful daisylike flowers in bright color combinations from early summer to frost, above attractive mounds of hairy leaves. They provide a long season of color in the sunny perennial border and make fine cut flowers.

Selected species and varieties: *G. x grandiflora*—yellow ray flowers surround yellow or purplish red disk flowers in a 3- to 4-inch daisy on stems up to 3 feet with large, hairy, gray-green leaves at the base; 'Goblin' bears red flowers with yellow margins on stems to 12 inches; 'Monarch Strain', flowers in varying combinations of red and yellow on 30-inch stems.

Growing conditions and maintenance: Space plants 18 inches apart. They tolerate hot, dry locations, poor soil, and seaside conditions. Crowns may die out in heavier soils, but roots will send out new plants, which can be dug and replanted in spring. Propagate by seed or division.

Galanthus
(ga-LANTH-us)
SNOWDROP

Galanthus nivalis 'Flore Pleno'

Hardiness:	Zones 3-8
Plant type:	bulb
Height:	6 to 12 inches
Interest:	flowers
Soil:	moist, well-drained, sandy
Light:	full sun to light shade

Snowdrops are one of the first signs of spring, often producing small white blooms before the last snow melts. Each blossom is composed of three longer petals almost concealing three shorter, inner petals tipped with green. A single flower dangles from a slender stem above two to three grassy leaves. Snowdrops rapidly naturalize under deciduous shrubs and are particularly well suited to a woodland border. They also are effective grouped in clumps at the edge of a shady perennial border.

Selected species and varieties: *G. nivalis* (common snowdrop)—1-inch flowers on 4- to 6-inch stems above 6-inch green leaves; 'Flore Pleno' produces globe-shaped double flowers.

Growing conditions and maintenance: Plant bulbs 3 inches deep and 3 inches apart in late summer or fall in soil that has been enriched with organic matter. They self-sow readily and can be propagated from seed or by lifting and dividing the clumps of bulbs that form.

Gardenia
(gar-DEE-ni-a)
GARDENIA

Gardenia augusta

Hardiness:	Zones 8-10
Plant type:	shrub
Height:	1 to 6 feet
Interest:	flowers, foliage, fragrance
Soil:	moist, well-drained, acid
Light:	full sun to partial shade

Each intensely fragrant, double, camellialike flower is creamy white, and is attractively displayed against the dark evergreen leaves in spring and summer. While hardy only to Zone 8 this shrub is worth the effort to grow wherever conditions allow. Where it is not hardy, it can be grown as a container plant.

Selected species and varieties: *G. augusta* [formerly *G. jasminoides*]—evergreen shrub, 3 to 6 feet tall and wide with a dense, rounded habit, with 3- to 4-inch glossy, oval leaves and double blooms up to 5 inches across; 'August Beauty' grows 4 to 6 feet tall with abundant 4- to 5-inch blooms; 'Radicans', to 1 foot tall and 3 feet wide with smaller foliage and flowers than the species.

Growing conditions and maintenance: Plant gardenias in acid soil enriched with organic matter. It thrives in hot weather, and requires monthly fertilizing during the growing season. Mulch to keep soil moist and protect shallow roots. Propagate by cuttings.

Geranium
(jer-AY-nee-um)
CRANESBILL

Geranium x magnificum

Hardiness: Zones 3-9

Plant type: perennial

Height: 10 to 48 inches

Interest: flowers, foliage

Soil: dry to moist, well-drained

Light: full sun to partial shade

Cranesbills are valued both for their dainty five-petaled flowers and neat mounds of lobed or toothed leaves, which often turn red or yellow in the fall, providing a long season of interest for the front or middle of a perennial border or naturalized in a shady bed.

Selected species and varieties: *G. endressii* 'Wargrave Pink' (Pyrenean cranesbill)—medium-green mounds to 15 inches tall, with 1-inch-wide salmon pink funnel-shaped flowers and broad, deeply notched petals; hardy to Zone 4. *G. himalayense* [also listed as *G. grandiflorum*]—10 to 15 inches tall with intense violet-blue flowers having darker veins and a reddish center; Zones 4-9. *G.* 'Johnson's Blue' has 1½- to 2-inch clear blue flowers traced with darker blue veins appearing profusely from spring to summer above 15- to 18-inch mats of lobed leaves; Zones 5-8. *G. macrorrhizum* (bigroot cranesbill)—clusters of magenta or pink flowers with prominent stamens in spring and summer on spreading

mounds of aromatic, maple-shaped leaves that turn red and yellow in fall; Zones 3-8. *G. maculatum* (wild geranium, spotted cranesbill)—loose clusters of lavender-pink flowers in spring on 1- to 2-foot stems with gray-green leaves; 'Album' bears white flowers; Zones 3-7. *G.* x *magnificum*—violet-blue flowers with darker veins from spring to summer on 24-inch stems and foliage that turns brilliant orange-scarlet in fall; Zones 4-8. *G.* x *oxoni-*

Geranium x oxonianum 'Claridge Druce'

anum 'Claridge Druce'—1½ to 3 feet tall with equal spread, gray-green foliage, and late spring-to-fall pink flowers with dark pink veins and white bases; Zones 4-9. *G. phaeum* (black widow)—large clumps from thick rhizomes, with bright green-lobed leaves often spotted reddish purple, and flowers that are dark purple-black or brownish, though sometimes pink or white, on 24-inch stems in summer; hardy to Zone 5. *G. psilostemon* (Armenian cranesbill)—vivid purplish red flowers up to 2 inches across with darker centers on plants 2 to 4 feet tall and equally wide; Zones 5-7. *G. sanguineum* (bloody cranesbill)—magenta flowers in spring and summer on 9- to 12-inch spreading mounds of leaves that turn red in fall; Zones 4-9.

Growing conditions and maintenance: Space Armenian cranesbill 3 to 4 feet apart, other varieties 1½ to 2 feet apart. Geraniums can grow in full sun or partial shade in cool regions, but need afternoon shade in areas where summers are hot. Propagate by division.

Gomphrena
(gom-FREE-na)
GLOBE AMARANTH

Gomphrena globosa

Hardiness: tender

Plant type: annual

Height: 8 to 24 inches

Interest: flowers

Soil: well-drained

Light: full sun

The colorful cloverlike flower heads of gomphrena top the upright stems from summer to frost. A native of India, this annual is easy to grow, and imparts a cheerful, informal appearance to gardens. Its flowers, which have a papery texture even when fresh, are excellent for both fresh and dried arrangements.

Selected species and varieties: *G. globosa*—erect, branched stems with somewhat coarse, hairy leaves, and 1-inch long globular flower heads that may be pink, white, magenta, orange, or red; 'Strawberry Fields' grows 2 feet tall with 1½-inch red flower heads.

Growing conditions and maintenance: Start seed indoors 8 to 10 weeks before last frost and transplant out after danger of frost has passed, or sow seed directly outside in late spring. Space plants 1 foot apart. Though slow to start, they are easy to grow once established. They thrive in warm weather.

Helenium
(he-LEE-nee-um)
SNEEZEWEED

Helenium autumnale

Hardiness: Zones 3-8

Plant type: perennial

Height: 2½ to 6 feet

Interest: flowers, foliage

Soil: moist, well-drained

Light: full sun

Sneezeweed's clumps of erect stems lined with willowy leaves provide a backdrop for shorter border plantings. Borne on multibranched stems, the daisylike blooms are composed of fan-shaped petals surrounding prominent centers and offer late-season color.

Selected species and varieties: *H. autumnale* (common sneezeweed)—stems to 6 feet tall with flowers up to 2 inches wide in summer, persisting through frost; 'Bruno' produces mahogany flowers on 4-foot plants; 'Butterpat', clear yellow-petaled flowers with bronze centers on 4- to 5-foot plants; 'Crimson Beauty', to 3 feet with bronzy red flowers; 'Moerheim Beauty', rusty red blossoms with brown centers on 4-foot stems.

Growing conditions and maintenance: Plant sneezeweed 18 to 24 inches apart. Taller types may need staking and early pinching helps promote more compact plants. Divide every 3 to 4 years to prevent crowding. Propagate by seed or division.

Heliotropium
(he-lee-oh-TRO-pee-um)
HELIOTROPE

Heliotropium arborescens 'Marine'

Hardiness: Zones 9-10

Plant type: annual or tender perennial

Height: 1 to 6 feet

Interest: flowers, fragrance

Soil: well-drained, fertile

Light: full sun, partial shade

Heliotrope is a tender perennial often grown as an annual. Large clusters of summer flowers range from deep purple to white and bear a vanillalike fragrance. Plant them in the foreground of a mixed border; they are especially effective in groups, located where their fragrance will be appreciated.

Selected species and varieties: *H. arborescens*—1 to 3 feet in the garden, though plants grown in a greenhouse may reach 6 feet with dark green, wrinkled foliage and five-petaled flowers that are ¼ inch across, occurring in clusters up to 12 inches wide; 'Marine' reaches 2 feet with large, deep purple flowers, but lacks intense fragrance.

Growing conditions and maintenance: Start seed indoors 10 to 12 weeks prior to last frost, or purchase young plants in spring. New plants also can be started from cuttings. Do not move into the garden until soil has warmed. Allow 12 inches between plants and keep well watered.

Helleborus
(hell-e-BOR-us)
HELLEBORE

Helleborus argutifolius

Hardiness: Zones 4-9

Plant type: perennial

Height: 1 to 2 feet

Interest: flowers, foliage

Soil: moist, well-drained, fertile

Light: full sun to partial shade

Hellebores are long-lived, consistent bloomers whose cup- or bell-shaped flowers rise above a clump of deeply lobed or toothed, usually evergreen leaves. They provide rich colors and early flowers for perennial beds and the foreground of shrub borders. All hellebores are poisonous to consume.

Selected species and varieties: *H. argutifolius*—to 2 feet with gray-green three-part leaflets that are ornamental much of the year with apple-green flowers; *H. orientalis* (Lenten rose)—cream, pale to deep pink, plum, brownish purple, chocolate brown, or nearly black flowers; 2 inches wide in early to midspring on 18-inch tall plants; Zones 4-9.

Growing conditions and maintenance: Grow in soil enriched with organic matter. Space smaller species 1 foot apart and larger species 2 feet apart. Apply a summer mulch. Propagate from seed or divide in early summer.

Hemerocallis
(hem-er-o-KAL-is)
DAYLILY

Hemerocallis 'Cherry Cheeks'

Hardiness: Zones 3-9

Plant type: perennial

Height: 10 inches to 4 feet

Interest: flowers, foliage, fragrance

Soil: moist, well-drained

Light: full sun to partial shade

Daylilies produce colorful rewards with minimal care. Planted in groups, they are an excellent choice for naturalizing or massing. Individually, they are outstanding specimens in a border. Pale-colored varieties, which tend to bleach in the sun, work extremely well in a shady border. The trumpet-shaped flowers are borne on tall, sturdy, branched stalks called scapes that rise from thick clumps of arching, grasslike foliage. Each scape bears multiple flower buds so even though each bloom lasts only one day, the buds continue to open over several weeks, providing a fine display. Daylilies are available in a wide range of flowering times, colors, and sizes, so with care in selection, you can have daylilies blooming in your yard from late spring until frost. Bloom colors span the rainbow with the exception of blue and white. Blooms are often bi- or tricolored.

Selected species and varieties: *H. citrina* (citron daylily)—extremely fragrant, 5- to 6-inch-long, light yellow,

narrow-petaled blooms that open in the evening. *H. fulva* (orange daylily, tawny daylily)—a vigorous plant developing a large clump with six to 12 flower trumpets per scape in midsummer; 'Europa' produces 5-inch orange flowers with a red eye; 'Kwanso', double flowers that bloom later than the species. *H.* hybrids—the following are but a few of the hundreds of varieties available; they are generally distinguished by their height, flower color, and season; 'Bountiful Valley' grows 28 inches tall and produces durable midseason lemon yellow flowers with lime throats; 'Cherry Cheeks', raspberry pink flowers on 28-inch stems late midseason; 'Eenie Weenie', 10- to 14-inch dwarf with yellow flowers over an extended season; 'Ruffled Apricot' blooms early midseason, bearing large and showy apricot flowers on 28- to 30-inch scapes.

Growing conditions and maintenance: Plant daylilies in spring or fall, spacing miniature varieties 18 to 24 inches apart, taller varieties 2 to 3 feet apart.

Hemerocallis 'Ruffled Apricot'

Daylilies compete well with tree roots and tolerate poor soil. They thrive in soil amended with organic matter. Avoid overfertilizing, which causes rank growth and reduces flowering. Propagate by dividing clumps, which is usually necessary every 3 to 6 years.

Heuchera
(HEW-ker-a)
ALUMROOT

Heuchera 'Chocolate Ruffles'

Hardiness: Zones 3-9

Plant type: perennial

Height: 1 to 3 feet

Interest: foliage, flowers

Soil: moist, well-drained, fertile

Light: full sun to partial shade

Alumroot produces a neat mound of leaves that make an attractive edging or foreground plant for a perennial bed. In late spring and summer flowers rise above the leaves.

Selected species and varieties: *H. americana* (rock geranium)—2 to 3 feet tall with mottled leaves turning solid green and greenish white flowers in late spring. *H.* 'Chocolate Ruffles' bears white flowers on 20-inch purple stems above ruffled leaves that are brown above and burgundy below;. *H.* x *brizoides* 'June Bride',white flowers on 15- to 18-inch stems. 'Mt. St. Helens' has blood-red blooms on 18-inch stems; 'White Cloud', white flowers on 24-inch stems; 'Coral Cloud', coral pink flowers on 18- to 24-inch stems.

Growing conditions and maintenance: Plant alumroot in spring in soil amended with organic matter, spacing plants 12 to 18 inches apart. In warm regions, it performs best in partial shade. Propagate by seed or division.

Hibiscus
(hy-BIS-kus)
MALLOW

Hibiscus syriacus 'Diana'

Hosta
(HOS-ta)
PLANTAIN LILY, FUNKIA

Hosta fortunei 'Albomarginata'

inches tall with lavender white flowers that barely clear the large, dark blue puckered leaves. *H.* x *tardiana* 'Halcyon'—12 inches tall and 16 inches wide with grayish blue heart-shaped leaves having wavy margins and parallel veins and lilac-blue flowers in late summer; 'Royal Standard' produces deeply veined green leaves and fragrant white blooms on 2- to 3-foot stems from late summer to early fall. *H. tardiflora* (autumn plantain lily)—glossy dark green leaves and large purple flowers in fall. *H. ventricosa* (blue hosta)—4-foot-high mounds of broad, glossy, dark green leaves and purple flowers with darker purple stripes. *H.* hybrids—'Fringe Benefit' grows 36 inches tall and 42 inches wide with broad, cream-colored margins on green heart-shaped leaves and pale lavender flowers in early sum-

---

Hardiness: Zones 5-9

Plant type: perennial or shrub

Height: 5 to 12 feet

Interest: flowers

Soil: moist, well-drained

Light: full sun to light shade

Hardiness: Zones 3-9

Plant type: perennial

Height: 6 inches to 4 feet

Interest: foliage, flowers, fragrance

Soil: moist, well-drained

Light: partial to full shade

Hosta x tardiana 'Halcyon'

The genus *Hibiscus* includes both woody shrubs and herbaceous perennials. Their showy flowers add color and a tropical appearance to borders or beds from summer to frost.

Selected species and varieties: *H. coccineus* (scarlet rose mallow)—a 5- to 8-foot-tall perennial with 6-inch-wide scarlet blooms from mid- to late summer; Zones 5-9. *H.* x 'Lady Baltimore' —crimson-eyed pink flowers. *H. syriacus* (rose of Sharon)—6- to 12-foot shrub with stiffly upright branches and 2½- to 4-inch flowers in shades of pink, red, purple, and white in late summer and fall; 'Diana' grows to 8 feet and bears 4- to 6-inch-wide single white blooms; Zones 5-8.

Growing conditions and maintenance: Both *H. coccineus* and *H.* hybrids are good choices for wet spots in the garden. Space 3 feet apart. Propagate by seed, cuttings, or division. *H. syriacus* requires well-drained soil. Allow 6 to 8 feet between plants and propagate by softwood cuttings in summer.

Hostas are valued chiefly for their foliage—mounds of oval or heart-shaped green, blue, white, and gold leaves in a variety of sizes. They are useful as edging or border plants, as ground covers, or for mass plantings. Tall, graceful spires of pale, lilylike flowers appear above the foliage in summer or fall.

Selected species and varieties: *H. fortunei* (giant plantain lily)—to 2 feet tall with funnel-shaped and lavender-tinged white flowers above dark green to blue-green foliage. *H. lancifolia* (narrow-leaved plantain lily)—a 2-foot-tall cascading mound of 4- to 6-inch-long leaf blades and 1- to 1½-inch blue-purple flowers in late summer. *H. sieboldiana* (Siebold plantain lily)—2½ to 3 feet tall with 10- to 15-inch-long glaucous gray to blue-green puckered leaves and lavender flowers that will bloom in midsummer; 'Frances Williams' grows 32 inches tall and 40 inches wide with round, puckered blue-green leaves having wide, irregular gold margins; *H. sieboldiana* var. *elegans*—36

mer; 'Golden Tiara', a low-growing mound 6 inches high and 16 to 20 inches wide, bearing yellow-edged, medium-green, heart-shaped leaves and purple flowers in midsummer.

Growing conditions and maintenance: Incorporate compost or leaf mold into soil prior to planting, and allow 1 to 3 feet between plants, depending on their eventual spread. Propagate by division in early spring.

Hyacinthus
(hy-a-SIN-thus)
HYACINTH

Hyacinthus orientalis

Hardiness: Zones 3-7

Plant type: bulb

Height: 8 to 12 inches

Interest: flowers, fragrance

Soil: moist, well-drained

Light: full sun

Hyacinth's flower spikes, crowded with 1-inch-long flowers whose petals curve backward, add color and sweet fragrance to the spring border. The spikes rise from a small bundle of canoe-shaped leaves. Hyacinths are impressive in mass plantings or mingled among other bulbs in beds and borders. They can also be forced to bloom indoors.

Selected species and varieties: *H. orientalis* (Dutch hyacinth, common hyacinth)—flowers in white, yellow, blue, purple, red, and pink, lasting up to 2 weeks in the garden; 'Anne Marie' has light pink flowers; 'Blue Jacket', navy blue flowers on black stems; 'Carnegie', cream flowers; 'City of Haarlem', pale yellow flowers.

Growing conditions and maintenance: Plant hyacinths in fall 4 to 6 inches deep and 6 to 8 inches apart in soil that has been enriched with organic matter. Bulbs produce their largest blooms the first year, smaller blooms thereafter. Bulbs should be replaced every 2 to 3 years.

Hydrangea
(hy-DRANE-jee-a)
HYDRANGEA

Hydrangea macrophylla 'Nikko Blue'

Hardiness: Zones 3-9

Plant type: shrub

Height: 3 to 6 feet

Interest: flowers, foliage, bark

Soil: moist, well-drained

Light: full sun to partial shade

Hydrangeas punctuate the border with huge flower clusters above coarse leaves that often color attractively in the fall. Older stems sometimes have peeling bark, adding winter interest.

Selected species and varieties: *H. arborescens* 'Annabelle'—3 to 5 feet tall and nearly as wide, with white flowers 10 to 12 inches across in summer; 'Grandiflora' (hills of snow hydrangea) bears white summer-to-fall flower clusters 6 to 8 inches across on shrubs 3 feet tall and wide; Zones 3-9. *H. macrophylla* (bigleaf hydrangea)—pink or blue summer flowers depending on soil pH on shrubs 3 to 6 feet tall with equal or greater spread; 'All Summer Beauty' grows to 3 feet tall; Zones 6-9. *H. quercifolia* 'Snow Queen'—to 8 feet tall and wide, large white blooms mature to a pale pink.

Growing conditions and maintenance: Plant in soil enriched with organic matter. Provide partial shade for *H. arborescens*. Propagate by softwood cuttings in spring.

Hypericum
(hy-PER-i-kum)
ST.-JOHN'S-WORT

Hypericum calycinum

Hardiness: Zones 3-9

Plant type: shrub or ground cover

Height: 1 to 4 feet

Interest: flowers, fruit, foliage, bark

Soil: poor, well-drained to dry

Light: full sun to partial shade

St.-John's-wort has bright yellow flowers over a long period of time and three-winged fruit capsules that persist all winter. It provides a long season of interest for the shrub border and combines very well with perennials.

Selected species and varieties: *H. calycinum* (creeping St.-John's-wort)—12 to 18 inches tall, spreading by stolons to 2 feet wide, with bright yellow, 3-inch-wide flowers throughout summer and dark semievergreen leaves; Zones 5-8. *H. frondosum* 'Sunburst'—2 feet tall and 4 feet wide with mounding blue-green foliage, reddish brown exfoliating bark, and 2-inch golden yellow flowers from late spring to early summer; Zones 5-8. *H. patulum* 'Sungold'—to 3 feet tall and wide, semievergreen to evergreen leaves and 2-inch yellow summer flowers; hardy to Zone 6.

Growing conditions and maintenance: St.-John's-wort prefers poor, rocky, dry soil. Prune in early spring. Propagate by cuttings in early summer.

Ilex
(EYE-lex)
HOLLY

Ilex x *'Sparkleberry'*

Hardiness:	Zones 3-9
Plant type:	shrub or tree
Height:	3 to 25 feet
Interest:	foliage, fruit
Soil:	moist, well-drained, acid
Light:	full sun to partial shade

Hollies are a diverse group of plants that include evergreen and deciduous trees and shrubs. Female hollies produce fruit in fall that is often highly ornamental, but most require male plants located within 100 feet for pollination to assure fruit set. They can be used as a background for herbaceous plantings or specimens in shrub borders.

Selected species and varieties: *I. cornuta* 'Burfordii' (Burford holly)—to 25 feet, may be maintained at 8 to 10 feet with pruning, rectangular leaves are shiny, dark evergreen with terminal spine, red, abundant fruit requires no pollination; Zones 6-9. *I. glabra* 'Compacta' (dwarf inkberry)—4 to 6 feet tall and wide, 2-inch evergreen leaves; Zones 4-9. *I.* x 'Sparkleberry'—to 12 feet, upright, deciduous, deep green leaves and bright red, prolific fruit; Zones 4-8.

Growing conditions and maintenance: Plant hollies in soil amended with organic matter. Fertilize in late winter and water during dry periods. Propagate by cuttings.

Impatiens
(im-PAY-shens)
IMPATIENS

Impatiens x *'New Guinea'*

Hardiness:	tender
Plant type:	annual
Height:	6 inches to 2 feet
Interest:	flowers, foliage
Soil:	moist, well-drained
Light:	shade to full sun

Impatiens brighten a garden with small single or double flowers in a wide range of colors from summer through frost. Most thrive in shade, and are perfect for scattering in a woodland border. Their uniform habit provides an ideal edging for beds and borders.

Selected species and varieties: *I.* x 'New Guinea'—to 2 feet, elongated leaves often variegated with purple, burgundy, yellow, or white; flowers up to 3 inches across in shades of pink, white, rose, red, and orange. *I. wallerana* (garden impatiens)—6 to 18 inches tall with a compact, mounded habit and 1- to 2-inch, flat-faced flowers available in single colors or bicolors.

Growing conditions and maintenance: Start indoors 3 to 4 months prior to the last frost, or purchase plants to transplant to the garden after danger of frost. Space plants 12 to 18 inches apart. Add organic matter to soil and water well. *I.* x 'New Guinea' requires more sun than garden impatiens.

Iris
(EYE-ris)
IRIS

Iris cristata *'Alba'*

Hardiness:	Zones 3-8
Plant type:	perennial
Height:	6 inches to 5 feet
Interest:	flowers, foliage
Soil:	well-drained to wet
Light:	full sun to light shade

Irises bloom in a rainbow of colors on zigzag stems rising from sword-shaped leaves. Each flower is composed of three drooping petal-like sepals called falls, three usually erect petals called standards, and three narrow, petal-like styles. Falls may be bearded with a tuft, crested with a ridge down the center, or beardless without a crest. With more than 200 species and thousands of varieties, irises vary widely in many respects including cultural requirements, height, and flower size, type, color, and season. All make lovely additions to herbaceous beds and borders.

Selected species and varieties: Tall bearded iris cultivars—28 or more inches tall with bearded flowers to 8 inches across in late spring to summer; *I. cristata* (crested iris)—grassy 6-inch leaves with early to midspring, typically blue-violet flowers with two yellow- or white-crested ridges along falls, effective in the front of a border or woodland garden; 'Alba' bears white flowers. *I. ensata* [also listed as *I. kaempferi*]

(Japanese iris)—beardless flowers up to 10 inches across in summer on stems to 4 feet; 'Great White Heron' bears semidouble petaled white blossoms; Zones 4-8. *I. laevigata* 'Variegata' (variegated rabbit-ear iris)—green leaves edged with cream, and lavender-blue summer flowers on 18-inch plants; hardy to Zone 5; 'Loop the Loop' produces violet-edged, white- petaled flowers; 'Navy Strut' has ruffled purple petals. *I. pallida* 'Aureo-variegata' (Dalmatian iris)—crinkled pale blue summer flowers and 3-foot, gray-green leaves striped with yellow; Zones 4-8. *I. pseudacorus* (yellow flag)—2-inch bright yellow flowers often with a brown blotch on falls, blooming in late spring to early summer on stalks to 5 feet; Zones 5-8. *I. sibirica* (Siberian iris)—clumps of slender, grasslike leaves and late spring flowers on stems to 4 feet; 'Caesar's Brother' produces blue-black flowers 36 inches tall; 'Dewful', 24 inches tall with blue flowers and pale blue styles; Zones 4-8.

Iris sibirica 'Caesar's Brother'

Growing conditions and maintenance: Plant iris in soil enriched with organic matter, spacing smaller types 12 inches apart, taller types 18 inches. Yellow flag and rabbit-ear iris require a wet soil, and can survive with roots submerged. Propagate by digging and dividing rhizomes after flowering. Divide Japanese and Siberian iris only when clumps show signs of reduced flowering.

Kalmia
(KAL-mee-a)
MOUNTAIN LAUREL

Kalmia latifolia 'Ostbo Red'

Hardiness: Zones 4-9

Plant type: shrub

Height: 7 to 15 feet

Interest: flowers, foliage

Soil: moist, well-drained, acid

Light: full sun to full shade

In early summer, mountain laurel bears rounded clusters of flowers set off by a background of dark, leathery leaves. It makes a fine addition to a mixed shrub border or a naturalized, shady bed.

Selected species and varieties: *K. latifolia*—variable height, usually to 15 feet with equal spread, leaves 2 to 5 inches long, evergreen, flower buds are deep pink or red and crimped, flowers to 1 inch across in 4- to 6-inch round, terminal clusters; 'Bullseye' has deep purple buds opening to creamy white flowers with a purple band; 'Ostbo Red', with red buds and pink flowers; 'Richard Jaynes', red buds and pink flowers that are silvery white inside.

Growing conditions and maintenance: Mountain laurel requires a moist, acid soil to which generous amounts of organic matter have been added. Mulch to maintain moisture. In Zones 7 to 9 protect plants from hot afternoon sun. Remove flowers after they fade.

Kerria
(KER-ee-a)
JAPANESE ROSE

Kerria japonica 'Pleniflora'

Hardiness: Zones 4-9

Plant type: shrub

Height: 3 to 8 feet

Interest: flowers, foliage, stems

Soil: well-drained

Light: partial to bright full shade

Airy mounds of foliage show off the kerria's yellow flowers in spring. The bright green leaves turn yellow in autumn and drop, revealing bare green stems that hold their color all winter. This shrub adds much interest to a shady border, and combines well with perennials.

Selected species and varieties: *K. japonica*—3 to 6 feet tall and wide with arching branches and glossy, heavily veined and coarsely toothed leaves 1½ to 4 inches long; 'Pleniflora' [also listed as 'Flore Pleno'] (globeflower kerria) grows semierect, 5 to 8 feet tall with double, pomponlike flowers 1 to 2 inches wide.

Growing conditions and maintenance: Kerria tolerates most soils but thrives in soil amended with organic matter. Excessive fertility will reduce the number of blooms. Remove winter-killed branches in early spring. Do other pruning just after flowering. Propagate by cuttings, layering, or division.

Lantana
(lan-TAN-a)
LANTANA

Lantana montevidensis

Hardiness: Zones 9-10

Plant type: annual or tender shrub

Height: 12 inches to 6 feet

Interest: flower, foliage, fragrance

Soil: well-drained

Light: full sun

Lantanas have somewhat stiff branches and a trailing habit that is particularly effective when stems cascade over the walls of raised beds or containers. The 1- to 2-inch flower clusters in shades of yellow, white, orange, red, lavender, and bicolors appear throughout the summer. Flowers and leaves have a slightly pungent fragrance.

Selected species and varieties: *L. camara* (yellow sage)—2- to 6-foot shrub with dark, hairy leaves and flat-topped clusters of tiny flowers that start yellow and turn orange-red; 'Confetti' bears white, pink, and red flowers all on the same plant. *L. montevidensis* [also listed as *L. sellowiana*] (weeping lantana)—to 30 inches with a greater spread, mounding habit, dark green wrinkled leaves and flower clusters similar to *L. camara.*

Growing conditions and maintenance: Space plants 18 inches apart. They can be trained to standards, and are easily dug and potted in fall for indoor winter flowering. Propagate from cuttings.

Lavandula
(lav-AN-dew-la)
LAVENDER

Lavandula angustifolia 'Munstead'

Hardiness: Zones 5-9

Plant type: shrub

Height: 1 to 3 feet

Interest: flowers, foliage, fragrance

Soil: well-drained

Light: full sun

Lavender is a small evergreen shrub. Both the gray-green leaves and flowers are extremely fragrant and add a welcome touch to the edge of a border. Lavender's soft colors and fine texture combine well with more brightly colored perennials.

Selected species and varieties: *L. angustifolia* (English lavender, true lavender)—whorls of lavender to purple ½-inch flowers in summer on compact, rounded plants 1 to 2 feet tall; 'Hidcote' grows to 3 feet tall, with deep purple flowers; 'Munstead' is extremely fragrant with lavender-blue flowers on 2-foot-tall plants; 'Munstead Dwarf' is 1 foot tall; Zones 5-8. *L. stoechas* (French lavender)—to 3 feet tall with gray-green leaves and purple or white flowers; Zones 7-9.

Growing conditions and maintenance: Plant lavender 12 to 18 inches apart in very well-drained soil that is not overly rich. Cut stems to 8 inches in early spring and remove old woody stems. Propagate by seed or division.

Lespedeza
(les-ped-EE-za)
BUSH CLOVER

Lespedeza thunbergii 'White Fountain'

Hardiness: Zones 4-8

Plant type: shrub

Height: 3 to 10 feet

Interest: flowers

Soil: well-drained to sandy, dry

Light: full sun

Bush clovers are deciduous shrubs valued for their late-season flowers. They are most attractive when massed or mixed in a sunny shrub border.

Selected species and varieties: *L. bicolor* (shrub bush clover)—6 to 10 feet, with trifoliate leaves along arching stems, and rosy purple flowers in 2- to 5-inch-long clusters arising from the current season's growth from mid- to late summer; Zones 4-8. *L. thunbergii* [also listed as *L. sieboldii*] (purple bush clover)—to 6 feet tall and 10 feet wide with slender arching stems that become weighted down by the 8-inch-long dark purple flower clusters from late summer to fall; 'White Fountain' has white flowers; Zones 5-8.

Growing conditions and maintenance: Because bush clovers tend toward legginess if allowed to grow unpruned, cut stems to the ground in early spring before growth begins. New stems will reach 3 to 4 feet by flowering time. Propagate by seed or stem cuttings.

Leucothoe
(loo-KO-tho-ee)
FETTERBUSH

Leucothoe fontanesiana 'Girard's Rainbow'

Hardiness: Zones 5-9

Plant type: shrub

Height: 2 to 6 feet

Interest: foliage, flowers

Soil: moist, well-drained, acid, fertile

Light: partial to full shade

With its clusters of creamy, urn-shaped flowers, lustrous evergreen leaves, arching branches, and spreading, broad-mounded habit, leucothoe looks stunning in the border, either as a specimen or planted in masses. It also makes an elegant ground cover for shady beds.

Selected species and varieties: *L. fontanesiana*—3 to 6 feet tall and wide, fountainlike, arching habit with 2- to 5-inch-long pointed leaves that are bronze when young, dark green in summer, turning bronze to purple in fall and winter. Fragrant white flowers are borne in drooping clusters in late spring; 'Girard's Rainbow' bears leaves that emerge variegated white and pink and mature to gold, copper, and green.

Growing conditions and maintenance: Plant leucothoe in a shady location in soil amended with organic matter. Mulch to keep roots cool and soil moist. Prune after flowering. Propagate by cuttings taken in midsummer.

Liatris
(ly-AY-tris)
GAY-FEATHER

Liatris spicata 'Kobold'

Hardiness: Zones 3-10

Plant type: perennial

Height: 2 to 6 feet

Interest: flowers

Soil: well-drained, sandy

Light: full sun to light shade

The flowers of gay-feather are borne on erect stems, and unlike most spike flowers, the top buds open first and proceed downward, creating a feathery bottlebrush. The tall stem arises from a tuft of grasslike leaves borne by a corm. It provides a striking vertical accent or specimen in the border.

Selected species and varieties: *L. scariosa* (tall gay-feather)—to 6 feet tall with mid- to late-summer flowers on a stout, erect stem; 'September Glory' produces deep purple flowers in early fall on 3- to 6-foot stems. *L. spicata* (spike gay-feather)—usually 2 to 3 feet tall, but may reach 5 feet tall with stout stems of purple or rose flowers in mid- to late summer; 'Kobold' is a dwarf form that grows 18 to 24 inches with bright purple flowers.

Growing conditions and maintenance: Plant gay-feather in spring in light soil, setting corms 3 to 4 inches deep and 18 to 24 inches apart. All but *L. spicata* 'Kobold' require staking. Propagate by seed or division.

Ligularia
(lig-yew-LAY-ree-a)
GOLDEN-RAY

Ligularia dentata 'Desdemona'

Hardiness: Zones 4-10

Plant type: perennial

Height: 2 to 6 feet

Interest: flowers, foliage

Soil: moist loam or boggy soil

Light: full sun to partial shade

Ligularias produce showy clumps of attractive, sometimes variegated leaves up to 4 feet tall and equally wide, providing a coarse texture to beds and borders. Many are prized for their flowers, some on stalks up to 6 feet tall.

Selected species and varieties: *L. dentata* (bigleaf golden-ray)—leathery, kidney-shaped leaves 20 inches wide forming mounds 3 to 4 feet high with yellow daisylike flowers on branched stalks; 'Desdemona' is more compact with mahogany red leaf stems and undersides; Zones 4-8. *L. stenocephala* 'The Rocket'—light green leaves 8 to 12 inches wide creating soft mounds with 4- to 6-foot black stalks of bright yellow summer flower spikes; Zones 5-8. *L. tussilaginea* [also listed as *Farfugium japonicum*]—leaves 12 inches wide in 2-foot tall clumps with pale yellow flower clusters; Zones 7-10.

Growing conditions and maintenance: Plant ligularias 2 to 3 feet apart in a cool, moist location. Propagate by division or seed.

Lilium
(LIL-ee-um)
LILY

Lilium 'Golden Splendor'

Hardiness: Zones 3-9	
Plant type: bulb	
Height: 2 to 6 feet	
Interest: flowers	
Soil: moist, well-drained	
Light: full sun to light shade	

Showy flower trumpets with prominent stamens make lilies outstanding border specimens. They are also excellent for massing in front of a shrub border or at the sunny edge of a woodland bed.

Selected species and varieties: Asiatic Hybrids—spring to summer 4- to 6-inch flowers sometimes bi- or tricolored on 2- to 4-foot stems; 'Gran Cru' is yellow with maroon flush. Trumpet Hybrids [also called Aurelian Hybrids]—trumpet, sunburst, or bowl-shaped flowers up to 12 inches across in summer on 4- to 6-foot stalks; 'Golden Splendor' has fragrant golden trumpets flushed with copper outside. Oriental Hybrids—fragrant late-summer flowers to 12 inches across on 2- to 8-foot stems; 'Casa Blanca', pure white trumpets with orange anthers.

Growing conditions and maintenance: Plant bulbs three times as deep as their height, 1 foot apart. Propagate by removing and planting bulblets.

Lobelia
(lo-BEE-lee-a)
LOBELIA

Lobelia siphilitica

Hardiness: tender or Zones 3-9	
Plant type: annual or perennial	
Height: 4 inches to 6 feet	
Interest: flowers	
Soil: moist, well-drained to wet	
Light: full sun to partial shade	

Lobelias range from compact annuals useful as a border edging to erect, moisture-loving perennials that may grow as tall as 6 feet and provide outstanding color.

Selected species and varieties: *L. cardinalis* (cardinal flower)—perennial usually 2 to 4 feet tall, but may reach 6 feet, with bright red flowers on 8-inch spikes in summer or fall; Zones 3-9. *L. erinus* (edging lobelia)—annual with spreading habit 4 to 8 inches tall and blue, pink, or white flowers throughout summer into fall. *L. siphilitica* (great blue lobelia)—perennial with blue tubular flowers on erect, 2- to 3-foot leafy stems from late summer to early fall; Zones 4-7.

Growing conditions and maintenance: Plant in soil amended with organic matter. Grow edging lobelia from seed, spacing plants 4 to 6 inches apart, cutting plants back when flowering slacks off to encourage blooms. Plant perennial types in moist areas, 12 inches apart. Propagate by seed or division.

Lupinus
(loo-PY-nus)
LUPINE

Lupinus 'Russell Hybrids'

Hardiness: Zones 4-6	
Plant type: perennial	
Height: 18 inches to 5 feet	
Interest: flowers	
Soil: moist, well-drained, acid	
Light: full sun to light shade	

Lupine's elongated spikes of small, butterfly-shaped flowers are packed tightly along the ends of stiff stalks above attractive palmate leaves. Their refined appearance enhances flower borders.

Selected species and varieties: *L. polyphyllus* (Washington lupine)—2 to 5 feet tall with deep blue flowers on long stalks throughout summer, white- and pink-flowered forms are available. *L.* 'Russell Hybrids'—plants to 4 feet tall with showy 18- to 24-inch-long summer-blooming flower spires that open from the bottom up in a multitude of colors and combinations, dwarf strains reach only 18 inches.

Growing conditions and maintenance: Lupines thrive in cool regions and do not tolerate heat. In warmer areas, they are best planted in fall and treated as annuals. Space plants 2 feet apart in acidic soil enriched with organic matter. Taller types may require staking. Propagate from seed or from root cuttings taken in the spring with a piece of the crown attached.

Lycoris
(ly-KOR-is)
SPIDER LILY

Lycoris squamigera

Hardiness: Zones 5-10

Plant type: bulb

Height: 12 to 24 inches

Interest: flowers, fragrance

Soil: well-drained, fertile

Light: full sun to light shade

Lycoris produces whorls of frilly blossoms from late summer to fall atop stout bare stems that provide a fine display in borders and beds. Clumps of narrow, strap-shaped leaves emerge in late winter to early spring, fading as the plants enter summer dormancy.

Selected species and varieties: *L. aurea* (golden hurricane lily)—yellow petals and filaments on 12- to 24-inch stems, late summer to early fall; Zones 7-10. *L. radiata*—12 to 16 inches tall, rose-red flowers. *L. squamigera* (resurrection lily)—extremely fragrant, 3-inch rose to lilac trumpets on 2-foot stalks in late summer, differing from other species by appearing after the foliage has died back; Zones 5-10.

Growing conditions and maintenance: Plant lycoris bulbs 3 to 5 inches deep and 6 inches apart. Propagate by removing the small bulblets that grow alongside mature bulbs. Disturbing clumps may delay blooming for a year or more.

Mahonia
(ma-HO-nee-a)
HOLLY GRAPE

Mahonia bealei

Hardiness: Zones 4-9

Plant type: shrub

Height: 20 inches to 12 feet

Interest: flowers, fruit, foliage, fragrance

Soil: moist, well-drained, acid

Light: partial to bright full shade

Mahonia's coarse texture and stiff habit provide year-round interest in a shrub border. Its spiny, compound, evergreen foliage has a scalloped outline and provides a dramatic foil for the fragrant flower clusters followed by showy fruit.

Selected species and varieties: *M. aquifolium* (Oregon grape)—broad and dense or upright and open, growing 3 to 6 feet tall with a similar spread, dark green leaves turn red-purple in winter, 3-inch-long clusters of tiny yellow spring flowers, and blue-black late summer berries. *M. bealei* (leatherleaf mahonia)—6 to 12 feet, upright habit with spiked, blue-green leaflets, fragrant yellow flowers in early spring and steel blue berries in midsummer; Zones 6-9.

Growing conditions and maintenance: Mahonias prefer partial shade and perform well under trees. Protect from drying winds, provide mulch, and water during dry spells. Propagate by digging and replanting suckers growing from roots.

Miscanthus
(mis-KAN-thus)
EULALIA

Miscanthus sinensis 'Morning Light'

Hardiness: Zones 5-9

Plant type: perennial grass

Height: 3 to 10 feet

Interest: foliage, flowers

Soil: well-drained to dry

Light: full sun

Miscanthus forms graceful clumps of narrow, arching leaves and tall flower plumes in summer and fall. They impart graceful movement and soft colors to a border either as a backdrop or as a specimen, keeping their appeal throughout the winter.

Selected species and varieties: *M. sinensis*—5 to 10 feet tall displaying narrow leaves 3 to 4 feet long with a prominent white midrib, and feathery, fan-shaped inflorescence in late summer to fall; 'Malepartus' has pink summer blooms silvering as they age and bronze fall foliage; 'Morning Light', white-striped leaves with reddish bronze fall flowers on stalks to 6 feet; var. *condensatus* 'Silberpfeil' grows to 6 feet with bronze plumes and leaves showing white vertical variegation.

Growing conditions and maintenance: Space clumps of miscanthus at least 3 feet apart, but 5 feet is better; plants spread to 6 feet across. Cut plants back to 6 inches in late winter before new growth begins. Propagate by division.

Nandina
(nan-DEE-na)
HEAVENLY BAMBOO

Nandina domestica

Hardiness: Zones 6-9

Plant type: shrub

Height: 1 to 8 feet

Interest: foliage, flowers, fruit

Soil: moist, well-drained

Light: full sun to partial shade

Nandina forms clumps of upright canes with compound leaves and late-spring panicles of creamy white flowers, followed by huge clusters of brilliant red berries that persist through winter, providing a long season of interest to any shrub border. Evergreen in warm regions, nandina is deciduous in colder zones

Selected species and varieties: *N. domestica*—6 to 8 feet tall with multiple stems from base and compound leaves 12 to 20 inches long that emerge bronze or pink in spring, become dark green in summer, and turn deep red in fall; 'Alba' produces white berries; 'Harbour Dwarf' grows 1 to 2 feet tall with a spreading habit.

Growing conditions and maintenance: Nandina is tolerant of most soils, but performs best in fertile soil where it is long-lived and virtually pest free. Remove oldest canes and cut back remaining canes to different heights in late winter. Transplant tiny plants from self-seeding parent.

Narcissus
(nar-SIS-us)
DAFFODIL

Narcissus 'Gigantic Star'

Hardiness: Zones 3-10

Plant type: bulb

Height: 4 to 20 inches

Interest: flowers, fragrance

Soil: well-drained

Light: full sun to partial shade

Daffodil flowers appear singly or in small clusters atop stout, hollow stems above narrow, grasslike leaves. Each bloom consists of an outer ring of six petals called the perianth and a raised center called a corona, which may be an almost flat, small cup, a large cup of medium length, or, when it is very long, a trumpet. The edges of the corona may be ruffled, fringed, flared, frilled, or split. The petals of the perianth may be pointed or round, overlapping or separate. Species narcissus are renowned for their sweet, intense fragrance. Hybrids of the species number in the thousands, and the genus is grouped into 12 divisions for identification. Plant daffodils in groups in perennial gardens or naturalize them. They make excellent cut flowers, but all parts of narcissus are poisonous.

Selected species and varieties: *N. bulbocodium* var. *conspicuus*—petals reduced to tiny pointed projections around yellow corona on 6- to 10-inch stems. Cyclamineus daffodils—solitary flowers on short stems with trumpet-shaped corona and perianth petals swept backward; 'February Gold' produces late winter yellow blooms; 'Tete-a-Tete', yellow petals and a corona flushed with orange on 6- to 8-inch stems. Double daffodils—one or more flowers per stem with doubled, ruffled, and frilled cups or perianths. Jonquilla daffodils—three to six fragrant flowers with small cups on 10- to 14-inch stems. *N. jonquilla*—clusters of 2-inch yellow flowers with flat coronas on 12-inch stems. Large-cupped daffodils—solitary flowers with the corona more than one-third but less than the full length of the petals; 'Carlton' has fragrant, soft yellow flowers with a frilled corona and broad perianth on 18- to 20-inch stems; 'Flower Record', white perianth with red-rimmed, yellow corona; 'Gigantic Star', large golden yellow blooms with a deeper yellow cup. Tazetta daffodils—three to 20 fragrant, nearly flat cupped flowers per 6- to 14-inch stem. Trumpet daffodils—one flower per stem, with the corona a trumpet as long as or longer than the

Narcissus bulbocodium var. conspicuus

perianth petals; 'Lunar Sea', yellow perianth and white trumpet on 18- to 20-inch stem.

Growing conditions and maintenance: Plant daffodils in fall at a depth one and a half times their height and 1 to 3 inches apart. After flowering, allow leaves to fade before trimming back. Propagate by digging and dividing bulb clumps.

Nicotiana
(ni-ko-she-AN-a)
FLOWERING TOBACCO

Nicotiana alata

Hardiness: tender

Plant type: annual

Height: 1 to 6 feet

Interest: flowers, foliage

Soil: moist, well-drained

Light: full sun to partial shade

Flowering tobacco produces loose clusters of fragrant, flat-faced flowers with elongated tubular throats at the tips of soft stems, and clumps of large, sticky leaves. It is useful as a border filler or specimen. Flowers of some varieties close in sunlight but open on cloudy days or in the evening. Leaf juices contain nicotine and are poisonous.

Selected species and varieties: *N. alata* (jasmine tobacco)—1- to 2-foot tall clumps with flowers that bloom from spring to fall above 4- to 10-inch leaves. *N. langsdorfii*—nodding green flowers with turquoise anthers at the tips of 5-foot stems. *N. sylvestris* (woodland tobacco)—white blooms tinged pink or purple on branching plants 3 to 6 feet tall.

Growing conditions and maintenance: Start seed indoors 6 to 8 weeks prior to the last frost, or sow seed directly outdoors in late spring after all danger of frost has passed. Do not cover the seed, it needs light to germinate. Space plants 1 to 2 feet apart.

Nigella
(nye-JEL-a)
LOVE-IN-A-MIST

Nigella damascena

Hardiness: tender

Plant type: annual

Height: 18 to 24 inches

Interest: flowers, seed heads

Soil: well-drained

Light: full sun

Love-in-a-mist adds a delicate, fine texture to any border or flower arrangement in which it is used. Its fernlike leaves are light green, and solitary flowers are nestled in a mist of foliage at the ends of stems throughout the summer. Interesting seed capsules replace the flowers and are attractive in dried flower arrangements. Seeds are edible.

Selected species and varieties: *N. damascena*—an erect multibranched habit with delicate leaves in threadlike segments. Flowers are 1 to 1½ inches across with blue, white, or pink notched petals, and papery 1-inch seed capsules that are pale green with reddish brown markings.

Growing conditions and maintenance: Start seed directly outdoors in early spring, and make additional sowings every 2 or 3 weeks until early summer to extend the flowering season. Plants are not easily transplanted. Thin to allow 6 to 10 inches between plants. Water during dry periods. Pods allowed to dry on plants will self-seed.

Ocimum
(OS-si-mum)
SWEET BASIL

Ocimum basilicum 'Purple Ruffles'

Hardiness: tender

Plant type: annual

Height: 1 to 2 feet

Interest: foliage

Soil: moist, well-drained

Light: full sun

This annual native of Asia and Africa has been cultivated for centuries as a culinary and medicinal herb. Its fragrant foliage and mounded form make it an exceptional edging for borders and beds. Basil also can be effectively combined with flowering plants in containers and window boxes.

Selected species and varieties: *O. basilicum*—rounded growth habit and square stems typical of the mint family, to which it belongs, with opposite, slightly crinkled, oval, leaves, and tiny white or purple flowers borne in terminal clusters; 'Purple Ruffles' grows to 2 feet with dark purple leaves having ruffled margins and lavender flowers that bloom in summer.

Growing conditions and maintenance: Start basil seed indoors 8 weeks prior to last frost to transplant outdoors after all danger of frost has passed. Allow 10 to 12 inches between plants. As they appear, flowers may be pinched out to promote leaf growth. Basil thrives in warm weather.

Paeonia
(pee-O-nee-a)
PEONY

Paeonia 'Gay Paree'

Hardiness: Zones 3-8

Plant type: perennial

Height: 18 to 36 inches

Interest: flowers, foliage, fragrance

Soil: fertile, well-drained

Light: full sun to light shade

Peonies decorate a border in spring and early summer with enormous showy blossoms up to 10 inches across. They have been extensively hybridized into several forms: single peonies with a single row of petals encircling centers with fluffy golden stamens; Japanese peonies with single or double rows of petals surrounding centers filled with modified stamens that look like finely cut petals; semidouble and double peonies with larger outer petals framing a fluffy pompon of frilled and ruffled inner petals. Peonies are further classified by their flowering season (early, mid, late). Lush mounds of compound leaves bear a rosy tint as they emerge in spring, then deepen to dark green in summer and remain attractive until frost.

Selected species and varieties: *P. lactiflora* hybrids (garden or Chinese peony)—hundreds of varieties offering a selection of flower type, season, and color; Double peonies—'Elsa Sass' has pure white petals; 'Mrs. Franklin D. Roosevelt', early midseason rosy pink

flowers that fade to white and are very fragrant. Japanese peonies—'Gay Paree' blooms midseason producing pink petals surrounding a white center. Single peonies—'Bowl of Beauty' has creamy centers surrounded by carmine pink petals borne in midseason; 'Sea Shell', early to midseason clear, bright pink flowers. *P. tenuifolia* (fern-leaf peony)—single, deep red flowers in late spring, and finely divided foliage on 18- to 24-inch stems; 'Plena' (double fern-leaf peony) grows 12 to 15 inches tall with early red blooms, and can be used as an edging for a border where its fine-textured foliage remains attractive throughout the growing season.

Growing conditions and maintenance: Peonies are long-lived plants that can be left undisturbed indefinitely, thus thorough soil preparation is vital. Incorporate generous quantities of organic matter into soil prior to planting but

Paeonia tenuifolia 'Plena'

do not allow manure to come in contact with the fleshy roots. Peonies are best planted in the fall. Plant Chinese peonies and hybrids 36 inches apart, fern-leaf peonies 18 inches apart. Be careful to set the roots so that the buds (eyes) are no more than 1 to 2 inches below the soil surface; setting them deeper delays flowering. Full sun will produce the most vigorous growth, but pastel flowers are often seen to best advantage in light shade. Divide clumps in late summer to early fall into sections containing 3 to 5 eyes each.

Papaver
(pa-PAY-ver)
POPPY

Papaver somniferum 'Double Black'

Hardiness: tender or Zones 3-8

Plant type: annual or perennial

Height: 1 to 4 feet

Interest: flowers

Soil: well-drained to dry

Light: full sun to light shade

Poppy's tissuelike flower petals surround prominent centers above clumps of coarse, lobed leaves. Flowers may be single or double and are available in shades of white, red, pink, and purple, providing early color.

Selected species and varieties: *P. nudicaule* (Iceland poppy, Arctic poppy)—perennial, often grown as an annual with fernlike gray-green foliage and 2- to 4-inch saucer-shaped late-spring flowers on 12- to 18-inch stems. *P. rhoeas* (corn poppy)—annual to 3 feet with wiry, branching stems and single or double late-spring flowers. *P. somniferum* (opium poppy)—3 to 4 feet tall with large flowers throughout summer, generally grown as an annual; 'Double Black' has dark maroon double flowers.

Growing conditions and maintenance: Start *P. nudicaule* indoors 10 weeks prior to the last frost or sow directly in the garden in late fall or early spring. Others are difficult to transplant, and are best sown in place. Many self-seed.

Pennisetum
(pen-i-SEE-tum)
FOUNTAIN GRASS

Pennisetum orientale

Hardiness: Zones 5-9 or tender

Plant type: hardy or tender perennial

Height: 2 to 4 feet

Interest: foliage, flowers

Soil: moist, well-drained

Light: full sun

Fountain grass forms large clumps of slender, arching leaves. In summer, numerous flower stalks arise from the clump, topped with spikes that resemble bottle brushes. Flowers last through fall, and foliage remains attractive through winter. Use fountain grass as a border specimen or backdrop.

Selected species and varieties: *P. alopecuroides* (Chinese fountain grass) —perennial with rosy silver flowers in 5- to 7-inch spikes above leaf mounds 3 to 4 feet wide and tall; 'Hameln' is a fine-textured 2-foot dwarf; Zones 5-9. *P. orientale* (Oriental fountain grass)— perennial forming 2-foot clumps of gray-green foliage with pink flower heads throughout summer; Zones 7-9.

Growing conditions and maintenance: Plant fountain grass 2 to 3 feet apart in any well-drained soil. Cut back to 6 inches above the ground before new growth begins in spring. Propagate by seed or division.

Perovskia
(per-OV-skee-a)
RUSSIAN SAGE

Perovskia atriplicifolia

Hardiness: Zones 5-9

Plant type: perennial

Height: 3 to 4 feet

Interest: flowers, foliage, fragrance

Soil: well-drained

Light: full sun

Russian sage adds cool colors, pleasing fragrance, and soft texture to any bed. Its silvery white mounds of aromatic foliage provide an effective filler and remain attractive through most of the winter. The flowers are lavender-blue and appear for several weeks in the summer. It is particularly well sited in a border among boldly colored plants.

Selected species and varieties: *P. atriplicifolia*—3 feet tall with equal spread, silvery white leaves and stems have a sagelike aroma when bruised, leaves are 1½ inches long, the two-lipped flowers are pale lavender-blue, appearing in branched spikelike clusters in summer; 'Longin' grows to 3 to 4 feet with a more upright habit and blue flowers.

Growing conditions and maintenance: Plant Russian sage 2 to 3 feet apart in full sun; shade causes floppy, sprawling growth. Cut plants back to within several inches of the ground in early spring to promote bushy growth. Propagate from seed or summer cuttings.

Petunia
(pe-TOO-nee-a)
PETUNIA

Petunia x hybrida 'Purple Wave'

Hardiness: tender

Plant type: annual

Height: 8 to 18 inches

Interest: flowers

Soil: well-drained

Light: full sun

Open flower trumpets appear in profusion from summer to frost along petunia's trailing or upright stems amid small, hairy, pointed leaves. Petunias are effective cascading over walls or banks or when massed as bedding plants; also excellent container plants.

Selected species and varieties: *P. x hybrida* (common garden petunia)— flowers from white through yellow to pink, red, purple, blue-purple, and lavender, often speckled, splotched, veined or striped in a contrasting color on compact, bushy, or trailing plants; 'Heavenly Lavender' has deep lavender double blooms; 'Purple Wave', burgundy purple flowers that grow to 4 inches tall and spread 3 to 4 feet, first ground cover petunia.

Growing conditions and maintenance: Start seed indoors 10 to 12 weeks before the last frost date. Pinch to develop bushy plants. Space petunias 6 to 8 inches apart, and deadhead regularly.

Phlox
(flox)
PHLOX

Phlox divaricata 'Fuller's White'

Hardiness: Zones 3-9

Plant type: perennial

Height: 6 inches to 4 feet

Interest: flowers, foliage, fragrance

Soil: moist, well-drained

Light: full sun to full shade

Clusters of dainty flowers appear above phlox's soft foliage in spring, summer, or fall. Taller species are suitable for fillers or massing; shorter species spread into ground-covering mats.

Selected species and varieties: *P. divaricata* (wild blue phlox)—to 15 inches tall with spring-to-summer flowers; 'Fuller's White' bears prolific creamy white blooms; Zones 4-9. *P. paniculata* (garden phlox)—4-foot stems tipped with flower clusters to 8 inches wide in summer and fall; 'Starfire' has cherry red flowers; Zones 3-8. *P. stolonifera* (creeping phlox)—6 to 12 inches with spreading habit, evergreen leaves, and many dense clusters of spring flowers; Zones 3-8.

Growing conditions and maintenance: Plant low-growing phlox 12 to 18 inches apart, tall species 2 feet apart. *P. divaricata* and *P. stolonifera* require moist shade. *P. paniculata* prefers full sun with ample moisture. Propagate by division or from cuttings.

Pieris
(PYE-er-is)
PIERIS

Pieris japonica 'White Cascade'

Hardiness: Zones 5-8

Plant type: shrub

Height: 2 to 12 feet

Interest: flowers, foliage

Soil: moist, well-drained, acid

Light: full sun to partial shade

An evergreen shrub with glossy, oval, pointed leaves and clusters of tiny urn-shaped spring flowers, pieris extends the season of bloom in a shrub border or provides a year-round backdrop.

Selected species and varieties: *P. floribunda* (fetterbush, mountain pieris)—rounded shrubs 2 to 6 feet tall with equal or greater width and 4-inch upright white flower clusters that are fragrant in midspring. *P. japonica* (lily-of the-valley bush, Japanese pieris)—upright shrubs to 12 feet and 6 to 8 feet wide with leaves that emerge bronzy pink in spring and become dark green in summer, and urn-shaped flowers in pendulous 3- to 6-inch clusters in early to midspring; 'Dorothy Wycoff' has red buds opening to pink flowers; 'White Cascade, profuse white flowers.

Growing conditions and maintenance: Plant pieris in soil enriched with organic matter. Provide mulch and protection from heavy winds. If necessary, prune after flowering. Propagate by softwood cuttings in summer.

Platycodon
(plat-i-KO-don)
BALLOON FLOWER

Platycodon grandiflorus 'Mariesii'

Hardiness: Zones 4-9

Plant type: perennial

Height: 10 to 36 inches

Interest: flowers, buds

Soil: well-drained, acid

Light: full sun to partial shade

Balloon flower gets its name from the round buds that pop open into shallow saucer-shaped flowers 2 to 3 inches across with translucent, pointed petals. The blue, white, or pink summer blossoms top erect stems growing in narrow clumps. Use balloon flowers as accents among lower-growing border plants or massed for a showy display.

Selected species and varieties: *P. grandiflorus*—24 to 36 inches tall with blue-green leaves forming neat clumps, and rounded, inflated flower buds that pop when squeezed; 'Apoyama' is a dwarf to 10 inches tall with violet-blue flowers; 'Mariesii' [also listed as var. *mariesii*], has bright blue flowers on compact 18-inch plants; 'Mother of Pearl' grows to 36 inches with soft pink, upward- facing blossoms.

Growing conditions and maintenance: Plant 18 inches apart in well-drained soil; they do not tolerate a soggy location. Late to emerge in spring. Mark their location to avoid injury or crowding. Propagate by seed or division.

Potentilla
(po-ten-TILL-a)
CINQUEFOIL

Potentilla fruticosa 'Abbotswood'

Hardiness: Zones 2-7

Plant type: perennial or shrub

Height: 1 to 4 feet

Interest: flowers, foliage

Soil: well-drained to sandy, dry

Light: full sun to partial shade

Cinquefoil's open, five-petaled flowers resemble wild roses, and are held above spreading mounds of palmately compound leaves. Low-growing types make effective ground covers and edgings while taller varieties combine well with perennials or shrubs in a border.

Selected species and varieties: *P. fruticosa* (bush cinquefoil)—1 to 4 feet tall, 2 to 4 feet wide, leaves emerge gray-green turning dark green, 1-inch flowers from early summer to late fall; 'Abbotswood' grows to 2 feet with white flowers; 'Primrose Beauty' produces primrose flowers with deeper centers on 3-foot plants; 'Tangerine', 2 to 4 feet tall with yellow flowers flushed with orange and copper tones; Zones 2-7.

Growing conditions and maintenance: Plant smaller cinquefoils 1 foot apart, larger types 2 feet apart. They flower best in full sun and with a not-too-rich soil. Propagate by seed or division.

Primula
(PRIM-yew-la)
PRIMROSE

Primula japonica 'Postford White'

Hardiness: Zones 3-8

Plant type: perennial

Height: 6 to 24 inches

Interest: flowers

Soil: moist to wet, well-drained, fertile

Light: partial to bright full shade

Primroses produce vividly colored flowers above a basal rosette of crinkled foliage in spring and early summer. Flowers have five petals and are borne in clusters atop naked stalks. Depending on the variety, primroses are excellent for mass plantings and in borders, rock gardens and along stream banks.

Selected species and varieties: *P. japonica* (Japanese primrose)—whorls of white, red, pink, or purple early-summer flowers on 2-foot stems; 'Miller's Crimson' has deep red flowers; 'Postford White', white blooms; Zones 6-8. *P. sieboldii* (Japanese star primrose)—nodding heads of pink, purple, or white flowers on 12-inch stalks; Zones 5-8. *P. vulgaris* (English primrose)—fragrant, solitary spring flowers in many colors often with darker centers on 6- to 9-inch stems; Zones 3-8.

Growing conditions and maintenance: Space primroses 1 foot apart in moisture-retentive soil. Water during dry periods. Propagate by seed or division.

Pulmonaria
(pul-mo-NAY-ree-a)
LUNGWORT

Pulmonaria longifolia 'Bertram Anderson'

Hardiness: Zones 4-8

Plant type: perennial

Height: 8 to 12 inches

Interest: flowers, foliage

Soil: moist, well-drained

Light: light to full shade

Pulmonaria's clusters of spring flower trumpets nod at the tops of stems rising from clumps of broadly oval, hairy leaves spreading twice their height. Grown primarily for their handsome foliage, they are effective as a ground cover in a shrub border or when used as accents in shady beds.

Selected species and varieties: *P. longifolia* (long-leaved lungwort)—tight clump of tapered, gray-spotted green leaves more than a foot long and deep blue-flowers; 'Bertram Anderson' has violet-blue flowers and silver-spotted leaves; Zones 5-8. *P. saccharata* (Bethlehem sage)—8 to 12 inches with 6-inch pubescent leaves mottled white and green in clumps with 12-inch stems of flowers that open pink and age to blue; 'Janet Fisk' produces leaves marbled almost to white with lavender-pink flowers; Zones 4-8.

Growing conditions and maintenance: Plant lungwort 12 to 18 inches apart in cool, moist location. Propagate by seed or division.

Punica
(PEW-ni-ka)
POMEGRANATE

Punica granatum

Hardiness: Zones 8-10

Plant type: shrub

Height: 2 to 10 feet

Interest: flowers, fruit, foliage

Soil: well-drained to dry

Light: full sun

Pomegranates are heat-loving deciduous shrubs with arching branches, slender, glossy leaves, and bright red or creamy yellow-and-red striped summer flowers followed by edible red fruit. They provide a lush backdrop for other flowers and have showy summer blooms and colorful fall foliage and fruit for shrub borders. Double-flowering selections do not bear fruit.

Selected species and varieties: *P. granatum*—1½- to 3-inch leaves emerge reddish in spring, mature to green, and turn yellow in fall with a fountainlike growth habit on plants to 10 feet, though dwarf forms may not exceed 3 feet, with single or double 1½- to 4-inch flowers with fleshy petals and 4-inch spherical reddish fruit.

Growing conditions and maintenance: Pomegranates are easy to grow in warm climates. They tolerate drought and alkaline soils. Prune to shape in early spring. Propagate by seed, suckers, or winter cuttings.

Rhododendron
(roh-doh-DEN-dron)
RHODODENDRON

Rhododendron schlippenbachii

Hardiness: Zones 3-9

Plant type: shrub

Height: 2 to 30 feet

Interest: flowers, foliage

Soil: moist, well-drained, acid

Light: full sun to partial shade

The genus *Rhododendron* includes more than 900 species commonly known as rhododendrons and azaleas. Distinguishing features between them are not always clear-cut, but most true rhododendrons are evergreen, while most azaleas are deciduous. Also, rhododendron flowers are usually bell-shaped, whereas the azalea's are funnel-shaped, and rhododendron leaves are often scaly, while azalea leaves are smooth. All are outstanding additions to mixed shrub and perennial borders and woodland beds.

Selected species and varieties: Deciduous species: *R. arborescens* (sweet azalea)—8 to 20 feet tall with equal spread, glossy green leaves turning red in fall, white fragrant blooms; hardy to Zone 4. *R. atlanticum* (coast azalea)—3 to 6 feet high and wide with pinkish white flowers and blue-green leaves; hardy to Zone 6. *R. calendulaceum* (flame azalea)—4 to 8 feet tall and wide with yellow, pink, orange, peach, or red flowers, leaves yellow to red in fall; Zones 5-7. *R. schlippenbachii* (royal azalea)—6 to 10 feet tall and wide with rosey pink spring flowers, and dark green leaves turning red, orange, and yellow in fall; Zones 4-7. Evergreen species: *R. catawbiense* (Catawba rhododendron)—6 to 18 feet with slightly less spread, leaves dark, dense habit, flowers lilac-purple with green or yellow markings in 5- to 6-inch trusses in late spring; Zones 4-8. *R. fortunei* (Fortune's rhododendron)—20 to 30 feet tall with fragrant pale pink, lilac, or white flowers and large, dark green leaves; hardy to Zone 6. *R. maximum* (rosebay rhododendron)—4 to 30 feet with open habit and rose to pink flowers in late spring; hardy to Zone 3. *R. vaseyi* 'White Find'—upright growth to

Rhododendron yakusimanum

12 feet tall, white flowers appear before leaves in spring; Zones 4-9. *R. yakusimanum*—3 to 4 feet tall and 8 feet wide with pink flower buds opening to white flowers; Zones 5-8. *R. hybrids*—'Boule de Neige' is an evergreen that grows 5 feet tall and up to 8 feet wide with white flowers in large trusses; Zones 5-8. 'Yaku Princess' grows 3 to 4 feet tall and slightly wider, evergreen with pale pink spotted flowers in ball-shaped trusses; Zones 4-8.

Growing conditions and maintenance: Plant rhododendrons and azaleas in well-drained soil amended with organic matter. Avoid setting plants too deep. In warmer zones provide partial shade. Propagate from seed or cuttings.

Ricinus
(RISS-i-nus)
CASTOR-OIL PLANT

Ricinus communis 'Carmencita'

Hardiness: tender

Plant type: annual

Height: 8 to 10 feet

Interest: foliage

Soil: well-drained

Light: full sun

Ricinus produces clumps of large, glossy leaves that make an effective, coarse-textured backdrop in sunny borders, and because the plants grow rapidly, they are also used as screens. They impart a bold tropical appearance to any bed. The somewhat insignificant flowers are followed by colorful, prickly husks filled with tiny brown seeds that are extremely poisonous.

Selected species and varieties: *R. communis* (castor bean)—broad leaves, emerging red-tinged and turning glossy green until frost, up to 3 feet across with narrow, pointed segments on plants to 10 feet tall and 3 or 4 feet wide; 'Carmencita' has early blooming, bright orange-red flowers and deep bronze-brown leaves.

Growing conditions and maintenance: Soak seed overnight before planting indoors 6 to 8 weeks prior to the last frost. From Zone 9 south, seed can be sown directly in the garden in mid-spring. Best in hot, humid climates.

Rosa
(RO-za)
ROSE

Rosa 'Touch of Class'

Hardiness: Zones 2-10

Plant type: shrub

Height: 3 inches to 20 feet

Interest: flowers, fragrance, fruit

Soil: well-drained

Light: full sun

Roses offer limitless choices for landscaping, from formal gardens to informal shrub or herbaceous border plantings, where they put on outstanding displays over a long season. They can be cultivated individually as specimens, massed as hedges, pegged as ground covers, or trained against fences and trellises, where they can serve as an elegant backdrop for beds. The often fragrant flowers bloom singly or in clusters on arching or stiff woody stems lined with small thorns, sometimes appearing in a single flush, sometimes one at a time from summer through fall. Flowers of many types are followed by brightly colored hips for a showy display in fall and early winter.

Selected species and varieties: Bush roses—hybrid tea roses, such as *R. 'Touch of Class'*, bloom singly over the season on 2- to 6-foot-tall shrubs; floribunda roses have small clusters of blossoms blooming over the season on plants to 10 feet. Climbing roses—a single flush or repeating blooms along

canes to 20 feet; large-flowered climbing roses have solitary flowers like hybrid tea roses; cluster-flowered climbing roses have smaller blossoms in multiples. Hybrid rugosa roses—single- or double-petaled fragrant flowers on arching canes; unclassified modern shrub roses are a variable group with flowers on spreading mounds or upright bushes. Miniature roses—tiny versions of hybrid tea and floribunda roses only 3 to 18 inches tall. Old garden roses—moss roses, such as *R. 'Louise Odier'*, with a single flush of flowers on soft, floppy stems; hybrid perpetual roses have fragrant rosettes up to 7 inches across on plants to 8 feet or more. Climbing tea roses—large sin-

Rosa 'Louise Odier'

gle flowers on stiff, arching canes to 10 feet. Shrub roses—English roses with large flowers in old-fashioned rosettes on plants to 8 feet; hybrid musk roses have wonderfully fragrant, almost ever-blooming clusters on shrubs to 8 feet. Wild roses—arching stems with single-petaled, often fragrant flowers.

Growing conditions and maintenance: Plant roses in sites with good air circulation and a slightly acidic soil enriched with organic matter. Mulch to suppress weeds and protect roots in winter. Propagate species from seed, by layering, or by dividing rooted suckers; propagate cultivars and species from softwood cuttings in spring, semihard-wood cuttings in midsummer, or hardwood cuttings in late fall or winter.

Rudbeckia
(rood-BEK-ee-a)
CONEFLOWER

Rudbeckia hirta

Hardiness: tender or Zones 4-9

Plant type: annual, biennial, or perennial

Height: 2 to 7 feet

Interest: flowers

Soil: well-drained

Light: full sun to light shade

Coneflowers have prominent dark centers fringed with petal-like ray flowers. These undemanding and rewarding performers bloom over a very long season in any sunny border. They combine particularly well with ornamental grasses in informal beds.

Selected species and varieties: *R. hirta* (black-eyed Susan)—annual, biennial, or short-lived perennial, 2 to 3 feet tall, single or double flower heads with drooping yellow rays surrounding dark centers. *R. maxima* (great coneflower)—perennial, 3 to 9 feet tall with large gray-green leaves and drooping yellow ray flowers. *R. nitida* 'Herbstsonne'—perennial, 2 to 7 feet tall, flower heads 3 to 4 inches across with drooping yellow rays surrounding green centers appearing from midsummer to fall.

Growing conditions and maintenance: Plant coneflowers 1½ to 2 feet apart. They tolerate heat and dry conditions. Propagate by seed or division; they often self-sow.

Salvia
(SAL-vee-a)
SAGE

Salvia splendens

Hardiness: tender or Zones 5-11

Plant type: annual, biennial, or perennial

Height: 8 inches to 5 feet

Interest: flowers, foliage, fragrance

Soil: well-drained

Light: full sun to light shade

Salvias produce spires of two-lipped, hooded flowers in whorls lining square stems. Many produce attractive, fragrant foliage. From rounded 8-inch annual clumps to erect 6-foot shrublike perennials, sages fit many landscape uses. The long-flowering annual salvias are particularly appropriate for edging beds or massing. Perennial salvias provide fillers and specimens for mixing in herbaceous borders, and tall types make dramatic background plantings.

Selected species and varieties: *S. argentea* (silver sage)—perennial grown primarily for its foliage with branching clusters of white flowers tinged yellow or pink on 2- to 3-foot stems above rosettes of woolly, silvery gray, 8-inch leaves; Zones 5-10. *S. farinacea* (mealycup sage)—perennial often grown as an annual with a bushy habit and slender 1½- to 3-foot stems bearing blue flowers from midsummer to frost; Zones 8-9. *S. guaranitica*—perennial commonly grown as an annual with deep blue, 2- inch flowers and dark green

leaves on shrubby 3- to 5-foot plants. *S. leucantha* (Mexican bush sage)—perennial often grown as an annual, 3 to 4 feet with gracefully arching stems, gray-green leaves and arching spikes of purple and white flowers in summer and fall; Zones 8-11. *S. sclarea* var. *turkestaniana*—biennial with rosy pink flower spikes topping 3-foot stems above wrinkled, hairy leaves. *S. splendens* (scarlet sage)—annual 8 to 30 inches with glossy green leaves and tubular red flowers in whorls on erect

Salvia sclarea var. turkestaniana

stems from early summer to frost. *S. x superba* (perennial salvia)—violet-purple flowers in dense whorls from late spring to early summer on rounded plants to 3 feet tall; 'Blue Queen' grows 18 to 24 inches tall; 'East Friesland' has deep purple flowers on 18-inch plants; 'May Night' grows to 24 inches with violet- blue flowers; Zones 5-8. *S. uliginosa*—annual with 5-foot stems tipped with azure blue flowers on branched spikes above broad leaves.

Growing conditions and maintenance: Plant smaller salvia varieties 18 inches apart, larger ones 2 to 3 feet apart in sites that will be dry in winter. Excessive moisture in winter causes perennial species to rot. Salvias tolerate dry conditions. Remove spent flowers to encourage reblooming, and cut back perennials to the ground in late fall or winter. Propagate annual salvias from seed. Propagate perennial species by division in spring or fall or by cuttings.

Santolina
(san-to-LEE-na)
LAVENDER COTTON

Santolina chamaecyparissus

Hardiness: Zones 6-8

Plant type: perennial

Height: 14 to 24 inches

Interest: flowers, foliage, fragrance

Soil: well-drained to dry

Light: full sun

Santolina produces tiny yellow flower buttons on slender stems above broad, spreading clumps of aromatic leaves. It makes an attractive edging for a bed, and can be sheared into a dense, low hedge. It is also useful as a low-growing specimen in a border or rock garden.

Selected species and varieties: *S. chamaecyparissus*—to 24 inches tall with equal or greater spread, forming a broad, cushionlike, evergreen mound, aromatic leaves are silvery gray-green, ½ to 1½ inches long, yellow flowers appear in summer but are often removed to maintain clipped hedge; 'Nana' is a dwarf that grows to 14 inches.

Growing conditions and maintenance: Plant lavender cotton 18 to 24 inches apart. It is a rugged plant, tolerant of drought and salt spray. It prefers dry soils of low fertility and becomes unattractive and open in fertile soils. Avoid excess moisture, especially in winter. Prune after flowering to promote dense growth. Propagate by seed or cuttings.

Sedum
(SEE-dum)
STONECROP

Sedum x 'Autumn Joy'

Hardiness: Zones 3-10

Plant type: perennial

Height: 6 inches to 2 feet

Interest: flowers, foliage

Soil: well-drained to dry

Light: full sun

Stonecrops bear large clusters of tiny flowers on stems lined with fleshy leaves that are often tinged purple or bronze. Trailing types can be used as ground covers or edgings, while taller varieties can be massed in a border.

Selected species and varieties: *S.* x 'Autumn Joy'—15 to 24 inches tall with gray-green new leaves in spring, rosy pink flower buds in midsummer, opening to bronzy red flowers in fall, turning golden brown in winter; Zones 3-10. *S. sieboldii*—dense clusters of pink flowers bloom in autumn; Zones 3-8. *S. spectabile* (showy stonecrop)—round clumps of 18- to 24-inch stems lined with fleshy leaves and tipped with a flat cluster of white, pink, or red summer-to-fall flowers. 'Carmen' has rosy pink blooms.

Growing conditions and maintenance: Space plants 1½ to 2 feet apart. Propagate by division in spring or stem cuttings in summer.

Spiraea
(spy-REE-a)
SPIREA

Spiraea prunifolia

Hardiness: Zones 3-8

Plant type: shrub

Height: 1 to 8 feet

Interest: flowers, foliage

Soil: well-drained

Light: full sun to partial shade

Spireas are carefree deciduous shrubs that produce an abundance of dainty flowers in spring or summer. Spring-blooming spireas bear flower clusters along the entire length of the stems; summer-blooming types at the ends of stems. All combine easily with other shrubs or perennials.

Selected species and varieties: *S.* x *bumalda* 'Anthony Waterer'—2 to 4 feet tall, 4 to 5 feet wide, leaves emerge bronze in spring, turning blue-green in summer, carmine-pink flowers in 4- to 6-inch clusters appear in summer. *S. japonica*—5 to 6 feet tall and wide with flat-topped clusters of pink flowers in summer; 'Alpina' grows only 12 inches tall; Zones 4-8. *S. prunifolia* (Bridal wreath spirea)—5 to 8 feet with white spring flowers on arching stems.

Growing conditions and maintenance: Spireas flower best in full sun. Deadhead 'Anthony Waterer' spirea to encourage rebloom. Propagate spireas by softwood cuttings.

<table>
<tr><td>

Syringa
(si-RING-ga)
LILAC

Syringa x laciniata

</td><td>

Tagetes
(ta-JEE-teez)
MARIGOLD

Tagetes patula

</td><td>

Taxus
(TAKS-us)
YEW

Taxus x media

</td></tr>
</table>

Hardiness: Zones 3-8

Plant type: shrub

Height: 6 to 15 feet

Interest: flowers, foliage, fragrance

Soil: moist, well-drained

Light: full sun

Hardiness: tender

Plant type: annual

Height: 6 inches to 3 feet

Interest: flowers, foliage

Soil: well-drained

Light: full sun

Hardiness: Zones 4-7

Plant type: shrub or tree

Height: 2 to 60 feet

Interest: foliage, fruit

Soil: moist, well-drained, fertile

Light: full sun to partial shade

Lilacs are old-fashioned, deciduous shrubs that produce fragrant, late-spring flowers in dense grapelike clusters. They are standouts in the mixed shrub border and serve well as backdrops for herbaceous flowers.

Selected species and varieties: *S.* x *laciniata* (cut-leaf lilac)—to 6 feet with rounded form, deeply cut, fine-textured leaves, and pale lilac flowers; hardy to Zone 4. *S. microphylla* 'Superba'—6 feet tall and 12 feet wide with dense, wide-spreading habit, medium-green leaves, and deep pink flowers; Zones 4-7. *S. vulgaris* (common lilac)—8 to 15 feet tall with a similar spread, heart-shaped leaves and extremely fragrant flowers borne in 4- to 8-inch panicles; Zones 3-7.

Growing conditions and maintenance: Plant lilacs in soil amended with organic matter and close to neutral pH. Cut oldest stems with fewest flowers to the ground immediately after bloom, and remove other faded flowers. Propagate by cuttings or suckers.

Marigolds provide a reliable display in the summer border with nonstop pale yellow to bright orange and burgundy flowers from early summer to frost. Depending on their size, they can be placed in the background of a border, used as an edging, or massed in a bed.

Selected species and varieties: *T. erecta* (African marigold)—10 to 36 inches tall with erect to rounded habit, and solitary single or double flower heads 2 to 5 inches across. *T. patula* (French marigold)—6 to 18 inches tall with a rounded habit and deeply serrated leaves; flower heads are solitary, single or double, to 2½ inches across; double flowers often display a crest of raised petals at their center.

Growing conditions and maintenance: Start seed indoors 6 to 8 weeks or sow directly outdoors 2 weeks prior to the last frost. Space plants 6 to 18 inches apart, depending on the variety, and pinch seedlings to promote bushiness. They thrive in moist, well-drained soil, but tolerate drought.

Yews are dark evergreen shrubs with flat, needlelike leaves that provide a dramatic contrast to brightly colored plants. They are effective in shrub borders, as specimens, or as backgrounds for herbaceous plantings.

Selected species and varieties: *T. baccata* (English yew)—highly variable form, 30 to 60 feet tall and 15 to 25 feet wide, with 1¼-inch-long needles; 'Adpressa' grows to 30 feet with very short needles; 'Repandens', 4 feet tall and up to 15 feet wide with very dark leaves. *T. cuspidata* (Japanese yew)—10 to 40 feet tall and wide with exfoliating reddish brown bark; 'Densa' grows 3 to 4 feet tall and twice as wide with a dense habit and abundant fruit. *T.* x *media*—a hybrid of the above two species; 'Densiformis' grows 3 to 4 feet tall and 4 to 6 feet wide with bright green leaves.

Growing conditions and maintenance: Plant yews in soil with excellent drainage. Protect from drying winds. Propagate from cuttings.

Tulipa
(TOO-lip-a)
TULIP

Tulipa 'New Design'

Hardiness: Zones 3-9

Plant type: bulb

Height: 4 inches to 3 feet

Interest: flowers

Soil: well-drained, sandy, fertile

Light: full sun

Rising singly or occasionally in clusters, from clumps of canoe-shaped leaves, tulips make cheerful spring accents in borders and beds. Tulips come in many forms, including lily-flowered, with pointed petals; Darwin, with curved petals arranged in deep cups; double- or peony-flowered, with multiple rows of overlapping petals; and parrot, with overlapping frilled petals. They bloom in most colors except blue, and are often splashed with a second hue. Tulip hybrids are classified by their parent species, flower form, or bloom time.

Selected species and varieties: Hybrid tulips: Darwin tulips—'Apeldoorn' bears cherry red blooms with black centers; 'Pink Impression', soft pink flowers that mature to a deep rose. Double early tulips—'Monte Carlo' has deep, clear yellow flowers. Double late tulips—'Angelique' is deep pink shading to pale pink. Fosterana tulips—'Juan' is orange with a yellow base. Greigii tulips—'Plaisir' has red flowers edged with creamy yellow.

Fringed tulips—'Fancy Frills' is ivory with a rosy fringe; 'Fringed Elegance', yellow flecked with pink. Lily-flowering tulips—'Red Shine' bears deep ruby red flowers; 'West Point' produces primrose yellow blooms. Parrot tulips—'Black Parrot' bears black flowers with elaborate fringe; 'Fantasy', salmon pink flowers. Single early tulips—'Bellona' produces fragrant golden yellow flowers; 'Couleur Cardinal' bears plum-tinged red blooms. Single-late tulips—'Dreamland' is a red and creamy white

Tulipa greigii 'Plaisir'

bicolor; 'Queen of Bartigons' bears clear salmon flowers. Species tulips: *T. bakeri* 'Lilac Wonder'—rosy purple cups with yellow bases on 6-inch stems. *T. clusiana* var. *chrysantha* [also called *T. chrysantha*]—deep saucers, yellow inside, crimson edged with yellow outside, 12 inches tall. Triumph tulips—'Negrita' has deep purple blooms; 'New Design', silvery pink flowers with deeper pink edges.

Growing conditions and maintenance: Set bulbs out in late fall. Plant three times the depth of the bulb's diameter, usually 4 to 8 inches deep. Space according to bulb size; tulips can be thickly planted with no ill effect and close spacing enhances their impact. Plant up to 40 hybrid bulbs or up to 60 smaller species bulbs per square yard. Treat tulips as annuals, or dig them up and replant every 2 to 3 years as flowering diminishes. Propagate by removing bulb offsets, which will grow to blooming size in 2 to 3 years.

Verbascum
(ver-BAS-cum)
MULLEIN

Verbascum chaixii 'Album'

Hardiness: Zones 4-9

Plant type: biennial, perennial

Height: 3 to 6 feet

Interest: flowers, foliage

Soil: well-drained

Light: full sun

Mulleins develop a rosette of coarse leaves and tall, sturdy spikes of long-lasting summer flowers. Plant them at the rear of a border or in a wildflower garden.

Selected species and varieties: *V. bombyciferum* (silver mullein)—a biennial with rosettes of oval leaves covered with silvery, silky hairs and 4- to 6-foot spikes of sulfur yellow flowers; Zones 5-9. *V. chaixii* (Chaix mullein)—perennial with ½- to 1-inch-wide yellow flowers with fuzzy purple stamens creating a prominent eye; 'Album' has white flowers and gray foliage; Zones 4-9. *V.* x 'Cotswold Queen'—4 feet tall and 1 to 2 feet wide with apricot flowers; 'Pink Domino' grows 3 to 4 feet tall with deep pink flowers.

Growing conditions and maintenance: Space mulleins 1 to 2 feet apart. Plants tolerate dry conditions. Propagate biennials from seed, perennials from seed or root cuttings in early spring.

Verbena
(ver-BEE-na)
VERVAIN

Verbena canadensis

Hardiness: tender or Zones 6-10

Plant type: annual or perennial

Height: 6 inches to 4 feet

Interest: flowers

Soil: moist, well-drained

Light: full sun

Vividly colored small flowers blooming from summer through frost in clusters on wiry stems with soft green foliage make verbenas useful as ground covers or fillers in the border.

Selected species and varieties: *V. canadensis* (rose verbena)—perennial with rose pink blossoms in rounded clusters on dense mats of creeping stems 6 inches tall; Zones 6-10. *V. x hybrida* (common garden verbena)—an annual, 6 to 12 inches tall spreading to 2 feet, with wrinkled leaves and small flowers in loose, rounded heads to 2 inches across in shades of pink, red, blue, purple, and white; 'Homestead Purple' produces 6- to 10-inch-tall ground cover, evergreen foliage, and rich purple flowers; Zones 6-9.

Growing conditions and maintenance: Space verbenas 1 to 2 feet apart. Water during dry periods. Perennial verbenas can be grown as annuals in colder climates. Propagate by seed or cuttings taken in late summer.

Veronica
(ve-RON-i-ka)
SPEEDWELL

Veronica incana

Hardiness: Zones 4-8

Plant type: perennial

Height: 10 inches to 4 feet

Interest: flowers, foliage

Soil: well-drained

Light: full sun to light shade

Veronica's tiny flower blossoms appear on dense spires held above the foliage on erect stems. They add intense color and a vertical accent to the perennial bed or border.

Selected species and varieties: *V. incana* (silver speedwell)—lilac-blue flowers on 12- to 18-inch stems above clumps of silver gray foliage. *V. longifolia* (long-leaf speedwell)—2 to 4 feet tall with flowers for 6 to 8 weeks from midsummer to fall. *V. spicata* (spike speedwell)—10 to 36 inches tall with flowers from late spring to midsummer; 'Blue Peter' grows to 24 inches with navy blue flowers; 'Red Fox' has rosy pink flowers on 10- to 16-inch stems; 'Snow White', white blossoms on 18-inch stems.

Growing conditions and maintenance: Plant speedwell 1 to 2 feet apart. Remove spent flowers to extend bloom. Taller types may need staking. Propagate by seed, cuttings, or division.

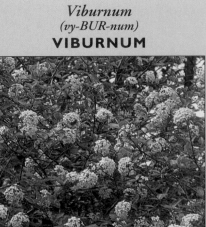

Viburnum
(vy-BUR-num)
VIBURNUM

Viburnum carlesii

Hardiness: Zones 4-8

Plant type: shrub

Height: 4 to 10 feet

Interest: flowers, fruit, foliage, fragrance

Soil: moist, well-drained

Light: full sun to partial shade

Deciduous or evergreen viburnums offer a choice of textures for specimens or backdrop plantings in shrub borders or woodland beds. Showy spring flowers are often followed by colorful fall fruit.

Selected species and varieties: *V. x carlcephalum* (fragrant viburnum)—6 to 10 feet tall and wide, deciduous, rounded, open habit with dark green leaves turning reddish purple in fall, pink buds opening to fragrant white flowers in 5-inch clusters; Zones 5-8. *V. carlesii* (Korean spice viburnum)—6 to 8 feet tall and nearly as wide, deciduous, with dense, rounded, upright habit, dark green leaves turning red in fall, pink buds opening to extremely fragrant white flowers; Zones 4-8.

Growing conditions and maintenance: Plant viburnums in soil amended with organic matter. When necessary, prune immediately after flowering. Propagate by cuttings.

Vitex
(VY-teks)
CHASTE TREE

Vitex agnus-castus

Hardiness: Zones 6-9

Plant type: shrub

Height: 3 to 15 feet

Interest: flowers, foliage, fragrance

Soil: well-drained

Light: full sun

The aromatic, soft, gray-green foliage of the chaste tree serves as a backdrop to fragrant spikes of flowers that tip stems from midsummer to fall. This fast-growing, deciduous shrub makes an attractive addition to the shrub border and serves as a backdrop to more brightly hued flowers.

Selected species and varieties: *V. agnus-castus*—grows 3 to 10 feet and similarly wide, palmately compound leaves with slender leaflets and prominent spikes of small, showy, fragrant, lavender flowers to 7 inches long; 'Alba' has white flowers; 'Rosea', pink flowers.

Growing conditions and maintenance: Plant vitex in loose, well-drained soil. Thrives in hot weather. In cold regions, it often dies to the ground, but grows 3 to 4 feet each season. Stems can be cut back to 6 to 12 inches in winter. Propagate by softwood cuttings.

Yucca
(YUK-a)
YUCCA

Yucca filamentosa 'Golden Sword'

Hardiness: Zones 4-9

Plant type: perennial or shrub

Height: 3 to 6 feet

Interest: foliage, flowers

Soil: well-drained to dry

Light: full sun

Yucca develops a rosette of sword-shaped evergreen leaves that provide a striking accent in rock gardens and perennial borders and among shrubs. Stiff stems bear white, nodding flowers in summer.

Selected species and varieties: *Y. filamentosa* (Adam's-needle)—2- to 3-foot-tall rosettes to 3 feet wide, leaves that bear a sharp terminal spine with threads curling off leaf margins, and flowers that are creamy white, 1 to 2 inches long, appearing in erect clusters on 3- to 12-foot scapes; 'Golden Sword' produces variegated leaves with yellow centers and green margins; Zones 5-9. *Y. glauca* (soapweed)—3 to 4-foot-wide rosettes of gray-green leaves with pale edges, and greenish white flowers on unbranched stalks to 6 feet; Zones 4-8.

Growing conditions and maintenance: Yuccas tolerate heat, drought, wind, and infertile soil. Remove flower stalks after blossoms fade. Propagate by separating offsets from the main plant.

Zinnia
(ZIN-ee-a)
ZINNIA

Zinnia elegans 'Peter Pan White'

Hardiness: tender

Plant type: annual

Height: 8 to 36 inches

Interest: flowers

Soil: well-drained

Light: full sun

Zinnias brighten beds or borders throughout summer with pompons of petal-like rays crowded around centers with yellow or green true flowers. Colors range from bright yellows, oranges, and reds to subdued pinks, roses, salmons, creams, and even maroon and purple.

Selected species and varieties: *Z. angustifolia* (narrowleaf zinnia)—compact, spreading habit to 8 inches tall with narrow, pointed leaves and 1-inch-wide, single orange flowers that make it excellent for an edging or ground cover. *Z. elegans* 'Peter Pan White'—10- to 12-inch large-flowered dwarf, free-flowering bushy plant with big double and semidouble flowers up to 3 inches across.

Growing conditions and maintenance: Start seed indoors 6 weeks prior to last frost, or sow directly outdoors after frost danger has passed. Space seedlings 6 to 12 inches apart, and pinch young plants to encourage bushiness. *Z. angustifolia* tolerates dry conditions.

Acknowledgments and Picture Credits

The editors wish to thank the following for their valuable assistance in the preparation of this volume:

Henry W. Art, Williamstown, Mass.; Jennifer Clark, Washington, D.C.; Catriona Tudor Erler, Vienna, Va.; Robert Hebb, Richmond, Va.; Adrian Higgins, Alexandria, Va.; Jennifer Jepson, Storey Communications, Pownal, Vt.; Jane Jordan, Alexandria, Va.; Anne Nottingham Kelsall, Landover Hills, Md.; Katya Sharpe, Fairfax, Va.; Robert Speziale, Time-Life Books, Alexandria, Va.; Karen Sweet, Time-Life Books, Alexandria, Va.

The sources for the illustrations in the book are listed below. Credits from left to right are separated by semicolons; credits from top to bottom are separated by dashes.

Cover: Kathlene Persoff. Back Cover insets: Michael S. Thompson/courtesy Libby McGeary—Art by Fred Holz—©Karen Bussolini/designed by Johnsen Design & Planning. End papers: © Crandall & Crandall. 1: Lefever/Grushow/Grant Heilman Photography, Inc. 2, 3: Roger Foley/designed by Oda Von Berg. 4: J. Paul Moore. 6, 7, 8: Derek Fell. 9: Michael S. Thompson/courtesy Libby McGeary. 10: Robert Perron/designed by Janet Cavanaugh. 11: ©Walter Chandoha. 12: Robert E. Lyons. 13: ©Karen Bussolini. 14: ©Walter Chandoha. 15: Robert E. Lyons. 16: ©Karen Bussolini/designed by Johnsen Design & Planning. 16, 17: ©Lynn Karlin/courtesy Stonewall Kitchen. 17: C. Colston Burrell. 19: Lefever/Grushow/Grant Heilman Photography, Inc.; ©Allan Mandell/designed by Dale Brous. 20: Art by Gordon Morrison. 21: Kathlene Persoff/designed by Cheryl K. Lerner. 22, 23: ©Walter Chandoha. 24: Charles Mann Photography/courtesy Dulcy Mahar. 25: ©Karen Bussolini/designed by Barbara Carr. 26, 27: Art by Elayne Sears/designed by Luanne Urfer, Muddy Knees Designs. 28: Michael S. Thompson/courtesy Byron and Sally Blanicinship. 29: ©Karen Bussolini—art by Gordon Morrison (2). 30: Art by Fred Holz. 31: ©Laurie Black Photography/designed by Northwest Landscape Industries/courtesy Rich and Peg Ackerman. 32: Roger Foley/designed by William Hoogeveen. 35: Thomas E. Eltzroth. 36, 37: Gay Bumgarner/courtesy Mechlin. 38: ©Crandall & Crandall/designed by Sassafras Gardens. 39: Jane Grushow/Grant Heilman Photography, Inc. 40: Cathy Wilkinson Barash. 40, 41: ©Crandall & Crandall/designed by Sassafras Gardens. 42: ©Crandall & Crandall/designed by Anne Roth. 43: Art by Gordon Morrison. 44, 45: Roger Foley/designed by Oda Von Berg. 45: ©Walter Chandoha. 46, 47: Art by Gordon Morrison. 48: Kathlene Persoff/designed by Linda Chisari. 49, 50: Walter Chandoha. 50,51: Art by Fred Holz. 52, 53: Roger Foley/designed by Mike Zajic. 54, 55: Jerry Pavia. 56, 57: Kathlene Persoff/designed by Nancy Goslee Power. 58, 59: Kathlene Persoff. 60, 61: ©Dency Kane/designed by Carol Mercer, Lisa Ver de Rosa/courtesy Carol Mercer. 62, 63: Jim Strawser/Grant Heilman Photography, Inc. 64, 65: Robert E. Lyons. 66: Michael S. Thompson/courtesy Patricia Chase. 67: Lefever/Grushow/Grant Heilman Photography, Inc. 68, 69: Art by Nancy Hull. 69: Michael S. Thompson/courtesy Marietta and Ernie O'Byrne. 70, 71: ©Christi Carter. 72: ©Ken Druse. 73: Stephen R. Swinburne/courtesy Cook's Garden. 74, 75: Art by Elayne Sears/designed by Luanne Urfer, Landscape Architect. 75: Drawing by Luanne Urfer, Landscape Architect—drawing by Anna Dewdney. 76: Drawing by Anna Dewdney. 76, 77: Art by Elayne Sears/designed by Luanne Urfer, Landscape Architect. 77: Drawing by Luanne Urfer, Landscape Architect. 78, 79: Art by Elayne Sears/designed by Luanne Urfer, Landscape Architect. 79: Drawing by Anna Dewdney—drawing by Luanne Urfer, Landscape Architect. 80, 81: Art by Elayne Sears/designed by Luanne Urfer, Landscape Architect. 81: Drawing by Anna Dewdney—drawing by Luanne Urfer, Landscape Architect. 82: Drawing by Luanne Urfer, Landscape Architect. 82, 83: Art by Elayne Sears/designed by Luanne Urfer, Landscape Architect. 83: Drawing by Anna Dewdney. 84: ©Walter Chandoha. 85: ©Dency Kane. 86, 87: Art by Elayne Sears/designed by Luanne Urfer, Landscape Architect. 87: Drawing by Luanne Urfer, Landscape Architect—drawing by Anna Dewdney. 88, 89: Art by Elayne Sears/designed by Luanne Urfer, Landscape Architect. 89: Drawing by Luanne Urfer, Landscape Architect—drawing by Anna Dewdney. 90, 91: Art by Elayne Sears/designed by Luanne Urfer, Landscape Architect. 91: Drawing by Luanne Urfer, Landscape Architect—drawing by Anna Dewdney. 92: Art by Nicholas Fasciano. 93: Art by Nicholas Fasciano. 94: Art by Nicholas Fasciano—art by Lorraine Mosley Epstein—art by Nicholas Fasciano. 95: Art by Lorraine Mosley Epstein (2)—art by Nicholas Fasciano—art by Lorraine Mosley Epstein. 102: Map by John Drummond, Time-Life Books. 104: ©Richard Shiell; Jerry Pavia. 105: Jerry Pavia. 106: ©R. Todd Davis Photography; Jerry Pavia (2). 107, 108, 109: Jerry Pavia. 110: Jerry Pavia; Charles Mann Photography; Jerry Pavia. 111: Jerry Pavia. 112: Jerry Pavia; Joseph Strauch; Carol Ottesen. 113: ©Dency Kane; Jerry Pavia (2). 114: Jerry Pavia (2); ©Peter Lindtner. 115: Jerry Pavia (2); judywhite. 116: Jerry Pavia (2); Robert E. Lyons. 117: Jerry Pavia. 118: Jerry Pavia (2); Derek Fell. 119: ©Peter Lindtner; Jerry Pavia (2). 120: Jerry Pavia (2); Thomas E. Elzroth. 121: Jerry Pavia. 122: ©Richard Shiell; Jerry Pavia (2). 123: Joseph Strauch (2); Robert E. Lyons. 124: Jerry Pavia; ©Richard Shiell; ©Peter Lindtner. 125: Jerry Pavia (2); ©Peter Lindtner. 126: ©Richard Shiell; Joseph Strauch; Derek Fell. 127: Jerry Pavia. 128: Joseph Strauch; Jerry Pavia (2). 129, 130: Jerry Pavia. 131: Derek Fell; Jerry Pavia; Derek Fell. 132: Jerry Pavia. 133: Jerry Pavia (2); ©Richard Shiell. 134: Jerry Pavia (2); Anita Sabarese. 135: Jerry Pavia; ©Richard Shiell; Joseph Strauch. 136: Jerry Pavia. 137: ©R. Todd Davis Photography; Jerry Pavia (2). 138: Roger Foley; Jerry Pavia (2). 139: Anita Sabarese; Jerry Pavia (2). 140: ©R. Todd Davis Photography; Joseph Strauch; Jerry Pavia. 141, 142: Jerry Pavia. 143: Joseph Strauch; Jerry Pavia (2). 144: ©Richard Shiell; Jerry Pavia (2). 145, 146: Jerry Pavia. 147: Joseph Strauch; Jerry Pavia (2). 148: Jerry Pavia. 149: Jerry Pavia (2); Joseph Strauch. 150: Jerry Pavia. 151: ©Richard Shiell; Jerry Pavia (2).

Bibliography

BOOKS:

Alexander, Rosemary, and Anthony du Gard Pasley. *The English Gardening School: The Complete Master Course on Garden Planning and Landscape Design for the American Gardener.* New York: Weidenfeld & Nicolson, 1987.

Appleton, Bonnie Lee. *Rodale's Successful Organic Gardening: Trees, Shrubs and Vines.* Emmaus, Pa.: Rodale Press, 1993.

Ashmun, Barbara. *The Garden Design Primer.* New York: Lyons & Burford, 1993.

Bailey, Liberty Hyde, Ethel Zoe Bailey and the Staff of the Bailey Hortorium at Cornell University. *Hortus Third* (rev. ed.). New York: Macmillan, 1976.

Bailey, Liberty Hyde, and the Staff of the Bailey Hortorium at Cornell University. *Manual of Cultivated Plants* (rev. ed.). New York: Macmillan, 1951.

Bales, Suzanne Frutig. *Burpee American Gardening Series: Annuals*. New York: Prentice Hall, 1991.

Brickell, Christopher, ed. *The American Horticultural Society Encyclopedia of Garden Plants*. New York: Macmillan, 1989.

Buczacki, Stefan. *Creating a Victorian Flower Garden*. New York: Weidenfeld & Nicolson, 1988.

Chatto, Beth. *The Green Tapestry*. New York: Simon and Schuster, 1989.

Cowley, Jill. *Beds and Borders for Year Round Colour* (*A Ward Lock Book*). London: Wellington House, 1995.

Cox, Jeff, and Marilyn Cox. *The Perennial Garden: Color Harmonies through the Seasons*. Emmaus, Pa.: Rodale Press, 1985.

Crockett, James Underwood, and the Editors of Time-Life Books:
Annuals (*The Time-Life Encyclopedia of Gardening*). New York: Time-Life Books, 1971.
Bulbs (*The Time-Life Encyclopedia of Gardening*). New York: Time-Life Books, 1971.
Evergreens (*The Time-Life Encyclopedia of Gardening*). New York: Time-Life Books, 1976.
Flowering Shrubs (*The Time-Life Encyclopedia of Gardening*). New York: Time-Life Books, 1972.
Landscape Gardening (*The Time-Life Encyclopedia of Gardening*). New York: Time-Life Books, 1971.
Perennials (*The Time-Life Encyclopedia of Gardening*). New York: Time-Life Books, 1972.

Damrosch, Barbara. *The Garden Primer*. New York: Workman, 1988.

Dirr, Michael A. *Manual of Woody Landscape Plants*. Champaign, Ill.: Stipes, 1990.

Druse, Ken. *The Natural Garden*. New York: Clarkson N. Potter, 1989.

Frances Lincoln Limited (London), Editors of, *Best Borders*. New York: Viking Penguin, 1995.

Gates, Galen, Chris Graham, and Ethan Johnson. *American Garden Guides: Shrubs and Vines*. New York: Pantheon, 1994.

Heriteau, Jacqueline, and André Viette. *The American Horticultural Society Flower Finder*. New York: Simon and Schuster, 1992.

Hill, Lewis. *Pruning Simplified*. Pownal, Vt.: Storey Communications, 1986.

Hobhouse, Penelope. *Color in Your Garden*. Boston: Little, Brown, 1985.

Hutson, June. *American Garden Guides: Annual Gardening*. New York: Pantheon, 1995.

Janick, Jules. *Horticultural Science* (2d ed.). San Francisco: W.H. Freeman, 1972.

Loewer, Peter. *Rodale's Annual Garden*. Emmaus, Pa.: Rodale Press, no date.

Marston, Ted, ed. *Hearst Garden Guides: Annuals*. New York: Hearst Books, 1993.

McGourty, Frederick. *The Perennial Gardener*. Boston: Houghton Mifflin, 1989.

Moore, Charles W., William J. Mitchell and William Turnbull, Jr. *The Poetics of Gardens*. Cambridge: MIT Press, 1988.

Murphy, Wendy. *Beds and Borders: Traditional and Original Garden Designs*. Boston: Houghton Mifflin, 1990.

Murray, Elizabeth, and Derek Fell. *Home Landscaping*. New York: Simon & Schuster, 1988.

Ortho Books, Editorial Staff. *Successful Flower Gardening*. San Ramon, Calif.: Ortho Books, 1990.

Phillips, C.E. Lucas, and Peter Barber. *Ornamental Shrubs*. New York: Van Nostrand Reinhold, 1981.

Phillips, Roger, and Martyn Rix. *The Random House Book of Shrubs*. New York: Random House, 1989.

Reader's Digest, Editors of:
Reader's Digest Illustrated Guide to Gardening. Pleasantville, N.Y.: Reader's Digest Association, 1978.
Reader's Digest Magic and Medicine of Plants. Pleasantville, N.Y.: Reader's Digest Association, 1986.

Roth, Susan A. *The Four-Season Landscape: Easy-care Plants and Plans for Year-round Color*. Emmaus, Pa.: Rodale Press, 1994.

Sinnes, A. Cort. *All About Perennials*. San Francisco: Ortho Books, 1981.

Smyser, Carol A., and the Editors of Rodale Press Books. *Nature's Design: A Practical Guide to Natural Landscaping*. Emmaus, Pa.: Rodale Press, 1982.

Still, Steven M. *Manual of Herbaceous Ornamental Plants*. Champaign, Ill.: Stipes, 1994.

Strong, Roy. *A Small Garden Designer's Handbook*. Boston: Little, Brown, 1987.

Tanner, Ogden, and the Editors of Time-Life Books. *Garden Construction* (*The Time-Life Encyclopedia of Gardening*). Alexandria, Va.: Time-Life Books, 1978.

Taylor's Guide to Perennials. Boston: Houghton Mifflin, 1986.

Thomas, Graham Stuart. *The Art of Planting: or The Planter's Handbook*. Boston: David R. Godine, 1984.

Time-Life Books, Editors of:
Bulbs (*The Time-Life Complete Gardener*). New York: Time-Life Books, 1995.
Combining Plants (*The Time-Life Complete Gardener*). New York: Time-Life Books, 1995.
Low Maintenance Gardening (*The Time-Life Complete Gardener*). New York: Time-Life Books, 1995.
Perennials (*The Time-Life Complete Gardener*). New York: Time-Life Books, 1995.
Shade Gardening (*The Time-Life Complete Gardener*). New York: Time-Life Books, 1995.
Wildflowers (*The Time-Life Complete Gardener*). New York: Time-Life Books, 1995.

Toogood, Alan. *Border Plants*. London: Ward Lock Limited, 1987.

Wasowski, Sally, and Andy Wasowski. *Gardening with Native Plants of the South*. Dallas: Taylor, 1994.

Wilkinson, Elizabeth, and Marjorie Henderson. *Decorating Eden: A Comprehensive Source Book of Classic Garden Details*. San Francisco: Chronicle Books, 1992.

Williamson, John. *Perennial Gardens: a practical guide to home landscaping*. New York: Harper & Row, 1988.

Wilson, Andrew. *Garden Style Source Book* (*A Quarto Book*). Secaucus, N.J.: Chartwell Books, 1989.

Wyman, Donald:
Shrubs and Vines for American Gardens. New York: Macmillan, 1973.
Wyman's Gardening Encyclopedia. New York: Macmillan, 1971.

Wyman, Donald, and the Editors of Time-Life Books. *Easy Gardens* (*The Time-Life Encyclopedia of Gardening*). Alexandria, Va.: Time-Life Books, 1978.

PERIODICALS:

"Beds & Borders," *Plants and Gardens: Brooklyn Botanic Garden Record*, Vol. 42, No. 1. Brooklyn, N.Y.: Brooklyn Botanic Garden, 1986.

Burrell, C. Colston, ed. *Brooklyn Botanic Garden Handbook No. 145: Woodland Gardens, Shade Gets Chic*. Brooklyn, N.Y.: Brooklyn Botanic Garden, 1995.

Hyland, Bob, ed. *Brooklyn Botanic Garden Handbook No. 141: Shrubs: The New Glamour Plants*. Brooklyn, N.Y.: Brooklyn Botanic Garden, 1994.

Lawlor, Robert. "The Measure of Difference." *Parabola, The Magazine of Myth and Tradition*, November 1991.

Lewis, Alcinda, ed. *Brooklyn Botanic Garden Handbook No. 143: Butterfly Gardens*. Brooklyn, N.Y.: Brooklyn Botanic Garden, 1995.

OTHER SOURCES:

André Viette Nursery catalog. Fisherville, Va.: 1994.

Appalachian Gardens catalog. Waynesboro, Pa.: 1996.

Beauty from Bulbs catalog. Bantam, Conn.: John Scheepers, Fall 1995.

Bluestone Perennials catalog. Madison, Ohio: 1995.

Breck's catalog. Peoria, Ill.: 1995.

Chiltern Seeds catalog. England: 1995.

Crownsville Nursery catalog. Crownsville, Md.: 1995.

Fairweather Gardens catalog. Greenwich, N.J.: 1995.

Jackson & Perkins Perennials catalog. Medford, Ore.: no date.

Joy Creek Nursery catalog. Scappoose, Ore.: 1995.

Kurt Bluemel Nursery catalog. Baldwin, Md.: 1994.

Limerock Ornamental Grasses catalog. Port Matilda, Pa.: 1995.

McClure & Zimmerman catalogs. Friesland, Wis.: Fall 1995 and Spring 1996.

Milaeger's Gardens Perennial Wishbook. Racine, Wis.: Spring 1996.

Niche Gardens catalog. Chapel Hill, N.C.: Spring 1996.

Nichols Garden Nursery catalog. Albany, Ore.: 1996.

Oakes Daylilies catalog. Corryton, Tenn.: no date.

Park's Seed—Flowers and Vegetables catalog. Greenwood, S.C.: 1996.

Park's Springtime Planting Book catalog. Greenwood, S.C.: 1996.

WE-DU Nurseries catalog. Marion, N.C.: 1994.

Weiss Brothers Nursery catalog. Grass Valley, Calif.: 1996.

White Flower Farm Garden Book catalogs. Litchfield, Conn.: Spring 1995 and Spring 1996.

Index

Time-Life Books is a division of Time Life Inc.

TIME LIFE INC.
PRESIDENT AND CEO: George Artandi

TIME-LIFE BOOKS
PRESIDENT: John D. Hall
PUBLISHER / MANAGING EDITOR: Neil Kagan

THE TIME-LIFE COMPLETE GARDENER
Designing Beds and Borders

EDITOR: Paul Mathless
MARKETING DIRECTOR: James Gillespie

Art Director: Kathleen D. Mallow
Associate Editor/Research and Writing:
Mary-Sherman Willis

Vice President, Director of Finance: Christopher Hearing
Vice President, Book Production: Marjann Caldwell
Director of Operations: Eileen Bradley
Director of Photography and Research:
John Conrad Weiser
Director of Editorial Administration: Barbara Levitt
Production Manager: Marlene Zack
Quality Assurance Manager: Miriam P. Newton
Library: Louise D. Forstall

Produced by Storey Communications, Inc.

PRESIDENT: M. John Storey
EXECUTIVE VICE PRESIDENT: Martha M. Storey
VICE PRESIDENT AND PUBLISHER: Pamela B. Art
CUSTOM PUBLISHING DIRECTOR: Amanda R. Haar

Project Managers: Megan Kuntze and Deirdre A. Lynch
Design: Mary B. Minella, Leslie H.R. Noyes, Lisa Richmond
Editor: Jacqueline Murphy
Associate Editors: Marjorie N. Allen, Mary Grace Butler, Susan Etkind
Copy Editor: Judith E. Storie
Indexer: Barbara E. Cohen
Special Contributors: Karen M. Elliott, Rita Pelczar, Elizabeth Toffey

Other Publications:

Do It Yourself
HOME REPAIR AND IMPROVEMENT
THE ART OF WOODWORKING
FIX IT YOURSELF

Cooking
WEIGHT WATCHERS® SMART CHOICE RECIPE COLLECTION
GREAT TASTE-LOW FAT
WILLIAMS-SONOMA KITCHEN LIBRARY

History
THE AMERICAN STORY
VOICES OF THE CIVIL WAR
THE AMERICAN INDIANS
LOST CIVILIZATIONS
MYSTERIES OF THE UNKNOWN
TIME FRAME
THE CIVIL WAR
CULTURAL ATLAS

Time-Life Kids
FAMILY TIME BIBLE STORIES
LIBRARY OF FIRST QUESTIONS AND ANSWERS
A CHILD'S FIRST LIBRARY OF LEARNING
I LOVE MATH
NATURE COMPANY DISCOVERIES
UNDERSTANDING SCIENCE & NATURE

Science/Nature
VOYAGE THROUGH THE UNIVERSE

For information on and a full description of any of the
Time-Life Books series listed above, please call 1-800-621-7026, or write:
Reader Information
Time-Life Customer Service
P.O. Box C-32068
Richmond, Virginia 23261-2068

Library of Congress Cataloging in
Publication Data
Designing beds and borders / by the editors of Time-Life Books.
p. cm.—(The Time Life complete
gardener)
Includes bibliographical references (p.
152) and index.
ISBN 0-7835-4115-5
1. Beds (Gardens) 2. Garden borders. 3.
Gardens—Design. 4. Plants, Ornamental. I. Time-Life Books. II. Series
SB423.7.D47 1996   635.9'63—
dc20   96-28538   CIP